D1431270

Between
EARTH
and
HEAVEN

Between
EARTH
and
HEAVEN

Shakespeare, Dostoevsky, and the
Meaning of Christian Tragedy

✍ BY ☙

ROGER L. COX

HOLT, RINEHART AND WINSTON
NEW YORK   CHICAGO   SAN FRANCISCO

*The following chapters have already appeared in some-
what altered form:*

Chapter 1 in *The Yale Review,* Summer 1968. Copyright © 1968 by Yale University.

Chapter 2 in *The Antioch Review,* Spring 1968. Copyright © 1968 by the Antioch Press.

Chapter 3 in *The Yale Review,* Spring 1966. Copyright
© 1966 by Yale University.

Chapter 4 in *Thought,* Spring 1969. Copyright © 1969
by Fordham University Press.

Chapter 9 in *Cross Currents,* Fall 1967. Copyright ©
1967 by Cross Currents Corporation.

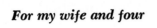

For my wife and four

Acknowledgments

∽ I AM INDEBTED to the American Council of Learned Societies, the Great Lakes Colleges Association—Carnegie Humanities Program, and DePauw University for grants of money and for released time from teaching. Without their help, this project would have taken much longer to complete than it actually did. I also wish to thank the editors of the Antioch Review, Cross Currents, Thought, and the Yale Review for permission to reprint here in slightly revised form the chapters which first appeared in those magazines. My largest personal obligation is to my friend and colleague, Robert H. King, with whom I have twice conducted a seminar in tragedy at DePauw University.

Grateful acknowledgement is also made to the following who have so generously granted permission to include in this book excerpts from the publications listed:

Mr. Edmund Brill, *Totem and Taboo*, by Sigmund Freud, translated by A. A. Brill; Cambridge University Press, New York, *The Interpretation of the Fourth Gospel*, by C. H. Dodd, 1954; Cross Currents Corporation, New York, "Pauline and Johannine

Theology: A Contrast," in *Cross Currents,* Summer 1965; Harper and Row, New York, "The Cosmology of the Apocalypse," by Paul S. Minear, from *Current Issues in New Testament Interpretation,* edited by William Klassen and Graydon F. Snyder, 1962; Macmillan and Company, London, *Shakespearean Tragedy: Lectures on Hamlet, Othello, King Lear, Macbeth,* 1960; Penguin Books, Hammondsworth, Middlesex, *Hamlet, Othello, King Lear, Macbeth,* in *The Pelican Shakespeare;* Random House, New York, *Crime and Punishment, The Idiot, The Brothers Karamazov,* Modern Library editions, 1950; Charles Scribner's Sons, New York, *Theology of the New Testament,* by Rudolf Bultmann, 1951; The World Publishing Company, Cleveland, *Existence and Faith,* by Rudolf Bultmann. Copyright © 1960.

I am myself indifferent honest, but yet I could accuse me of such things that it were better my mother had not borne me: I am very proud, revengeful, ambitious, with more offenses at my beck than I have thoughts to put them in, imagination to give them shape, or time to act them in. What should such fellows as I do crawling between earth and heaven?

HAMLET, III, i, 122–128

Contents

xi

Preface

❧ From a literary viewpoint, the question of Christian tragedy is not theoretical, but practical. Speculative thinkers may argue endlessly about whether or not there can be any such thing as Christian tragedy; but if their discussion remains purely abstract, the answers they reach will throw very little light upon actual works of literature. No one particularly cares whether Christian sonnets exist as a genre; but when we encounter a poem like "God's Grandeur," by Gerard Manley Hopkins, we notice two things about it: first, that it is a sonnet, and second, that the thought and feeling which underlie it and unify it are unmistakably Christian. Until we perceive at least that much about the poem, we cannot truthfully claim to understand it from either a literary or an intellectual point of view. It might be cogently argued, I suppose, that "what is essential to the Christian cannot even emerge" within the narrow confines of a sonnet; but all such discussion would seem trivial and irrelevant to the person who could sympathetically contemplate the fourteen lines called simply, "God's Grandeur."

The idea of Christian tragedy presented in these chapters does not involve a new "theory of tragedy." On the contrary, it springs from the conviction that all such theories, as long as they remain rigid and dogmatic, hinder our understanding of particular tragedies far more than they help. When a reader approaches a piece of tragic literature with preconceived definite notions as to what such a piece *should* be like, and then fails to find what he is looking for, he may do any one of four things in an effort to be consistent: he imposes (sometime unconsciously) his own conception of form or meaning upon the work; he finds reasons for regarding it as a failure; he qualifies his praise by saying that of course it is not *really* a tragedy; or, he revises his theory. Unfortunately for both themselves and the general public, most critics would rather pursue one of the first three possibilities than go to all the work of revising their theory.

Hamlet criticism has followed the pattern just described. Many commentators, utterly baffled by the play, have used it as a vehicle for expressing their own views on man and the world without being aware that they do so. Among the more conscientious readers, T. S. Eliot found ample reason for thinking it a bad play, an "artistic failure." And E. M. W. Tillyard, unable to fit *Hamlet* into his theory, concludes disappointingly that it is not really a tragedy, but a "problem play." This book proposes that we choose the remaining alternative and revise our theory of tragedy to include meaningfully the work that many regard as the greatest tragedy written since classical times. A "tragic theory" is, after all, no more than a series of generalizations about such works as *Hamlet*.

Any substantial piece of imaginative writing necessarily raises at least two questions for the serious reader: (1) What kind of work is it? and (2) What thought or feeling informs it and gives it meaning? If in relation to a particular work, we can answer the first question by common consent with the word *tragedy,* and if we can answer the second, by careful and convincing argument, with the word *Christian,* then the abstract debate as to whether or not Christian tragedy can even exist may be relegated to its proper place as a matter for speculative thinkers rather than for students of literature. No one can predict what special characteristics a work would have to possess in order to qualify as

Christian tragedy. Even in retrospect, we cannot establish a set of necessary and sufficient characteristics, but this should not be unduly disturbing. Witness the case of Greek tragedy: Aristotle's *Poetics* simply fails to illuminate some of the plays by Aeschylus, Sophocles, and Euripides; but we do not refuse for that reason to call them Greek tragedies. With postclassical literature, all we can do is to accept the judgment of countless readers and playgoers that such works as *Hamlet* and *King Lear* are tragedies, and then attempt to discover the fundamental character of the thought and feeling that make them coherent works of art. If we find that these works are definitely more comprehensible when interpreted by means of biblical writings than by any other frame of reference, it is pointless for us to insist that they are not Christian tragedies merely because we have decided in advance that no such thing exists.

The term *Christian tragedy* does not designate a subdivision or an offshoot of pure and essential tragedy. It closely parallels the term *Greek tragedy*, in which the adjective indicates not only the national origin of certain plays but also the cultural matrix from which they spring. In English the only commonly used adjectives that we have for describing tragedy are *Shakespearean*, which parallels *Sophoclean*, and *Elizabethan*, which parallels *classical*. We are allowed to speak of French classical tragedy, but we are left, unfortunately, with no acceptable term for describing a work such as *The Brothers Karamazov*, which approximates tragedy very closely and which would be almost unintelligible apart from the Christian thought and feeling that infuse and transform the whole story. If upholding a theory which declares that Christian tragedy cannot exist hinders our understanding of the book which Sigmund Freud, André Gide, and Arnold Bennett called the greatest novel ever written, then by all means let us discard or at least revise the theory.

One can never be entirely certain what a critic means when he declares, as if he were stating an indisputable fact, that Christian tragedy cannot exist. If he means only that tragedy produced during the Christian era is not identical with Greek tragedy, no one would argue with him—any more than one would argue against the claim that English literature is not identical with Greek literature. But if most of our authorities on literature insisted that English literature ("if it may be said to exist") is very different from its Greek counterpart and that Greek literature is the only genuine article, then someone would have to attempt a responsible reply. By the same token, when our most respected commentators on tragic literature repeatedly assert that the term *Christian tragedy* is completely self-contradictory and can only mislead the student of literature, then someone must interpret the works in question very carefully to show that the opposite is true and that we are misled by arbitrarily divorcing works written during the Christian era from the matrix of Christian thought. Christian tragedy *does* exist, and we gain nothing by continuing to insist that it does not and cannot. We not only gain nothing; we lose a great deal as far as understanding is concerned.

The bible is regarded in this book not as holy scripture but as a literary document, perhaps the most important and influential one the Western world has produced. We shall treat it as we would treat any other book; and when its influence seems unmistakable and illuminating, we shall take advantage of that fact. Unless otherwise noted, all bible quotations are from the Revised Standard Version, primarily because it is more readable than the older translations. This practice is consistent with the use of a modern edition of the Shakespeare plays and an English translation of the Dostoevsky novels. All bible passages cited in connection with Shakespeare have been checked against *The New Testament Octapla,* edited by Luther A. Weigle (New York, T. Nelson, 1962); and in no case is a point argued which is not supported by the wording of at least one major version of the English bible which was available to Shakespeare at the time he wrote the plays (Geneva Bible, 1560; Bishops' Bible, 1568; Rheims New Testament, 1582). Occasionally the King James Version is cited, either because its wording is more nearly consistent with the older translations than is the Revised Standard Version on the point in question, or because the meaning of one of Dostoevsky's self-confirmed references is lost in the newer version. Bible quotations within passages quoted from other writers are transcribed verbatim regardless of the version involved. All Greek tragedy quotations are from the University of Chicago's *Complete Greek Tragedies*, edited by David Grene and Richmond Lattimore; all Shakespeare quotations are from *The Pelican Shakespeare*, edited by Alfred Harbage; and all Dostoevsky quotations are from the Modern Library Edition of his novels, translated by Constance Garnett.

In the chapters that follow, we make only two assumptions: that *Hamlet, King Lear,* and *Macbeth* are tragedies, and that the New Testament is Christian. The terms *tragedy* and *Christian* quickly become almost meaningless unless we make those two assumptions. All else, however, stands in doubt. We shall challenge any generalization about tragedy, no matter how widely accepted it may be, if it contradicts the evidence provided by the tragic paradigms. Our sole criterion for judging whether or not something is specifically and genuinely Christian will be the extent to which it reflects the language, the thought patterns, and the imagery of the New Testament. This procedure, which is purely literary, will keep us from becoming entangled with the inconsistencies of traditional, authoritarian statements about tragedy and the intricacies of historical theology, both of which are fundamentally irrelevant to the main question.

It is of course pointless to "Christianize" pagan literature in the way that people tried to do centuries ago with Virgil's Fourth Eclogue, just as it is pointless, for the same reason, to offer (except for biographical purposes) detailed Freudian interpretations of particular literary works written before 1900, as if those works had been produced by minds fully conscious of Freud's special insights. As we shall see in connection with *Macbeth*, sexual imagery and symbolism may sometimes be central to the meaning of a Shakespeare play. There is nothing "Freudian," however, about such a pattern of imagery, just as there is nothing "Christian" about the religious implications of Greek tragedy—although some critics might be strongly tempted to use Christian categories in analyzing a play such as *Alcestis*. Freud himself sometimes made illuminating general statements about older literature; but the systematic application of Freud's psycho-analytic discoveries to individual works written before his time serves mainly as a vehicle for the critic's own comments about life; and however closely related they may be, literature and life are not the same thing.

On the other hand, if an important twentieth-century writer possessed a thorough knowledge of Freud's work and made use of that knowledge in his own writing (one thinks, for instance, of Ralph Ellison's *Invisible Man*), then we would be foolish to ignore that relationship simply because we had personal objections to Freudian psychology or because we cherished a theory that no significant work could be both literary and Freudian. Aeschylus, Sophocles, and Euripides knew about religion, but they never heard of Christ; and Shakespeare knew about sex, but he never heard of Freud. A third fact, also perfectly obvious though usually ignored, is that Shakespeare and Dostoevsky *did* read the New Testament, and they apparently knew parts of it extremely well. Richmond Noble's book, *Shakespeare's Biblical Knowledge and Use of the Book of Common Prayer*, demonstrates the frequency if not the depth of Shakespeare's reliance upon biblical material; and Ernest Simmons's *Dostoevski: The Making of a Novelist* reminds us that during the four years of Dostoevsky's imprisonment at Omsk, "the New Testament was the sole book allowed him." If we willfully close our eyes to these facts, then we deliberately ignore literary evidence of the most significant kind.

The assertion that Christian tragedy can and does exist implies that the arguments advanced to support the opposite claim are basically unsound. We would gain very little, however, by merely recapitulating those arguments and setting forth counter-arguments. To do so would be to keep the dispute on a purely theoretical level, where it has already foundered. Instead, let us apply the same practical method of criticism to the gospel narratives that we apply in later chapters to three of the Shakespeare plays. In these latter cases, we make the initial assumption that the works in question are tragedies and then show that the thought and feeling which underlie them are radically and identifiably Christian. Reversing this procedure, we may assume that the thought and feeling which underlie the gospel narratives are indisputably Christian; and if we analyze those narratives by comparing their content with that of the commonly accepted literary tragedies, we find that they are basically tragic. If so, we ought to refrain from insisting, on theoretical grounds, that genuinely Christian tragedy cannot exist. Let us therefore begin by turning to the conception of tragedy and then to the gospel narratives themselves.

Roger L. Cox

Greencastle, Indiana
April 4, 1969

I

Tragedy and the Gospel Narratives

*Justice so moves that those
only learn who suffer.*
AGAMEMNON, 250–251

*"Whoever does not bear his own
cross and come after me,
cannot be my disciple."*
LUKE 14:27

⇜ PHILOSOPHERS, literary critics, and theologians often contradict each other's conclusions, but upon one matter they have reached almost universal agreement—that there can be no such thing as *Christian tragedy*. In *Tragedy Is Not Enough*, Karl Jaspers asserts that "no genuinely Christian tragedy can exist," and he further claims that "what is essential to the Christian cannot even emerge in tragedy." [1] Walter Kaufmann's *Critique of Religion and Philosophy* denies that the book of Job is tragic and insists that there can never be "any Jewish or Christian tragedy." [2] Richard Sewall, in *The Vision of Tragedy*, relegates to footnotes (presumably because they are almost self-evident) such statements as this: "Christian tragedy, to put it briefly, is not Christian; if it were, it would not be tragedy." [3] And Edmond Cherbonnier contends in an article called "Biblical Faith and the Idea of Tragedy" that "at nearly every point [biblical philosophy] stands in flat contradiction to tragedy." [4] Many thoughtful people share such a view, including Reinhold Niebuhr, who sums it up clearly and finally in his statement, "Christianity stands beyond tragedy." [5] These assertions admit of no qualifica-

1

tion; they totally exclude Christian literature from the category of tragedy.

When we contemplate a play which nearly everyone regards as belonging to the most select company of tragic dramas and we strongly suspect that the world view which it embodies is genuinely and specifically Christian, we wonder whether the claims of Jaspers and others are actually true. Do their statements have the status of fact, supported by a staggering amount of empirical evidence? Are they generalizations which, though they cannot be absolutely proven, seem to be justified by what evidence we have? Or, are they statements of private belief by men better acquainted with Christian doctrine than with tragic literature, or the reverse? If these statements are true, we should be able to verify them; and if we cannot verify them, we should hesitate to accept them unqualifiedly. They are not, after all, articles of faith; they are merely conclusions as to the relationship between Christianity and literature.

A persistent doubt about the assertion that no literary work can be both Christian and tragic leads to the more basic question, are not the gospel narratives themselves fundamentally tragic stories? They certainly seem so to the disinterested observer: the main character, who possesses both courage and integrity, conducts his life as he believes he must, even in the face of overwhelming opposition; and as a direct result of this behavior, he is put to death. Indeed, the similarity of the gospel narratives to the pattern of tragedy is so obvious that it is curious why no one has ever seriously advanced such an interpretation. It is also curious, since no one has done so at all systematically, why Jaspers and Niebuhr take such pains to deny that the gospel stories are tragic in any significant sense. In discussing failure as an aspect of tragedy, Jaspers remarks that "Christ is the deepest symbol of failure in this world, yet he is in no sense tragic." [6] And Niebuhr observes that "Jesus is, superficially considered, a tragic figure; yet not really so." [7] Against whom and to what purpose are they arguing? They are asserting, in effect, that appearances are deceptive and that their conception of tragedy is incompatible with their interpretation of the New Testament;

but they fail to convince anyone (except persons who already agree with them) that *any* valid conception of tragedy inevitably conflicts with *any* serious view of the New Testament.

A strongly partisan tone characterizes the arguments of those who most energetically deny the possibility of any Christian tragedy; and each commentator is doing his best to show either that tragedy is "superficial" when compared to the Christian gospel, or else that Christianity, because it offers the believer a way out of any desperate situation, never really comes to grips with tragic conflict. Edmond Cherbonnier creates the impression that only a dilettante, who relishes emotions which are "to be savored by the connoisseur for their psychological effect," [8] can respond sympathetically to literary tragedy. Walter Kaufmann, with equal sarcasm, takes the opposite position: "By what is today called religion one cannot live, nor could one die for it. How much more profound is the outlook of the great tragic poets! What is there to prevent a man from living and dying like Antigone?" [9] But Cherbonnier seems serenely confident that no Christian will merely "savor" Christ's suffering and death from a comfortable distance, secure in the knowledge that his sacrifice was all-sufficient, while Kaufmann fails to indicate how it happens that Antigone can show us the way to live and die when Christ cannot. Obviously, both men are passionate believers, and each scoffs at what the other believes in. Since both are concerned to assert the superiority of their own position, both feel compelled to demonstrate the supposed differences between Christianity and tragedy; and, as one might expect, both conclude that there can be no such thing as Christian tragedy.

The belief that Christianity and tragedy are mutually exclusive has a highly unfortunate double effect: The Christian, consciously or unconsciously, avoids the tragic implications of the gospel narratives; and the skeptic who admires tragedy is confirmed in thinking that the Christian takes a facile and unrealistic view of the world. The believer who sees nothing really tragic in Christ's suffering is not disquieted by the words, "Whoever does not bear his own cross and come after me, cannot be my disciple" (Luke 14:27; cf. Matt. 10:38 and 16:24, Mark 8:34, Luke 9:23). The command "Render therefore to Caesar the things that are Caesar's, and to God the things that are God's" (Matt. 22:21, Mark 12:17, Luke 20:25) holds no terror for him, because he somehow assumes that Caesar and God will never make contradictory demands upon him as Creon and the Greek gods did upon Antigone or as political authority and religious imperative did upon Jesus himself. To him Christ's words upon the cross, "My God, my God, why hast thou forsaken me?" (Matt. 27:46, Mark 15:34) seem to reflect only momentary discouragement, since we all know that the resurrection soon makes everything right again.

No small part of the gospel's power lies in its historicity, in our knowledge that a man did live and die in the way that Matthew, Mark, Luke, and John describe. On the other hand, when a person identifies himself totally with an imaginary character or an abstract ideal, he tends to divorce himself from meaningful existence: the *tragic hero* invites him to indulge in the kind of fantasy that James Thurber represents so well in "The Secret Life of Walter Mitty." For this reason, the skeptic who ignores Christ in favor of Antigone ends by identifying himself with a dramatic character in much the same way that a Christian behaves when he professes belief in Christ; and, because the character in question is purely imaginary, the skeptic moves toward a position which is laden with sentimentality. He is rather like the patriotic American who prefers the image of Davy Crockett (or even Paul Bunyan) to that of Abraham Lincoln, who was often awkward and sometimes ridiculous. Thus, the Christian who avoids the tragic implications of the gospel narratives concludes, with smug self-satisfaction, that Christ's sacrifice guarantees the salvation of all "true believers" without any real suffering on their part; and the skeptic who admires tragedy but rejects the gospel narratives as moralistic finally takes a stand that seems sentimental rather than tragic.

Since the confusion about Christianity and tragedy thrives upon partisanship—acceptance of Christianity and rejection of tragedy, or vice versa—it should not be surprising that a key to understanding the problem should come from a man whose primary interest was neither religious nor literary. I refer to Sigmund Freud's brief discussion of tragedy in *Totem and Taboo*. His remarks about "the oldest Greek tragedy" are highly significant and should be quoted verbatim rather than paraphrased.

A group of persons, all of the same name and dressed in the same way, surround a single figure upon whose words and actions they are dependent, to represent the chorus and the original single impersonator of the hero. Later developments created a second and a third actor in order to represent opponents in playing, and off-shoots of the hero, but the character of the hero as well as his relation to the chorus remains unchanged. The hero of the tragedy had to suffer; this is to-day still the essential content of a tragedy. He had taken upon himself the so-called "tragic guilt," which is not always easy to explain; it is often not a guilt in the ordinary sense. Almost always it consisted of a rebellion against a divine or human authority and the chorus accompanied the hero with their sympathies, trying to restrain and warn him, and lamented his fate after he had met with what was considered fitting punishment for his daring attempt.

But why did the hero of the tragedy have to suffer, and what was the meaning of his "tragic" guilt? We will cut short the discussion by a prompt answer. He had to suffer because he was the primal father, the hero of that primordial tragedy the repetition of which here serves a certain tendency, and the tragic guilt is the guilt which he had taken upon himself in order to free the chorus of theirs. The scene upon the stage came into being through purposive distortion of the historical scene or, one is tempted to say, it was the result of refined hypocrisy. Actually, in the old situation, it was the members of the chorus themselves who had caused the suffering of the hero; here, on the other hand, they exhaust themselves in sympathy and regret, and the hero himself is to blame for his suffering. The crime foisted upon him, namely, presumption and rebellion against a great authority, is the same as that which in the past oppressed the colleagues of the chorus, namely, the band of brothers. Thus the tragic hero, though still against his will, is made the redeemer of the chorus.

When one bears in mind the suffering of the divine goat Dionysos in the performance of the Greek tragedy and the lament of the retinue of goats who identified themselves with him, one can easily understand how the almost extinct drama was reviewed in the Middle Ages in the Passion of Christ.[10]

Though his discussion is helpful, there are at least two ambiguities in the tragic situation which Freud apparently misses. One of these is reflected in his statement that "the tragic hero, *though still against his will,* is made the redeemer of the chorus." In Greek tragedy the hero frequently becomes the instrument for "punishing" himself—Antigone hangs herself, and Oedipus puts out his own eyes. This being the case, it does not quite make sense to say that the hero acts "against his will" in doing so. It would be far more accurate to say that the hero *voluntarily though reluctantly* becomes the redeemer of the chorus. Unless we make this qualification, we get into an absurd discussion such as the one in Act V of *Hamlet,* where the gravediggers argue about whether or not Ophelia "drowned herself wittingly." Because Ophelia was mad, it is true that she did not have her wits about her when she drowned herself, but we certainly cannot argue about whether or not Oedipus "put out his eyes wittingly." There is no question of insanity, and there is no question of the brooches' coming to him and putting out his eyes "against his will." Even Walter Kaufmann, who has no interest in revising such a statement as this one of Freud's to make it fit the passion narrative, says that "the downfall and death of the tragic hero was originally, if we remember the genesis of tragedy, a self-sacrifice. The guilt which the hero takes upon himself transcends his own person: by accepting the guilt as his own and paying for it with his own destruction he sacrifices himself for others." [11] The other ambiguity, which involves the hero's being "to blame for his suffering," we shall analyze fully in a moment.

When those who deny the possibility of Christian tragedy attempt to describe the main features of tragic drama, their generalizations apply at least as well to the gospel narratives as they do to any literary tragedy. Ironically, this happens just as surely when the skeptic (Kaufmann) tries to analyze tragedy to show why it is more meaningful than Christianity as it does when the Christian (Niebuhr, Cherbonnier) tries to differentiate tragedy from Christianity to show the latter's superiority. Only by juxtaposing representative tragedies and the gospel narratives without any attempt to demonstrate that one is superior to the other, whether in kind or merely in degree, can we gain significant insight into the intimate connections between the two. By this procedure we can begin to evaluate the claim, which we hear on every side, that there can be no such thing as Christian tragedy.

A *tragedy* is a literary work, predominantly somber in tone, in which the main character encounters some significant misfortune for which he himself is partly, though not wholly, responsible. If misfortune is treated comically throughout, then the somber tone is lost, and the work is not tragic no matter what the degree of the main character's responsibility. Unless the protagonist encounters significant misfortune, the plot of the work would be indistinguishable from that of pure comedy; and unless the main character is partly though not entirely responsible, his misfortune would be indistinguishable from sheer accident on the one hand and from quite reasonable punishment on the other. That is to say, tragedy deals basically with the timeless problem of necessary injustice; and since it involves the *mis*fortune of a person who is at least partly good rather than with anyone's *unmerited good* fortune, it deals with necessary suffering. The human condition is such that when human suffering is seen in a literary work to be the product of absolute necessity, it affords some insight, some liberation—if not to the hero, at least to the audience. This insight or liberation is apparently what Aristotle means by *catharsis* and what Jaspers means by *transcendence*.

Most misunderstandings about tragedy arise from a failure to comprehend the fundamentally double meaning of two terms in the preceding paragraph, the first of which is *responsible*. When we say that an individual is responsible for something, we are designating his action as a cause, but we are not indicating whether that cause is *sufficient* or merely *necessary*. The difference here leads to whether or not we attach blame to the person in question. For example, Antigone's determination to bury her brother Polyneices leads directly to her suffering, but it does so only because Creon has declared that anyone who buries Polyneices must die. Her action is therefore a necessary but not a sufficient cause of her suffering, since under other circumstances her insistence upon the rite of burial for her brother could only be regarded as the proper fulfillment of a religious duty. As she says in one of her final speeches, "I stand convicted of impiety,/ the evidence my pious duty done" (lines 924–925). Similarly, Oedipus suffers because of his determination to discover the identity of Laius's murderer and thereby free his people from the plague. It is only proper that he as head of the government should do this; but his being the murderer (though he does not know it at the time) functions in this play, just as Creon's edict does in *Antigone,* to create a situation in which his admirable determination to do right leads to his own suffering.

Antigone and *Oedipus the King* both involve three significant elements, and the differences of construction result from the manner in which these elements are combined or separated within each of the two plays. Both works contain (1) a virtuous act by the protagonist, (2) an act which is an offense against the state, and (3) an edict which is designed to punish that offense. There are, moreover, three chief differences between the plays. First, in *Antigone* elements 1 and 2 are combined: Antigone's virtuous act (burying her brother) *is* an act which is an offense against the state; whereas in *Oedipus the King* elements 1 and 3 are combined: Oedipus's virtuous act as chief of state *is* the proclamation of an edict which is designed to punish an offense against the state. Secondly, as a consequence of the first difference, in *Antigone* a separate character (Creon) must be introduced into the play to proclaim the edict, whereas in *Oedipus* the protagonist performs this function himself. Hence, some people have mistakenly concluded that Creon is the main character in *Antigone;* Creon may be potentially a tragic hero, but he is *not* the hero of Sophocles' play. Thirdly, also as a consequence of the first difference, in *Antigone* element 3 (the edict) is beyond the control of the protagonist, whereas in *Oedipus* element 2 (the offense against the state) is beyond the protagonist's conscious control—he simply does not know that he is guilty of the offense. This third difference makes *Antigone* a battle of wills (Antigone versus Creon), while *Oedipus* represents a struggle for self-knowledge. In both cases, however, the protagonist performs at the beginning of the play an act that leads directly to his own suffering, and in both cases that act springs from a virtue, not a fault. The character is therefore *responsible* for his suffering —he causes it, but he is not *to blame* for it (hence the ambiguity which Freud fails to recognize).

The other term which involves double meaning is *necessary*. This word points specifically to the tension which exists between the poles of fate on the one hand and personal choice on the other, between external and internal causes, between destiny and freedom. *Necessary* suffering results when the protagonist makes a decision (often a forced decision), and one of the alternatives leads directly to suffering while the other, which would normally be open to him, is eliminated because it would require him to deny his own identity. Antigone might easily have avoided suffering simply by denying her obligation to Polyneices—that is, by denying her identity as his sister. This, of course, is what Ismene does; and consequently she does not suffer in the same manner as Antigone, nor does she attain Antigone's heroic stature.

In *Oedipus the King* the situation is more complex, but the relationship between fate and freedom is fundamentally the same. The events which are regarded as inevitable or fated (the hero's killing his father and marrying his mother) are represented as having taken place in the remote past. Thus, they are utterly beyond the power of human beings to do anything about them. The hero, however, lives happily and prosperously for a long time afterward. His downfall and the tragedy itself result not merely from these events, but from the attitude which he takes toward them. When he carries through his determination to know all about the events over which he now has no control, Jocasta begs him, "O be persuaded by me, I entreat you;/do not do this." But Oedipus replies, "I will not be persuaded to let be/ the chance of finding out the whole thing clearly" (lines 1064– 1065). Everyone urges him to leave well enough alone, not to bring down upon himself and Thebes the consequences of such a discovery; but he forces the truth out of all concerned: Jocasta,

Teiresias, and the herdsman who disposed of the baby. In short, though the events which are the background for the action of the play are "inevitable," the hero's fall and the tragedy itself come about because Oedipus finds it "necessary" to pursue the knowledge which is his undoing. He cannot do otherwise without denying his identity; such is the case by definition, since the knowledge that he feels compelled to pursue *is* the knowledge of his own identity.

Shakespearean tragedy reflects a similar attitude toward the questions of free will and determinism. Hamlet, like Oedipus and Antigone, could easily avoid the whole tragic situation. He might simply ignore the ghost's commands and return to Wittenberg, but such an alternative would require him to deny his identity as the elder Hamlet's son. Also, it is precisely the meaning of Hamlet's apology to Laertes that Hamlet is responsible for what has happened in the limited sense which we have been describing —he has *caused* the suffering which the play represents, but he is not completely "to blame" for it: "If Hamlet from himself be ta'en away,/And when he's not himself does wrong Laertes,/ Then Hamlet does it not, Hamlet denies it./Who does it then? His madness" (V, ii, 223–226). Yet this apology has been so widely misunderstood that one nineteenth-century critic (E. H. Seymour, 1805) concluded that the passage was an interpolation because "the falsehood contained in it is too ignoble." [12]

In *King Lear*, the protagonist (without fully realizing that he does so) denies his identity at the very beginning of the play by resigning his position as king and father because of his desire "To shake all cares and business from our age,/Conferring them on younger strengths while we/Unburdened crawl toward death" (I, i, 39–41). He soon discovers that he cannot abdicate in this manner and still retain "The name, and all th' addition to a king" (I, i, 136); and the rest of the play is devoted to the suffering he encounters in trying to reclaim his former identity. Because he is not compelled to abdicate, he might easily have avoided the whole situation; but because he does abdicate, he may be said to cause the suffering he encounters. It is also true, however, that his willful abdication is not a sufficient cause of his suffering, since that suffering is created in part by his daughters' reaction, which is completely beyond his conscious control and his ability to predict. In this respect, Cordelia's rigid truthfulness and innocence contribute no less directly to the suffering than do Goneril and Regan's hypocrisy and greed, even though it is finally Cordelia who "redeems nature from the general curse/ Which twain have brought her to" (IV, vi, 202–203).

From this analysis it begins to be clear that several of the widely received generalizations about tragedy are meaningless or misleading. Karl Jaspers asserts, for instance, that "absolute and radical tragedy means that there is no way out whatsoever." [13] Because the world operates in terms of cause and effect, there is some truth to this statement; but it really tells us nothing about the essential nature of tragedy. Jocasta and Teiresias repeatedly offer Oedipus a "way out," and each time he refuses to take it. What is the function of Ismene's role in *Antigone* if not to show that there is a very simple "way out" for the protagonist? Why is Hamlet so distressed at his failure "to be" if indeed "not to be" is an avenue which is completely closed to him? And why is Lear's abdication represented as being so arbitrary if he cannot do otherwise? If Jaspers means that once the causes are established, then the effects must follow, what he is saying is true though perfectly obvious. If, however, he means that not only the effects but also the causes are completely beyond the control of the characters in tragedy, then what he is saying is simply false. Misfortunes that befall someone when the causes are completely beyond his control are not tragic but pathetic. Unless the main character is in some significant sense responsible for the suffering which according to Freud is the "essential content of a tragedy," the pain (like that of a toothache) is meaningless, not tragic from a literary point of view. Jaspers' statement that "absolute and radical tragedy means that there is no way out whatsoever" is true only when we add the words "unless the protagonist irrevocably denies or abandons his identity."

Moreover, the Aristotelian doctrine of *hamartia* is completely misleading. Classicists are beginning to reexamine it after centuries of trying to discover the "flaw" in Greek tragic characters.

In his book *Story Patterns in Greek Tragedy*, Richmond Lattimore says, "I find, of the thirty-two extant plays, fifteen in which
the Tragic Fault has little or nothing to do with the main
action, and ten more where one could establish it as a major
theme only by straining the dramatic facts." [14] Interestingly,
Sophocles' *Antigone* and Euripides' *Hippolytus* are two of the
plays to which, according to Lattimore, the *hamartia* doctrine
may be said to apply. Of *Antigone* he says, "The Chorus charges
the heroine with the fault of stubbornness. She is stubborn. It
destroys her, of course, but it is not in the whole view seen as
weakness, fault, or flaw. Few, certainly, will argue that this is
meant to be Antigone's inner weakness which destroys her." [15]
Of *Hippolytus* he writes, "Euripides shows the flaw of self-satisfaction and pedantry in the young hero, but I am not sure he
means to. He could equally well be trying—as Sophocles may be
in *Ajax*—to show a man too good for the world he lives in; and
what the world does to such a man." [16] Lattimore indicates that
the word *hamartia* as used by Aristotle in the *Poetics* "cannot
signify a permanent characteristic in a person, pride, quickness
to anger, etc., but must refer to a mistaken or wrong act or to a
mistake that has been made." [17] He concurs with Else in thinking
that "Aristotle, in his context, must be talking about something
much more narrow and specific, namely, the misidentification of
a person." [18]

This reinterpretation of *hamartia* is not very helpful though—
what "misidentification of a person" is there in *Antigone* or *Hippolytus*? And how, if at all, does such a view illuminate those
works as tragedies? The problem cannot be solved merely by re-
defining a word in Aristotle's *Poetics*, because the difficulty is
much deeper than that. The doctrine of *hamartia* is simply an
attempt to take into account the protagonist's partial responsibility for the suffering which is essential to tragedy. This particular attempt is bound to be unsuccessful because it seeks to
reconcile the meaningfulness of tragedy with the assumption that
we live in a nontragic world. Aristotle seems to take it for granted
that in the real world virtue always produces happiness, and evil
conduct or error inevitably leads to suffering. If, in a literary

tragedy, an apparently good man suffers, then it must be because of some *hamartia*, peculiar to him as an individual. Whether we take *hamartia* to mean "tragic fault" or simply "misidentification of a person," the conception still rests on the idea that the hero somehow blunders in a way that a really virtuous man ought to be able to avoid, and he is therefore "to blame" for the suffering which his action partly causes.

The moralistic nature of Aristotle's thought emerges very clearly in a sentence that appears in the same section of the *Poetics* as the *hamartia* statement: "Good and just men are not to be represented as falling from happiness into misery; for such a spectacle does not arouse fear or pity in us—it is simply revolting." [19] It follows from this that unless we can find some kind of *hamartia* in such characters as Antigone and Hippolytus, the plays in which they appear are not tragedies at all—just revolting spectacles. But Antigone speaks the unvarnished truth when she says, "I stand convicted of impiety,/the evidence my pious duty done." And Artemis is correct when she tells Hippolytus, "The nobility of your soul has proved your ruin" (line 1390). Aristotle derives the *hamartia* doctrine not from the tragedies but from his own moral views, and it remains true that no moralizing can ever touch the real meaning of tragedy. As Walter Kaufmann rightly observes, "Tragedy occurs where men have come to see that even an exemplary devotion to love, truth, justice, and integrity cannot safeguard a man against guilt." [20]

In attempting to describe the nature of tragedy, we are forced back to our own statement that characterizes any given tragedy as "a literary work, predominantly somber in tone, in which the main character encounters some significant misfortune for which he himself is partly, though not wholly, responsible." Tragedy centers upon the idea of *necessary suffering*, and we must bear in mind the essentially double meaning of the two words, "responsible" and "necessary." The suffering which a tragedy represents is neither accidental nor inevitable; the hero's action is, to be sure, one cause of the suffering, but the effect goes far beyond what we can explain by means of that one cause. Nevertheless, the hero accepts the suffering voluntarily though reluctantly. He takes the guilt upon himself, and in so doing he "frees the chorus of theirs."

The central event recorded in the gospels is the crucifixion, and it is here that the obvious similarity to the tragic pattern lies. When St. Paul reduces his message to its simplest form, it is this event that he emphasizes: "When I came to you, brethren, I did not come proclaiming to you the testimony of God in lofty words or wisdom. For I decided to know nothing among you except Jesus Christ and him crucified" (I Cor. 2:1–2). Whatever else it may also have been, the crucifixion was for Christ a "significant misfortune," which he accepted "voluntarily though reluctantly." This conclusion is borne out by his Gethsemane prayer: "My Father, if it be possible, let this cup pass from me; nevertheless, not as I will, but as thou wilt" (Matt. 26:39; cf. Mark 14:36, Luke 22:42). Peter, upon whom the church is built (Matt. 16:18), thought the events leading up to the crucifixion so disastrous that he three times denied having any connection with Jesus (recorded in all four gospels). The crucifixion involves a self-sacrifice which, from the Christian viewpoint, redeems all who believe in Christ. In this sense, the words of John the Baptist, "Behold, the Lamb of God, who takes away the sin of the world!" (John 1:29) seem closely related to Freud's statement that the protagonist in tragedy takes the guilt upon himself "in order to free the chorus of theirs." All this seems relatively obvious. Our task will be to establish whether, according to the gospel writers, Jesus himself was "partly though not wholly responsible" for the crucifixion, whether the suffering he underwent was "necessary" in our sense of the word, and (as a separate matter) whether the resurrection destroys or even significantly diminishes the tragic meaning of that event.

According to all four gospel writers, Jesus repeatedly predicted his own suffering and death, but all four of them treat the effect of these predictions in a way that seems strange at first. Both Mark and Luke record the predictions in completely unambiguous terms and then add the words: "But [the disciples] did not understand the saying, and they were afraid to ask him" (Mark

9:30–32, Luke 9:44–45, 18:31–34). Matthew makes the same point dramatically rather than narratively: after Christ makes his prediction, Peter exclaims, "God forbid, Lord! This shall never happen to you"; and Jesus responds, "Get behind me, Satan! You are a hindrance to me; for you are not on the side of God, but of men" (Matt. 16:21–23). John treats the matter least directly of all; and, as narrator, he gets ahead of his story in doing so. He offers Christ's statement about the rebuilding of the temple in three days as a prediction of his death and resurrection, and then says, "When therefore he was raised from the dead, his disciples remembered that he had said this; and they believed the scripture and the word which Jesus had spoken" (John 2:18–22). Furthermore, according to Luke, it is only *after* the crucifixion and resurrection that Jesus flatly declares that his suffering and death were "necessary": "And he said to them, 'O foolish men, and slow of heart to believe all that the prophets have spoken! Was it not necessary that the Christ should suffer these things and enter into his glory?' And beginning with Moses and all the prophets, he interpreted to them in all the scriptures the things concerning himself" (Luke 24:25–27). Likewise, it is after the fact that Peter is represented as saying that Jesus was "delivered up according to the definite plan and foreknowledge of God" (Acts 2:23).

This manner of proceeding raises the question, why did the gospel writers insist first of all upon the fact that Christ made these predictions and at the same time upon the disciples' refusal to believe them until much later? The answer is perfectly clear. The gospel narrators were striving to present Christ as the agent of destiny and yet to preserve his freedom in embracing that destiny. They sought to convince their readers that his self-sacrifice was of cosmic significance and that it was at the same time freely offered. In order to do this, they had to show that the disciples arrived at such an understanding of Christ's role only retrospectively, whereas Christ himself was fully conscious of this destiny at a much earlier point.

Such an attitude on the part of the gospel writers has some interesting implications. It means, for instance, that from their point of view Christ conducted his life with full consciousness of his destiny and that when he took decisive action, knowing what the consequences would be, he acted in a way to *fulfill* that destiny, not to avoid it. (Cf. Oedipus's flight from Corinth in an effort to escape his fate.) The extent to which one acts with consciousness of the probable results is precisely the measure of one's freedom. And the greater one's freedom in acting, the greater his responsibility for what happens. Thus, paradoxically, Christ is in a highly significant way represented as being "responsible" for his own crucifixion, though he dreaded the event, though "his sweat became like great drops of blood falling down upon the ground" (Luke 22:44), and though he prayed that "this cup might pass from him." At the same time, of course, one cannot say that he was "fully responsible" for the obvious reason that it was people's reaction to Christ which finally determined the catastrophic conclusion—in different circumstances, his behavior would not have led to his crucifixion. That is to say, Christ's action as a whole was a necessary but not a sufficient cause of his suffering and death; or, in other words, Christ is represented in the gospels as being partly though not fully responsible for the significant misfortune which he encounters.

This conclusion is no trick of argument or rhetoric; it is an undeniable corollary of the gospel writers' attitude. Indeed, it is the ordinary, traditional mode of thinking which contains the trick of argument. That line of thought runs this way: the tragic hero's responsibility for what happens to him is to be explained in *moral* terms, by his *hamartia*—and this *hamartia* is of course some kind of fault or error; Christ has no fault and he commits no error; therefore, he is not a tragic figure. Strangely, no one who endorses this kind of thinking seems bothered by the obvious implication that if this is so, then Christ has no responsibility whatever for what happens to him, in which case he is the protagonist in the most naturalistic story ever written, crushed by forces he finds it utterly impossible to control or to avoid. Such a view makes Christ nontragic, not by placing him *above* the tragic level, but by reducing him far below it. It takes him out of the tragic realm and makes him merely pathetic. No believer, I think, would be willing to accept this view, and yet it follows necessarily from the denial of Christ's partial responsibility for his own crucifixion. And any believer who insists, on the contrary, that Christ was totally *free* (and therefore totally responsible for his own crucifixion) misses the whole point. Quite clearly, the gospels represent the Sanhedrin condemning Jesus because his claim was blasphemy, pure and simple (Matt. 26:65–66; Luke 22:70–71).

At least two other points need to be stressed: first, the question which Freud articulates when he asks, "But why did the hero of the tragedy have to suffer?" and secondly, the more technical meaning of the word *necessary*, as opposed to *accidental* on the one hand and *inevitable* on the other. For our purposes it will not be sufficient merely to quote the words of Jesus in which he *says* that it was "necessary that the Christ should suffer these things." Our task is rather to show the basis for that assertion and why the gospel writers considered it an essential part of the story.

Freud's answer to his own question about the necessity for the tragic hero's suffering is very simple: "He had to suffer because he was the primal father." It might be objected that this answer is not very helpful because it leads to the further question, "But why did the primal father have to suffer?" Nevertheless, as far as it goes, Freud's statement applies beautifully to the gospel narratives. It calls to mind the words of Jesus, "I and the Father are one" (John 10:30); and it drives home the point that it was this claim, which Jesus refused to withdraw even before the high priest, that led to his guilt in the eyes of the Jewish leaders. Thus, from the believer's viewpoint, Christ had to suffer as the result of a chain of facts: he was put to death because he would not renounce his claim to being the Messiah; and he could not renounce that claim because he actually was the Messiah.

The chain of facts does not imply, however, that Christ's suffering was either accidental or inevitable. Because Jesus was at least partly responsible for what happened, his suffering cannot be described as accidental. The emphasis that the gospel writers place upon Christ's being an agent of destiny precludes this possibility. They make it perfectly clear that Christ knew his course of action would lead directly to a collision with the authorities, hence the predictions of his suffering and death. But on the other hand, the collision was not inevitable, because Jesus was at all times free to abandon his mission—that is, to change his conception of his role as Messiah by accepting an immediate earthly kingdom rather than preparing the way (by his suffering) for the establishment of the future kingdom of God. This is perhaps the deepest meaning of his being tempted in the wilderness (Matt. 4; Luke 4). Such a change was the only "way out" for him; but unless we allow him that one, we deny that his self-sacrifice was freely given. In other words, we deny the meaning of the gospel itself. There was in fact no way whatsoever that he could have avoided the crucifixion and retained his earlier conception of himself as the Christ.

Furthermore, we cannot argue that though there may have been no other way out for him as he faced suffering and death, by his doing so he provided one for us, since his sacrifice was all-sufficient. If that were the case, it would hardly be necessary, as Jesus said it was, for anyone to "take up his cross daily" in order to follow Christ (Luke 9:23). Nor can we argue that he transcends the crucifixion by means of the resurrection, and that therefore the whole series of events is no longer tragic. One of the categorical statements which Jaspers makes is this one: *"There is no tragedy without transcendence"* [21] (italicized in Jaspers' text). If so, it would appear that the resurrection, far from diminishing the tragic character of those events, is one of the features which mark them as genuinely tragic, since without the resurrection the crucifixion would be meaningless—we would probably never have heard of it. Jaspers' argument defines tragedy right out of existence, because it asserts that *without* transcendence these events remain below the level of tragedy, and *with* transcendence they stand above the tragic level.

The content of the gospel narratives thus lends itself to the same kind of analysis as does the content of literary tragedy because both Christianity and tragedy recognize that unmerited suffering is sometimes necessary suffering. *For the moralist,* suffering that goes far beyond anything the sufferer may be said to deserve is ultimately meaningless; and its narrative or dramatic representation is, in Aristotle's words, "simply revolting." Unless he can somehow convince himself that the punishment fits the crime, the moralist will be uncomfortable. But tragedy has at its center figures like Antigone and Hippolytus, Hamlet and Lear, who suffer and who cause others to suffer in a way that cannot be explained simply in terms of what any of them deserve; and Christianity has at its center a suffering God. That is, both tragedy and Christianity perceive a meaning in unmerited but necessary suffering which is bound to escape the moralist. Since the Christian clings to belief and hope no matter what happens, instead of being immune to tragic experience, he is peculiarly susceptible to it, because the number of things which he can dismiss as meaningless is greatly reduced. To him, any disaster that brings suffering and death to his fellow human beings takes on the character of tragedy, though no tragic poet could ever use such a catastrophe for the end of his play.

In *Christianity and Tragedy*, Reinhold Niebuhr differentiates Christ from the tragic hero by means of a simple comparison: he recalls Christ's words, "Weep not for me. Weep for yourselves and for your children"; he then asserts that "one weakness of the tragic hero is that he is always crying 'Weep for me.' " [22] According to Niebuhr, "There is in other words an inevitable element of self-pity in classic tragedy." But one quotation is enough to cast doubt upon this generalization. In the first episode of *Antigone*, which consists entirely of dialogue between the heroine and her sister, Ismene exclaims: "Oh my poor sister. How I fear for you!" Antigone replies, "For me, don't borrow trouble. Clear your fate" (lines 82–83). Such a response suggests the opposite of self-pity. It may be true that romantic tragedy often involves an element of self-pity, but to insist that there is "an *inevitable* element of self-pity in *classic* tragedy" is to distort the truth.

Occasionally, someone embarks upon a more systematic comparison of the bible and tragedy in an effort to prove that no

Christian tragedy can exist. Edmond Cherbonnier makes such an attempt in "Biblical Faith and the Idea of Tragedy." His most interesting and complex argument is based upon the "double perspective," which he identifies as "the basis of the tragic view of life, from Aeschylus to Sartre." [23] According to Cherbonnier, "The philosophical stage setting for tragic drama . . . consists of two shifting backdrops: the *ultimate perspective* of the detached observer, of the aesthete, in which all differences cancel each other out and in which no discord is possible; and the *finite perspective* of the man of action, in which strife and contradiction are the rule." [24] He describes the implications of this double perspective at some length:

> The spectator thus becomes part of the act, deliberately maintaining a conscious ambivalence. The moment he relaxes the tension between the two perspectives, the tragic effect dissolves. If he adopts the finite perspective to the exclusion of the ultimate, tragedy becomes either a morality play or a picture of unrelieved frustration. If he relinquishes the finite in favor of the ultimate perspective, and allows himself to view the hero's world *sub specie aeternitatis,* he realizes that the whole play is really "much ado about nothing." [25]

Cherbonnier's own attitude toward all of this soon becomes clear. He repeatedly makes such statements as the following: "What this really constitutes is an invitation to maintain a schizophrenic oscillation between the two perspectives, and thereby to become a party to one's own hypnosis." [26]

Taken as a whole, however, his analysis of this aspect of tragedy is fairly accurate. The astonishing part of the argument comes in his interpretation of the bible. He contends that in opposition to the double perspective of tragedy,

> biblical philosophy acknowledges no such convenient pretext for equivocation. Throughout the Bible there runs a single criterion of both truth and goodness, equally applicable "on earth as it is in heaven." This is the philosophical significance of the concept of God as Creator. . . . Whereas tragedy regards this present world as the negation of the "divine," the Bible asserts that there is no necessary incompatibility between it and the very nature of God himself. . . .

Even if the Old Testament accounts of God's walking on the earth are not historically true, the point remains that he is the *kind* of God who *could* do so, if he chose. And in the New Testament, he did so choose.[27]

What Cherbonnier never satisfactorily explains is why, if "there is no necessary incompatibility between [this present world] and the very nature of God himself," God's walking upon the earth, as described in the New Testament, should culminate in the long walk to Golgotha under the weight of a heavy cross. Cherbonnier asserts that tragedy attempts "to reconcile the spectator to [evil and suffering] by persuading him that they are necessary" and concludes that "all such attempts to explain evil only end by explaining it away." [28] And again, "In holding that human disaster *need* not happen, the Bible takes a far more serious view of it than tragedy, which either capitulates in resignation or exhausts itself in futile protest." [29] Jaspers is helpful at this point because he makes it perfectly clear that a view which regards evil as unnecessary is definitely untragic—his term for this view is "pre-tragic." He describes tragic knowledge and goes on to say: "No such tragic outlook develops wherever man succeeds both in achieving a harmonious interpretation of the universe and in actually living in accord with it. That is to a great extent what happened in ancient, especially in pre-Buddhist, China. In such a civilization, all misery, unhappiness, and evil are merely temporary disturbances which never need occur." [30]

The weakness in Cherbonnier's argument is not difficult to locate. He uses the terms "this present world" and "the world which the Bible describes" interchangeably, and he seems to assume that "the world which the Bible describes" is fully represented in the first chapter of Genesis. That is, he makes no distinction between the *created order* and the *fallen order*. According to Genesis 1, God created the world, and he "saw that it was good." Then, according to Genesis 3, Adam sinned; and from then on a different order of human existence obtained in the world. This distinction is perfectly clear in the first chapter of the fourth gospel: "The true light that enlightens every man was coming into the world. He was in the world, and the world was made through him, yet the world knew him not. He came to his own home, and his own people received him not" (John 1:9–11). As the created order, the world was Christ's "own home"; but as the fallen order, the world into which he came "knew him not." If a person is forcibly ejected from his own home and disowned by his own family, there is a real sense in which the home and family are no longer his, though he may have built the house with his own hands and populated it with his own flesh. It is for this reason that Jesus, according to more than one of the gospel writers, says, "Foxes have holes, and the birds of the air have nests; but the Son of man has nowhere to lay his head" (Matt. 8:20, Luke 9:58). Genesis 3 is, after all, no less important to understanding "the kind of world the Bible describes" than is Genesis 1.

Cherbonnier's argument culminates in this statement: "Where tragedy tends to call one and the same event both good, from one perspective, and evil, from the other, there is no trace of such ambivalence in the Bible." [31] In the light of the New Testament, this assertion is simply amazing. What does the crucifixion mean to the Christian if not that it is at one and the same time a disaster and a miracle, the worst failure and the greatest success in world history? At one stroke, God abandoned his own son and redeemed the world. Yet, this attitude is possible only for the believer, who sees the crucifixion as both the epitome of the problem of evil and as the source of the world's salvation. To the unbeliever, who refuses to engage in what Cherbonnier scornfully calls "a constant flirtation with two perspectives at once," [32] it is neither of these. St. Paul understood the matter clearly: "For the word of the cross is folly to those who are perishing, but to us who are being saved it is the power of God" (I Cor. 1:18).

Behind this double meaning of the crucifixion stands the double nature of Christ himself: from one perspective he is man, from the other he is God. Historically, Christianity has erred in proportion as it has lost sight of this two-fold nature of Christ. At times the church has stressed the divine aspect to such an extent that it seemed to many Christians almost presumptuous to seek to emulate him—he is God, and we are clay. At other times it has emphasized the human element so strongly that to many he became a sentimentalized conception of the good man. Either view robs the gospel narrative of its power, since that power depends finally upon the double perspective which, we are told, is characteristic of tragedy but utterly foreign to the bible. We identify with Christ in his suffering because, like us, he is a man; and we are able to bear those sufferings only because he, unlike us, is God.

The double perspective from which the Christian views Christ as both man and God thus requires the cooperation of the believer no less than the double perspective of literary tragedy requires it of the sympathetic observer. The believer "must be willing to hold both perspectives before him in a kind of tension," and maintain "a conscious ambivalence. The moment he relaxes the tension between the two perspectives, the tragic effect [and, we argue, the power of the gospel] dissolves." [33] If he sees Jesus merely as a man, he must reject the resurrection; and the gospel narrative becomes "a picture of unrelieved frustration." If he sees Jesus purely as God, then surely his "sufferings" were not in any sense unbearable to him—they seem really to be "much ado about nothing." Were we to take the same uncharitable view of the believer which Cherbonnier takes of the person who enters into the experience of literary tragedy, we could say that as long as one wears these "bifocal lenses" of belief, he is able to identify with Christ "sufficiently to derive a vicarious sense of dangerous living," and at the same time remain "secure in the knowledge" that Christ's sacrifice guarantees his (the believer's) salvation.

According to Cherbonnier, "Perhaps the furthest penetration by the tragic view of life into Christian usage . . . is the famous liturgical phrase, *felix culpa.*" [34] Following Professor Lovejoy's commentary on Milton's *Paradise Lost*, he indicates that "whereas in the early part of the poem the fall of Adam is deplored as a 'ruinous enormity,' by the time the reader arrives at the Twelfth Book, Adam begins to describe his transgression as a ground for self-congratulation!" [35] Cherbonnier does not, however, explain how this change of attitude is any different from the one which Peter undergoes between the occasion when he denies Christ not once but three times and the occasion when he preaches the sermon urging his listeners to be baptized in the name of Jesus, who had been "delivered up according to the definite plan and foreknowledge of God." Apparently, Peter regarded his connection with the final events of Jesus' life as a "ruinous enormity" at the time those events occurred, but as "a ground for self-congratulation" at some later point.

Such arguments as the ones we have just examined appear to have been devised as rationalizations for a conclusion that was formed on some other basis. One suspects that this other basis consists of two self-evident facts: (1) in retrospect, Christ upon the cross seems to the Christian triumphant rather than defeated, and (2) because the writers who devised and first exploited the tragic mode in literature lived before the time of Christ, they used that mode to convey insights which are pre-Christian. The first of these two facts is accounted for by the believer's acceptance of the double perspective which characterizes the observer's relation to tragedy in any form, and the second fact is obvious but irrelevant. If we conclude that there can be no Christian tragedy because tragedy is older than Christianity, we might almost as reasonably conclude that because the Greek language was devised before the Christian era to convey pre-Christian ideas, Greek could not be used (as it is in the New Testament) to communicate "what is essential to the Christian."

The relationship between Christianity and tragedy must be stated as a paradox. The same Jaspers who asserts that "no genuinely Christian tragedy can exist" provides the key to this relationship, though he apparently does so unconsciously. He ends one chapter by saying that "Christ is the deepest symbol of failure in this world, yet he is in no sense tragic. In his very failure he knows, fulfills, and consummates." The first paragraph of the next chapter contains this sentence: "Paradoxically, however, when man faces the tragic, he liberates himself from it." [36] Even from these two statements we can see that Christ submits himself so totally to tragic experience that in the end he totally liberates himself from it. Though it may seem that "what is essential to the Christian cannot even emerge in tragedy," the truth is that *everything* which is essential to the Christian actually *does* emerge in the tragic narrative which we have in the four gospels. If some Christians believe that literary tragedy is incapable of communicating what is essentially Christian, it is only because the tragedy recorded in the New Testament seems to them so powerful that all other tragedies are trifling and pale in comparison.

We can say, then, with Niebuhr that Christianity stands beyond tragedy—but not because Christianity is untragic. On the contrary, it does so only because Christianity is so profoundly and uncompromisingly tragic that it ends by seeming to lose its tragic character, by coming out on the other side. That is to say, its catharsis is almost total. But in order to be a Christian, the individual must in turn submit himself to the tragic just as Jesus did. How else may we understand the words, "Whoever does not bear his own cross and come after me, cannot be my disciple"? Christian tragedy *can* exist then, because even if "Christianity stands beyond tragedy," the raw material of literature is experience, and for anyone who accepts Christ's life as the model, experience is fundamentally tragic. Jesus himself framed the paradox with which we are confronted: "He who finds his life will lose it, and he who loses his life for my sake will find it" (Matt. 10:39). Losing one's life out of loyalty requires total submission to the tragic; no one can surrender his life in this way and remain serenely confident that all is well. If we are ever tempted to think otherwise, we should remember the words of Jesus upon the cross, "My God, my God, why hast thou forsaken me?"

This analysis does not pretend to demonstrate that literary Christian tragedy does exist, nor, if it does, what form such tragedy takes. It merely shows that the arguments advanced to support the contention that "no genuinely Christian tragedy can exist" are basically unsound. It reopens a question that many people, both believers and skeptics, would have us regard as closed. If as Jaspers indicates, "A Christian is bound to misunderstand, say, Shakespeare," [37] then we would be foolish to interpret *Hamlet* and *King Lear* as if they had any direct connection with historical Christianity. But we suspect that this assertion makes no better sense than saying that "an ancient Greek was bound to misunderstand, say, Sophocles." No one claims that it is grossly misleading to interpret Sophocles in the light of Greek religion, and no really good reasons have been adduced for believing that we will surely be misled if we try to understand Shakespearean tragedy in the light of Christianity. On the contrary it seems more likely that we will be led astray by denying categorically that Christianity is relevant to understanding Shakespearean drama, than by admitting the possibility that the New Testament may illuminate, for instance, Hamlet's dilemma.

II

The Two Sources of
Christian Tragedy

Therefore, if any one is in Christ,
he is a new creation;
the old has passed away, behold,
the new has come.
II CORINTHIANS 5:17

And this is the judgment,
that the light has come into the world,
and men loved darkness rather than light.
JOHN 3:19

⚜ Christian tragedy, despite innumerable assertions
to the contrary, not only *can* exist, but *does* exist; and our failure
to recognize this fact has led to serious confusion about some of
the most important works in Western literature. Critics who insist most emphatically upon interpreting Shakespearean tragedy
within the author's own historical context often ignore one of the
most easily accessible parts of that context, the English bible;
and others who profess to understand Dostoevsky attach no real
significance to the biblical knowledge he acquired during the
four years of his imprisonment at Omsk, when "the New Testament was the sole book allowed him." [1] On the one hand, a few
critics have sought to establish a connection between Christianity
and Shakespearean tragedy; but they have set forth no convincing
evidence, primarily because their methods are essentially nonlit-
erary. On the other, Dostoevsky commentators have hesitated to
assign any special importance to his intensive reading of the
bible, apparently because the elements of doubt and unbelief re-

main prominent in all his work. The assumption, however, that for the "real Christian" there is no continuing tension between faith and doubt is almost entirely baseless.

The relationship of Shakespeare and Dostoevsky to Christianity is both direct and deep; that is, they are indebted specifically to the New Testament, not to biblical commentators or religious reformers, and what they have borrowed is not merely random phrases or quotable verses, but the very fabric of biblical thought with its characteristic patterns of language and imagery. The New Testament as read by Shakespeare and Dostoevsky is, for our purposes at least, a literary document like any other; and we can hardly assess its influence upon them without examining it thoroughly. But the bible, for all its accessibility, presents special problems. We all know people who can quote scripture at length but who, Polonius-like, seem not to understand the implications of what they are saying, and one soon learns as a teacher of literature that he cannot expect the majority of college students to recognize even the most obvious biblical allusions and references. We must, therefore, immerse ourselves in the New Testament if we are to evaluate its impact upon these two writers, not treat it as a reference work to be explored only by means of a concordance. We must deal with it as a whole, showing which parts of it are relevant to literary tragedy, which parts are not, and what it is that accounts for this difference of relevance.

The New Testament itself falls more or less naturally into four main blocks of material. The first of these divisions includes the *synoptic* writings, which set forth most of the information we have about the life and teachings of Jesus and the activities of the early apostles. The second consists of the genuinely *Pauline* letters, which provide the intellectual basis for Christian theology. The third takes in the *deutero-Pauline* books, some of which were traditionally ascribed to Paul and all of which show the later development of Pauline thought. The last block consists of the *Johannine* writings, which are predominantly symbolic and imagistic in character, rather than intellectual in any systematic way. The only uncertainty about this method of classifying the New Testament books arises in connection with Ephesians and

Colossians; conservative scholars ascribe them to Paul himself, whereas some modern critics place them in the deutero-Pauline group. Disputes as to whether or not it was the same John who wrote the gospel, the letters, and the book of Revelation (also called the Apocalypse) do not affect the grouping; the Johannine writings may be regarded as constituting a single category no matter how many authors were actually involved.[2]

Though the synoptic writings no doubt govern any reader's response to the New Testament as a whole, these materials—together with the deutero-Pauline books—have not had as direct an influence upon tragic writers as certain other parts of the New Testament have had. The deutero-Pauline literature merely repeats Paul and adds some things which do not lend themselves to use in tragedy. It consists mainly of practical advice to young churches. The synoptic writings, too, though they contain the stuff of tragedy (particularly the passion of Christ and the experience of the first martyrs), have only a limited usefulness to the tragic writer. He would turn to them if he wanted to use actual story material from the New Testament; but when he does so, he has only two alternatives: he may retell a story which has already been adequately told, or else he may attempt to rework the story in contemporary terms. If he merely retells the old stories, he runs the risk of either distorting them until they are no longer recognizably Christian or of sticking so close to them that he will be regarded as having nothing new or significant to say. If he tries to modernize or adapt them, he often produces as the main character some sort of Christ-figure who suffers by comparison with the original from which he is drawn. Thus, whether he offers an historical version of the story, or a modern parallel, he is likely to defeat his own purpose. For these reasons the synoptic books, which are devoted primarily to storytelling, have had relatively little impact upon tragic literature.

The two sections of the New Testament which remain to be considered, the Pauline and Johannine writings, are the ones that have provided the basis for important literary tragedy. They are quite different from each other, though they are equally biblical and therefore equally authentic as sources for Christian tragedy, but historically, where the one tradition tends to be important, the other falls into obscurity. The Western church stresses the Pauline heritage, which represents the believer as a "new creation" in Christ, and pays scant attention to the apocalyptic vision of St. John the Divine; Eastern Orthodoxy strongly emphasizes Johannine revelation, and attaches less significance to Pauline intellectualism. The relationship of Shakespeare and Dostoevsky to these two traditions goes a long way toward explaining Shakespeare's anthropology and his conception of evil as well as Dostoevsky's mysticism and his idea of time. The two writers represent two fundamentally different modes of Christian tragedy, Shakespeare's being Pauline and intellectual, Dostoevsky's Johannine and prophetic.

Stated as simply as possible, our hypothesis is this: Shakespearean tragedy derives some of its principal motifs and conceptions from the letters of St. Paul, and the great Dostoevsky novels depend in similar fashion upon the Johannine writings. Different as they are, these two sources have contributed importantly to the production of two easily distinguishable but equally authentic varieties of Christian tragedy. Our present purpose is simply to clarify the differences between the two sources and to indicate briefly their relevance to certain works of Shakespeare and Dostoevsky.

In an article called "Pauline and Johannine Theology: A Contrast," Pierre Benoit juxtaposes the two biblical writers in a way that is extremely helpful.[3] Before comparing the two viewpoints in detail, he makes this general statement:

> The combined action of the Word and the Spirit of God appears to us in the Old Testament under two correlative but distinct aspects: creation and revelation. After having illustrated this idea textually, I will present for your consideration the thesis that Paul has retained more the aspect of creation, while John stresses revelation. These two different points of departure, this twofold illumination, disparate yet converging, seems to furnish a satisfying explanation of the agreements and differences of the two systems.[4]

Benoit draws primarily upon John's gospel, as we would expect a Westerner to do, in representing the Johannine viewpoint, though he ranges freely through the Pauline writings, including Ephesians and Colossians, for his Pauline examples. He mentions the letters of John occasionally; but he makes almost no reference to the Apocalypse. He concludes his introductory generalization with these words:

> It remains true, therefore, to say that in the final analysis salvation for John consists more in a re-birth to the life of a truly illuminated knowledge of God, while for Paul salvation essentially consists in the transition from death to life by means of a re-creation of the whole being.[5]

This broad distinction clarifies the fundamental difference between the two kinds of Christian tragedy, and a detailed analysis will make the distinction easier to understand and appreciate. For the moment, we may say that in Alyosha Karamazov we witness "a re-birth to the life of a truly illuminated knowledge of God," whereas in Lear we see the "re-creation of a whole being."

The first point at which Benoit distinguishes between the two views has to do with the conception of sin, and we can hardly overemphasize the importance of this difference. Since Benoit articulates the matter succinctly and well, let us begin by considering his statement:

> For Paul, *Hamartia* [sin] denotes an evil force, a personified power which characterized the old world and which by abiding in his flesh and giving him over to death, dominates and enslaves man. The sole means of destroying sin is to destroy this "sinful flesh" which has been made its docile instrument. This is to be achieved by a death which kills the sinner yet frees and prepares man to receive the Spirit. . . . Sin entered the world by the transgression of the First Adam and has been driven out by the obedience of the New Adam. In this New Adam, God has remade His work and created a New Man who no longer lives according to the flesh but according to the Spirit (Rom. 5–8).
>
> John's conception of sin is quite different. . . . In John's thought, sin is a refusal of the Truth, a refusal of the Light, a refusal to be-

lieve. . . . Sin is blind and, what is worse, is not aware of its blindness (9:41). . . . Sin, then, clearly consists in not believing Him whom God has sent, in not listening to His words, and in preferring darkness to the light (8:42–43, 45, 47; 3:18–21). For John sin is an offense against the light, whereas for Paul it is a disorder introduced in the first creation which the second creation seeks to correct.[6]

This brief comparison is perfectly adequate; but it is so condensed that it requires considerable explanation.

We observe, for instance, that Paul regards sin as "an evil force, a personified power." His most characteristic statement on the subject represents sin as a power which takes over the individual, subjugates his will, and destroys him as a free agent: "Now if I do what I do not want, it is no longer I that do it, but sin which dwells within me" (Romans 7:20). Thus Paul, despite the adjective which Benoit uses, does not simply equate sin with moral evil; instead he finds its effects in a man's persistent inability to convert his intention into successful action. In his *Theology of the New Testament*, Rudolf Bultmann makes precisely this point about Paul and relates it to the Pauline attitude toward "the flesh." [7] Explicating the same chapters which Benoit cites in his summary (Rom. 5–8), Bultmann says that

> this language stamps *flesh and sin as powers to which man has fallen victim* and against which he is powerless. The personification of these powers expresses the fact that man has lost to them the capacity to be the subject of his own actions. . . . It is . . . significant that "I" and "my flesh" can be equated. Under the viewpoint of "doing," they are identical; but if they can be opposed to each other in regard to "willing," then it is apparent that the subject-self, the true self of a man, is inwardly split. . . . Therefore "I" and "I," self and self, are at war with each other; i.e., to be innerly divided, or not to be at one with one's self, is the essence of human existence under sin.[8]

It is a paradoxical implication of this view, then, that the person who seeks to establish a reign of terror over his fellow human beings but who, for reasons that he himself cannot explain, fails in his purpose, clearly illustrates the Pauline conception of sin— *not* because of his evil intention, but purely because of his inability to achieve the goal which he sets for his own activity. The importance of this view, which separates the religious conception of sin from the moral conception of evil, is far-reaching. When all is said and done, Hamlet, a paragon of princely virtue, and Macbeth, a villain of the deepest dye, are "sinners" in exactly the same way: both know perfectly well what they want to do, and both find themselves divided and incapable of consistently effective action.

As both Benoit and Bultmann indicate, "flesh" and "death" are closely linked with Paul's idea of sin. "For I know that nothing good dwells within me, that is, in my flesh," writes the apostle in the passage quoted above. And again, he speaks of sin as "working death in me through what is good, in order that sin might be shown to be sin" (Rom. 7:13). The same association between "sullied flesh" and "death" runs through the great Shakespearean tragedies. Hamlet articulates it in his first soliloquy:

> O that this too too sullied flesh would melt,
> Thaw, and resolve itself into a dew,
> Or that the Everlasting had not fixed
> His canon 'gainst self-slaughter. (I, ii, 129–132)

When Gloucester cries, "O, let me kiss that hand," Lear replies, "Let me wipe it first; it smells of mortality" (IV, vi, 131–132). And Macbeth, his hand reddened by Duncan's murder, asks:

> Will all great Neptune's ocean wash this blood
> Clean from my hand? No, this my hand will rather
> The multitudinous seas incarnadine,
> Making the green one red. (II, ii, 59–62)

The flesh, recognized as the "docile instrument" of a force that divides and ruins the self, inspires horror in all three protagonists.

John conceives of sin, however, as "an offense against the light"; and the darkness which permeates the Dostoevsky novels has its origin in this conception. In the Johannine writings, Jesus himself is "the true light that enlightens every man" (John 1:9); and the evildoing of men springs from the darkness which prompts men to believe that they are self-sufficient and therefore have no need of Christ's light. Again, Bultmann helps to clarify matters:

> Before the light's coming all were blind. "Those who see" are only such as imagine they can see. "The blind" are such as knew of their blindness or know of it now that the light encounters them. The "blind" and the "seeing," accordingly, are not two groups that were already present and demonstrable before the light's coming. Now, and not before, the separation between them takes place in that each one is asked whether he chooses to belong to the one group or the other—whether he is willing to acknowledge his blindness and be freed from it or whether he wants to deny it and persist in it.[9]

Unlike Paul, John has no particular interest in the question of sin apart from a man's relation to Christ—he does not trace it historically to "the Old Adam," nor to anything else before the appearance of Christ. The metaphor itself precludes any such possibility, since the concept of "darkness" has no meaning apart from the concept of "light." But the dualism that pervades Johannine thought (light-darkness, sight-blindness, life-death) does not make it any more moralistic than Paul's view. John too sees man as being externally determined in his behavior, unable by any simple choice to cast off his blindness or to embrace life rather than death.

The complexity of John's idea of sin resides in the way that it reconciles the fact of determinism with the possibility of choice. According to Bultmann,

> Man cannot act otherwise than as what he is, but in the Revealer's call there opens up to him the possibility of *being* otherwise than he was. He can exchange his Whence, his origin, his essence, for another; he can "be born again" (Jn. 3:1 ff.) and thus attain to his true being. In his decision between faith and un-faith a man's being definitively constitutes itself, and from then on his Whence becomes clear. The "Jews," who are asserted to be "from below" (8:23) and are reviled as children of the devil, are those who by refusing to believe have anchored themselves to their sins (8:44). The children of God and the children of the devil are henceforth recognizable by whether one "does right" and "loves his brother" (I Jn. 3:10)—for

brother-love is the fulfilment of the "new" commandment (13:34; I Jn. 2:7 ff.).[10]

In other words, John does not simply equate sin with moral evil any more than Paul does. For him, evil-doing is a by-product, a deterministic result of the darkness which engulfs any man who has no contact with the light of Christ. As Bultmann indicates, in the Johannine view "sin is not an occasional evil occurrence; rather, in sin it comes to light that man in his essence is a sinner, that he is determined by unreality, Nothing." [11] Sin is therefore equivalent to acting in darkness and is represented as the result of failure to believe in Christ.

The relevance of this conception to Dostoevsky's way of representing the world is immediately obvious. In *Crime and Punishment, The Idiot,* and *The Brothers Karamazov,* there is no clear and easy distinction between "saints" and "sinners"; the only distinction is between those who *know* that they are sinners and those who do not. This second group, which includes such major characters as Raskolnikov, Ippolit Terentyev, and Ivan Karamazov, is not regarded with condescension or distaste. On the contrary, they are often the center of interest; and they, like "Marie" and Myshkin's fellow patient in Switzerland, are represented not "as guilty but only as unhappy," not as "mad" but as "frightfully miserable." In these novels almost everything is shrouded in darkness; and the righteous man, like Christ himself, "shines forth" as a guide to others. Father Zossima, in words obviously calculated by the author to apply to Ivan Karamazov, gives this idea its fullest expression:

> If the evil doing of men moves you to indignation and overwhelming distress, even to a desire for vengeance on the evil-doers, shun above all things that feeling. Go at once and seek suffering for yourself, as though you were yourself guilty of that wrong. Accept that suffering and bear it and your heart will find comfort, and you will understand that you too are guilty, for you might have been a light to the evil-doers, even as the one man sinless, and you were not a light to them. If you had been a light, you would have lightened the path for others too, and the evil-doer might perhaps have been saved

by your light from his sin. And even though your light was shining, yet you see men were not saved by it, hold firm and doubt not the power of the heavenly light. Believe that if they were not saved, they will be saved hereafter. And if they are not saved hereafter, then their sons will be saved, for your light will not die even when you are dead. The righteous man departs, but his light remains.

(*The Brothers Karamazov*, p. 386)

For Dostoevsky, as for John, the question of believing is always central; and a character's "unhappiness" is directly proportional to his inability either to believe or to love.

The second point at which Benoit distinguishes between Paul and John has to do with their attitude toward the Law, the Mosaic code, by means of which the conscientious Jew sought to live uprightly before God. Since John's position is the more conservative, Benoit deals with that first.

In John the notion of Law appears relatively rarely and remains basically faithful to the Old Testament concept of an expression of the divine will appealing to the spirit of man and soliciting his obedience. The Law is to be observed (John 7:19) and its commandments executed (7:22–23). . . . In announcing the coming of Christ, the Law entrusted to Moses appears as an early intimation of the grace and truth that God's only Son was to bring in His plenitude (1:14–17).

This testimonial nature of the Law is certainly recognized in Paul's writings, but there it is understood in the more restricted sense of moral knowledge revealing the commands which lead to uprightness (Rom. 7:12). Moreover, he mercilessly denounces the Law because of its negative and restrictive nature. . . . The Law is likened, then, to Sin and is considered as its docile partner. . . . Though it was the strength of the old creation, the Law disappears in the new creation in order to make place for the "law of faith" (Rom. 3:27), the "law of Christ" (Gal. 6:2), the "law of the Spirit" (Rom. 8:2) where uprightness flourishes in love (Gal. 5:14; Rom. 13:8 ff.) through obedience to the Spirit (Rom. 8:2).[12]

Thus, John seeks to show that there is a significant continuity between the Old Testament and the coming of Christ by representing the law as prefiguring his arrival: "Philip found Nathanael, and said to him, 'We have found him of whom Moses in the law and also the prophets wrote, Jesus of Nazareth, the son of Joseph' " (John 1:45). Paul on the other hand, asserts boldly that "Christ is the end of the law" (Rom. 10:4), and goes on to say that " 'All things are lawful for me,' but not all things are helpful" (I Cor. 6:12; cf. 10:23).

Paul's attitude toward the Law is of the utmost importance for understanding the situation in *Hamlet*. The apostle regarded the Law as being conducive not to life, but to death: "I was once alive apart from the law, but when the commandment came, sin revived and I died; the very commandment which promised life proved to be death to me" (Rom. 7:9–10). The revenge code in *Hamlet*, like the Jewish Law as understood by St. Paul, requires obedience and promises fulfillment; yet it leads only to death. Hamlet is preoccupied with death not because he is afflicted with some form of melancholy, but because he tries sincerely to live under the requirements of the revenge code. It may seem odd at first to designate the "immoral" revenge code as the equivalent of the "moral" Jewish Law; but from a Pauline point of view, both are open to the same objection: the people who place their faith in either one seek to take matters into their own hands, to set themselves up as judges, and to "establish their own righteousness" (Rom. 10:3–4). The moralist assumes, whether he realizes it or not, that man is indeed capable of "establishing his own righteousness"; and if he prefers the Jewish Law to the revenge code, he is merely saying that the former provides a good way for man to take matters into his own hands, whereas the latter offers a bad way. For St. Paul, however, the two ways would be equally disastrous: man is justified by *faith,* not by anything he might *do* in obedience to any code whatsoever.

The concepts which operate in *Macbeth* are closer to those in *Hamlet* than we might at first suppose. In both cases the protagonist is "inwardly split," unable to achieve his goal. And in both cases the hero attempts to act on the basis of information that comes to him from a supernatural source. Macbeth, who is on a moral level with Claudius in the earlier work, places his faith not in a revenge code but in the witches' utterances. Everything they say is perfectly true; and Macbeth stakes all on what they tell him, not realizing that when he takes their indicative statements as imperatives, he is moving toward death rather than toward life. If *Macbeth* is less puzzling to audiences and readers than is *Hamlet*, it is only because a moralistic explanation is less obviously absurd when applied to *Macbeth* than when applied to *Hamlet*. We are all more willing to see a bad man come to disaster than a good one; but if it were actually true that Macbeth suffers simply because he is evil, then the play would not be a tragedy by either Aristotelian or Christian standards. Macbeth suffers for much the same reason that Hamlet does; the moral difference between them only *seems* to change the case.

As Benoit indicates, the Law is not nearly so difficult a problem for John as it is for Paul; and Dostoevsky's attitude toward matters connected with the Law is therefore quite different from Shakespeare's. For his religious characters, such as Myshkin and Zossima, the law presents no difficulty at all; and for his atheists, such as Raskolnikov and Ivan, it becomes a problem not because they try to obey it, but because they regard themselves as being above the law in a way that ordinary men are not. Shakespeare's heroes strive with all their might to obey the Law as they see it, whatever we (the audience) may think of their particular "law," which seldom coincides with the traditional law of the land as it does in Dostoevsky. They place their trust in a mode of conduct which they follow as rigorously as they can; and later they are shattered to discover that it leads them not to life, but to "dusty death." For Dostoevsky, however, this problem simply does not exist. He never represents the Law as being a code that reflects in some special way the personality of his hero or the historical times in which his works are set and that promises life as the reward for obedience. Instead, he offers for our consideration a perfectly respectable body of law, descended from the ancients and refined by modern man to fit the needs of society. He is therefore concerned with crime in the usual sense, as Shakespeare never is, even in *Macbeth*. Dostoevsky's characters either obey the law as if it were second nature to them; or else they cynically deny that the law applies to them, while insisting that the mass of humanity must "live in submission" to the law whether they like it or not. Dostoevsky ultimately shows that this latter attitude is the product of "Satanic pride," which alienates a person from the rest of mankind and causes him to be "frightfully miserable."

Those Dostoevsky characters who believe themselves to be above the law do not claim to have an unconditional license to kill and to steal whenever they please. They may sacrifice the lives and property of others only in so far as it is "necessary" for achieving their great "humanitarian" purpose. To that extent, it is not only their privilege to transgress the law; it is also their *duty*, since otherwise humanity in general would not benefit from their ability to "utter *a new word*." Raskolnikov articulates this all very clearly under Porfiry's questioning:

> I maintain that if the discoveries of Kepler and Newton could not have been made known except by sacrificing the lives of one, a dozen, a hundred, or more men, Newton would have had the right, would indeed have been in duty bound . . . to *eliminate* the dozen or the hundred men for the sake of making his discoveries known to the whole of humanity. But it does not follow from that that Newton had a right to murder people right and left and to steal every day in the market. Then, I remember, I maintain in my article that all . . . well, legislators and leaders of men, such as Lycurgus, Solon, Mahomet, Napoleon, and so on, were all without exception criminals, from the very fact that, making a new law, they transgressed the ancient one, handed down from their ancestors and held sacred by the people.
>
> (*Crime and Punishment,* pp. 254–255)

As Razumihin, another character in the novel, points out, much of this has been said before by other people. "But what is really *original* in all this," he continues, "and is exclusively your own, to my horror, is that you sanction bloodshed *in the name of conscience*, and, excuse my saying so, with such fanaticism" (p. 258). That is, Raskolnikov's thinking elevates certain kinds of crime to the level of virtuous behavior; and it leads him into becoming not an "extraordinary" or "great" man, but a common thief and murderer, totally alienated from his fellow human beings, one who cannot honestly claim that there were extenuating circumstances connected with his crime.

In *The Brothers Karamazov* this same line of argument is more eloquently presented by the Grand Inquisitor. No wild-eyed young radical like Raskolnikov, the Inquisitor is an ascetic old man, who speaks with the wisdom of experience. An eminently respectable churchman, his visage reflects the "great sadness" which, according to Raskolnikov, all "really great men" must have on earth (*Crime and Punishment*, p. 259). His terminology is different from Raskolnikov's, but his division of humanity into two categories, his belief that most men are a distinctly inferior breed, and his "humanitarian" motives for taking the law into his own hands are exactly the same. He condemns Christ for removing "the rigid ancient law" so that "man must hereafter with free heart decide for himself what is good and what is evil, having only Thy image before him as his guide" (*The Brothers*, p. 302). The Inquisitor himself can do very well without "the rigid ancient law," but the "weak and vile" masses of men cannot. He will therefore take it upon himself to create a nontragic world in which these numberless inferior people will be delivered from their troubles:

> And all will be happy, all the millions of creatures except the hundred thousand who rule over them. For only we, we who guard the mystery, shall be unhappy. There will be thousands of millions of happy babes, and a hundred thousand sufferers who have taken upon themselves the curse of the knowledge of good and evil. Peacefully they will die, peacefully they will expire in Thy name, and beyond the grave they will find nothing but death. But we shall keep the secret, and for their happiness we shall allure them with the reward of heaven and eternity. Though if there were anything in the other world, it certainly would not be for such as they. It is prophesied that Thou wilt come again in victory, Thou wilt come with Thy chosen, the proud and strong, but we will say that they have only saved themselves, but we have saved all. We are told that the harlot who sits upon the beast, and holds in her hands the *mystery*, shall be put to shame, that the weak will rise up again, and will rend her royal purple and will strip naked her loathesome body. But then I will

stand up and point out to Thee the thousand millions of happy children who have known no sin. And we who have taken their sins upon us for their happiness will stand up before Thee and say: "Judge us if Thou canst and darest."

(The Brothers Karamazov, p. 308)

If there were a Razumihin present at this interview between Christ and the Inquisitor as there had been at the one between Porfiry and Raskolnikov, he might very well say that he had heard much of it before; but what is really *original* about it is the Inquisitor's sanctioning tyranny *in the name of religion,* "and, excuse my saying so, with such fanaticism."

The main difference between this interview and the earlier one is that the irony is much deeper here. The Inquisitor is represented as being a product of Ivan's mentality, a distillation of his beliefs and attitudes. He carries to its final conclusion the assumption that "all is permitted" to one whose purpose is, at least in his own judgment, noble and humanitarian. This "justifying purpose" is not really essential to the argument, however, since the real reason that "all is permitted" (at least as far as Ivan is concerned) is that without a belief in God and immortality there is nothing to prevent a man from doing whatever he pleases—"there is no virtue if there is no immortality," as Ivan says repeatedly. The important question always hinges upon belief in immortality, which for Dostoevsky is closely related to an obvious fact of life: if it does not matter tomorrow what I do today, then it does not matter today either. And conversely, if what I do today *does* matter right now, then it also matters tomorrow and the day after—it matters, indeed, forever. In short, my action is either significant in a way that time does not affect, or else it has no genuine significance at all. (Cf. the words of St. Paul, from whom the formula "all things are lawful for me" is borrowed: "If the dead are not raised, 'Let us eat and drink, for tomorrow we die,'" I Cor. 15:32.) Alyosha sees through the Inquisitor's "justifying purpose" just as Porfiry had seen through Raskolnikov's: "Your inquisitor does not believe in God, that's his secret!" And Ivan replies, "What if it is so! At last you have guessed it. It's perfectly true that that's the whole secret" (*The Brothers Karamazov,*

p. 310). But Ivan insists upon the "justifying purpose" because otherwise—and this is the supreme irony of the novel—he could not conceal from himself that he is simply articulating the rationale for the behavior of the very people he despises, those who torture innocent children. If he (and the Inquisitor) are "above the law," why should the torturers not also be "above the law"? The "justifying purpose" is no answer, since the individual himself decides whether or not his purpose really justifies what he is doing.

Dostoevsky saw great danger in the Pauline assertion, "All things are lawful for me," probably because it was a view that a person could easily adopt without ever believing in Christ as Paul did, in which case it led not to freedom but to anarchy. In his novels, the conception of freedom is antithetical to both the bondage implied by slavish obedience to any code and the anarchy produced by willful rebellion against legitimate authority. The freedom Dostoevsky advocated was nothing more nor less than "freedom in Christ," a freedom that brings with it the conviction that "we are all responsible for all." Men who possess such freedom obey "the law" not in order to justify themselves; they obey it willingly, even unconsciously, because otherwise they could not discharge their responsibility to and for others. We see Dostoevsky's Johannine attitude very clearly in his choice of John 12:24 as the epigraph for *The Brothers Karamazov* and his representation of Ivan as a modern Cain (Genesis 4; *The Brothers Karamazov*, p. 275). The novelist takes it to be a fact that "unless a grain of wheat falls into the earth and dies, it remains alone"; and Ivan, who refuses to be responsible for his brother, is driven "away from the ground" like Cain and becomes spiritually "a fugitive and a wanderer on the earth." Clearly, in this case Dostoevsky regards "the Law entrusted to Moses" as prefiguring "the grace and truth that God's only Son was to bring in His plenitude."

Benoit makes his third distinction between Paul and John by comparing their views on "justification" and "judgment." He treats Paul only briefly, but he has a good deal to say about John.

The closely allied theme of Justification is too well known in Paul to require long exposition. . . . To consider justification only in terms of a divine decision made known to the human intelligence and thereby to neglect the present change in the human condition that justification implies, would be to misconceive the Pauline problematic of an actual re-creation realized totally in Christ and inchoatively in the Christian. Justification for Paul is not a matter of knowledge; it is an intrinsic renewal of a person's being.

[In John, this] theme is encountered in the closely related idea of the Judgment which has been entrusted to the Son by the Father and which takes place in the very manifestation of the Light (Jn. 3:18–21). . . .

The judgment which justifies or condemns a man is again elevated by John to the realm of revelation so dear to him. . . . Elsewhere the Christ of the Johannine gospel says, "Now is the judgment of this world; now will the prince of the world be cast out" (12:31). This statement leads us to another aspect of the theme of justification in John, . . . namely, the great struggle between Jesus and the Prince of this world. The latter would suppress his antagonist and condemn Him to the cross (6:70; 8:44; 13:2, 27); however he can do nothing against him (14:30). He himself will be condemned by that very cross because once Jesus has been elevated from the earth He will draw all things to Himself (12:32). . . . The Johannine conception of the justice of the divine judgment thus clearly presents itself as a manifestation of defeat and victory: the defeat of the Father of lies and of those whom he deludes, and the victory of the truth-bringing messenger of the Father and of those who believe in Him.[13]

This third one is the last of Benoit's headings that we shall use for comparing the two biblical writers; and we shall deal with it more briefly than we did with the concepts of sin and the Law.

The Pauline emphasis upon re-creation, which is "realized totally in Christ and inchoatively in the Christian," is reflected in both Hamlet and King Lear as they appear in the last act of each play. It takes place only "inchoatively" in the two protagonists, but it is there none the less. Most critics are perfectly willing to leave unexplained the obvious change which we see in Hamlet after his return from "exile"; and indeed Shakespeare gives us no clear hint as to why it should have taken place. That it *does* take place, however, no one denies; and A. C. Bradley's assumption that it reflects the development of a "fatalistic" attitude is not satisfactory.[14] If we acquiesce in Bradley's conclusion, then the end of the play becomes arbitrary and meaningless, little more than a theatrical flourish to retrieve a faltering play. No one who takes *Hamlet* seriously will accept this implication; yet it follows necessarily from what Bradley says.

In *King Lear* the "re-creation of a whole being," which had occurred off stage and without explanation in *Hamlet,* becomes the center of dramatic interest. When the play opens, Lear is not only unable to return Cordelia's love, he is totally incapable of even comprehending it. The words *love* and *loved* are spoken more frequently in the first scene of *King Lear* than in any one scene of *Romeo and Juliet*; and Cordelia embodies from the very beginning a conception that St. Paul sets forth in I Corinthians 13, the classic text on Christian love. The agony Lear suffers in the course of the play comes about not because Goneril and Regan are "ungrateful," but because Lear, prior to any occasion for their ingratitude, is unable to love except in a self-seeking way. Lear utters magnificent poetry, and he gives away his entire kingdom; but still, as the Fool tells him very pointedly, he is "nothing" (I, iv, 185). St. Paul explains why this is so: "If I speak in the tongues of men and of angels, but have not love, . . . I am nothing. If I give away all I have, . . . but have not love, I gain nothing" (I Cor. 13:1–3). When he is finally reunited with Cordelia, Lear begins to comprehend his daughter's devotion, and to that extent he is "a new creation." The absence of any direct reference to Christ in *Hamlet* and *King Lear* does not alter the fact that both plays are permeated with Pauline thought.

Benoit's description of the Johannine attitude toward judgment and justification provides a perfectly appropriate framework for understanding "The Grand Inquisitor" and the views of Prince Myshkin. It is completely accurate to say that "The Grand Inquisitor" represents "the great struggle between Jesus and the Prince of this world." The Inquisitor, in a manner consistent with the historical time in which he appears, condemns Christ not to the cross but to the flames of an *auto-da-fé;* but in the end, as he shows by his reaction to Christ's kiss, "he can do nothing against him." On the contrary, "he himself is condemned" by the judgment he renders against Jesus, because the latter "draws all things to Himself." Alyosha points out the irony of Ivan's position as author of "The Grand Inquisitor" when he cries, "Your poem is in praise of Jesus, not in blame of Him—as you meant it to be" (*The Brothers Karamazov*, p. 309). So pervasive is the Johannine view in Dostoevsky that all of the characters reflect it even when they are trying their best to deny its validity. When they do deny it, they are represented as "refusing the light"—not because they want to, but because they are in the grips of a determinism that renders them unwilling and therefore unable to "exchange their Whence, their origin, their essence, for another." Dostoevsky does not condemn them; he merely shows the determinism working itself out to the end.

In *The Idiot*, Myshkin offers another crystal-clear example of Johannine imagery and thought when he exclaims near the end of the story, "Our Christ whom we have kept and they have never known must shine forth and vanquish the West" (p. 519). This one sentence reflects at least three distinctively Johannine features: the word *vanquish* comes from the line of thought which Benoit describes as representing "the justice of the divine judgment . . . as a manifestation of defeat and victory"; the phrase *shine forth* derives from the conception of Christ as "the light of the world"; and the division into "we" and "they" is also characteristically Johannine, the two terms corresponding to "the children of God" and "the children of the devil." Like his counterpart Ivan in *The Brothers Karamazov*, Ippolit Terentyev also uses Johannine language and imagery even to deny his belief in Christianity. He consciously echoes and imitates the Apocalypse in his "Essential Explanation"; indeed, the whole novel bears the impress of this final book of the bible.

These three categories, involving the conceptions of *sin, the Law,* and *judgment* or *justification,* provide a convenient way of comparing the Pauline and Johannine views; but they do not exhaust the contribution which the two blocks of biblical writings have made to the two principal forms of Christian tragedy. Other, less obviously theological conceptions may also be traced to these sources. Let us take, for instance, the parallel notions of time which emerge in statements about judgment, some of which we have already cited. Again, the biblical sources are easily distinguishable from each other; and the two kinds of tragedy reflect this difference. Since Paul is more historical than John in his orientation, he tends to deal more straightforwardly with past, present, and future, emphasizing their separateness as well as their interdependence. John, however, thinks in terms of a continuous present, which contains both past and future within a single inclusive moment. It is this feature, as much as any, which distinguishes John's gospel from the so-called synoptic gospels (Matthew, Mark, and Luke), all three of which tell stories that unfold in chronological order.

Paul's conception of time is revealed more clearly than anywhere else in what he says about Israel in relation to universal salvation (Rom. 9–11). He argues that Israelites will not be saved merely because they are descended from Abraham, since "it is not the children of the flesh who are the children of God, but the children of the promise are reckoned as descendants" (Rom. 9:8). Salvation depends upon belief in Christ (Rom. 10:9), whom Israel has rejected; but, says Paul, "through their trespass salvation has come to the Gentiles, so as to make Israel jealous" (Rom. 11:11). When they see what has happened among the gentiles, the Israelites will relent and become believers: "I want you to understand this mystery, brethren: a hardening has come upon part of Israel, until the full number of the Gentiles come in, and so all Israel will be saved" (Rom. 11:25–26). Thus, Israel is to be saved by a process which will operate through history. Paul represents the judgment of God, then, as being neither fully accomplished in the past nor completely revealed in the present, but as unfolding gradually with the passage of time.

John likewise discloses his idea of time in what he says about judgment. Even the verb tenses reflect his difference from Paul on this point: "And this is the judgment, that the light has come into the world, and men loved darkness rather than light, because their deeds were evil" (John 3:19). One of the verses cited by Benoit makes this difference even clearer: "Now is the judgment of this world, now shall the ruler of this world be cast out" (John 12:31). In both clauses the initial and emphatic word is *now*. In the first, everything that is said about "judgment" is contained in that one word; in the second, the implications of "judgment" are stated a little more fully, but the word *now* retains its emphatic position. Even a brief look at the analytical concordance confirms our suspicion that almost all of the Greek forms which are translated by the English word *now* occur significantly more often in John than in any other book of the New Testament. The Apocalypse reinforces this emphasis upon a continuous present; twice in the first chapter it refers to God as the one "who is and who was and who is to come" (Rev. 1:4, 8). And the Johannine letters, which read very much like the discourses of Father Zossima, show the same attitude toward time: "Beloved, we are God's children now" (I John 3:2). Thus for John, time is not so much a framework within which events take place and history unfolds as it is a continuous present which offers the possibility of knowledge and decision and action.

Hamlet and *Macbeth* both reflect the Pauline notion of time. In *Hamlet* the present is regarded primarily as the interim between an offense which had taken place in the past (Claudius's killing of the elder Hamlet) and the expiation of that offense, which marks the end of the play (the death of all the major characters). The initial murder has created a situation in which "the time is out of joint"; and Hamlet takes it upon himself to "set it right." Time in the ordinary sense continues to pass as the play progresses, but the hero's activity is to no real purpose —the "time" remains "out of joint" until the final scene. Hamlet attempts to bring about the expiation by his own industry, through obedience to the law of revenge. But for reasons which Paul makes clear in his discussion of the Law and sin, Hamlet finds himself "inwardly split" and incapable of achieving his purpose—hence his delay, which is simply a prolongation of the interim between offense and expiation. Because man is constituted as he is, the expiation cannot take place until the person

in question surrenders himself to Providence and ceases to be
"one that would circumvent God" (V, i, 75). Only when Hamlet
realizes that, as far as he himself is concerned, "The readiness is
all," does he distinguish clearly between present and future: "If
it be now, 'tis not to come; if it be not to come, it will be now;
if it be not now, yet it will come" (V, ii, 209–211). Once he submits himself willingly to the occasion which offers itself, the
"time" is finally "set right."

Similarly in *Macbeth,* time is dislocated through most of the
play, again because of offenses that require expiation. In this
play, however, the offender himself is elevated to the protagonist's role; and his task is therefore the opposite of Hamlet's.
Instead of trying to "set it right," he seeks to "beguile the time"
(I, v, 61) and to "mock the time" (I, vii, 81). That the attitudes
of the two heroes are parallel tends to be borne out by the
structure of the plays. In both cases, the protagonist articulates
his relation to time in the last lines of Act I, while speaking to
his alter ego: Hamlet tells Horatio that he must "set it right";
and Macbeth tells his lady that she, like him, must "mock the
time with fairest show." Ironically, Macbeth is no less "inwardly
split" then Hamlet in trying to reach his goal. He exerts himself
just as strenuously, and he examines his own conduct just as
painfully, but like Hamlet he finds that his greatest efforts are
in vain. Consequently, he becomes convinced that the days creep
on,

> To the last syllable of recorded time,
> And all our yesterdays have lighted fools
> The way to dusty death. (V, v, 21–23)

Not until Macduff, who was "from his mother's womb/Untimely
ripped," slays the tyrant, can it be truthfully said that "the time
is free" (V, viii, 55). Both heroes try to interfere with the historical process—the one to speed it up, to "set the time right," and
the other to arrest it, to "mock the time," and both fail, though
the one who finally surrenders to Providence becomes instrumen-
tal in removing what is "rotten in the state of Denmark."

The Johannine conception, which almost repudiates the historical character of time, is taken over by Dostoevsky without change. At the moments of Myshkin's greatest insight, when "his mind and his heart were flooded with extraordinary light" by the onset of an epileptic fit, he perceives the world in this way:

> "At that moment," as he told Rogozhin one day in Moscow at the time when they used to meet there, "at that moment I seem somehow to understand the extraordinary saying that *there shall be no more time*. Probably," he added, smiling, "this is the very second which was not long enough for the water to be spilt out of Mahomet's pitcher, though the epileptic prophet had time to gaze at all the habitations of Allah."
>
> *(The Idiot, pp. 214–215)*

As we learn later in the novel (p. 365), the "extraordinary saying" about time is quoted from the Apocalypse (Rev. 10:6, K.J.V.); and this phrase epitomizes the Johannine conception. It is because past and future are contained in the present that "we are all responsible for all," since it would hardly make sense that we should all be held responsible for all at the *final* judgment unless we are similarly responsible right now. From this point of view, the word *final* means not last in time, but supremely important. That is, the assertion that "we are all responsible for all" is simply another way of saying, "Now is the judgment of this world" (John 12:31). (Incidentally, these words appear only a few lines after the verse which serves as the epigraph for *The Brothers Karamazov*, John 12:24.) Except for the element of plot, historical time almost disappears in Dostoevsky. It is partly for this reason that his novels leave an impression upon the reader's mind which more closely resembles that of an immensely elaborate conversation than that of a story which unfolds gradually through time.

Because each set of conceptions is closely integrated, it is not surprising that Paul and John, both of whom seek to present a unified view of human experience, should be easily distinguishable from each other on every major point. It is inconceivable that a historical view of sin as something which "entered the world by the transgression of the First Adam and has been driven

out by the obedience of the New Adam" (Paul) should be combined with an attitude toward time which regards past and future as being, in some "final" way, incorporated into the present
(John). And it would be equally inconsistent to associate a view
which "mercilessly denounces the Law because of its negative and
restrictive nature" (Paul) with the assumption that man is
justified by the victory of one whom Moses had described in the
Law itself (John). What does come as a surprise to many, however, is that Shakespeare and Dostoevsky, different as they are
from each other on all of these major points, should both be
thoroughly biblical in their thought, the one taking his cue
consistently from Paul and the other from John. So completely
and unconsciously Pauline is the Western idea of man that we
long failed to identify the source of Shakespeare's anthropology.
Some critics even go so far as to claim that Hamlet is "the first
modern man," as though the conception of man that he embodies
had not existed before 1600. And so unfamiliar are we with the
Johannine tradition that we have usually regarded Dostoevsky's
Christianity as being something eccentric and personal, not to
be confused with "real Christianity." Both of these attitudes
must be surrendered in the light of purely literary evidence that
Shakespeare and Dostoevsky derived basic conceptions of man
and the world as well as highly significant patterns of language
and imagery from two sources within the New Testament itself,
the Pauline and Johannine writings.

III

Hamlet's *Hamartia*

I do not understand my own actions. . . .
I can will what is right,
but I cannot do it.
ROMANS 7:15–18

◄§ Oᴜʀ understanding of *Hamlet* has long been inadequate because we try to explain the four crucial elements of the
play by four entirely different frames of reference. We seek to
illuminate the hero's "tragic flaw" by means of Aristotle's *Poetics.*
We bring the insights of psychology, both Renaissance and
modern, to bear upon his "madness." We put forward his in-
tellectuality, his moral sensitivity, or even the nature of Renaissance revenge plays in an effort to understand his "delay." And
we turn to Senecan dramatic tradition or Christian doctrine to
explain the appearance of a ghost in a play which is obviously
relevant to the problems of twentieth-century life. As a result of
this interpretive fragmentation, the modern reader or viewer is
almost forced to adopt one or the other of two attitudes: either
the play itself is ultimately fragmented and therefore unsatisfactory, or it is mysteriously unified by the power of Shakespeare's
genius in a way that we can never hope to understand. But both
attitudes finally imply that the play is incomprehensible. The
only difference between them is that the first one attributes this
incomprehensibility to some fault of Shakespeare's, while the
second attributes it to some fault of our own.

Even more disconcerting than our inability to interpret the
play as a coherent whole is the fact that our partial explanations
fail to resolve the limited problems which they treat. The psy-

chological view of Hamlet's madness significantly illustrates this failure. Though the Freudian commentators have contributed heavily to the modern view of Hamlet's dilemma as a psychological problem, they did not initiate the psychological approach to the play; non-Freudian critics still carry on a running dispute as to whether the hero's madness is feigned or real.[1] Neither alternative is convincing, because if the critic insists that Hamlet's madness is feigned, then his apology to Laertes (V, ii, 215–233) is a lie or a feeble excuse at best; and if one claims that the madness is psychologically genuine, he is perplexed by the comparison with Ophelia's derangement, which Laertes unironically calls "a document in madness" (IV, v, 177). Any *general* psychological interpretation of the protagonist's character explains very little about Hamlet's particular case, while any *special* or detailed psychological view fails to account for the almost universal tendency of readers and viewers to identify themselves with the hero. In *The Heart of Hamlet,* Bernard Grebanier avoids these inconsistencies by denying categorically that Hamlet is insane or that he ever pretends to be, but Grebanier makes no attempt to explain why Hamlet should use the word "madness" in his apology to Laertes.[2] In short, he denies that the "sore distraction" which Hamlet himself calls "madness" is insanity, but he neglects to say what it is.

The effort to specify Hamlet's "tragic flaw" in terms of Aristotle's *Poetics* has been no more successful than the attempt to understand his "sore distraction" by means of psychology. The undertaking is hazardous from the outset because Aristotle, to the dismay of translators and commentators, does not clarify the word *hamartia* in the *Poetics.* The word is translated variously as "error or frailty" (S. H. Butcher), "error of judgement" (Ingram Bywater), and "inadequacy or positive fault" (Preston H. Epps). This ambiguity permits the critic to designate whatever shortcoming he finds in Hamlet as the "flaw" which causes his undoing. The main problem here is that some very distinguished critics, including E. E. Stoll, assert that Hamlet has no flaw that would account for his fall.[3] A statement in Section 14 of the *Poetics* further compounds the difficulty of interpreting *Hamlet* by means of Aristotle. Discussing the least tragic possibility, Aristotle writes: "Of all the possibilities, the worst is the situation in which some one, aware of the relationship [between himself and his intended victim], is about to do another a deadly injury, and does not do it. The situation is revolting to our sense of natural affection; and it is not tragic—pity is not aroused —because the intended victim does not suffer" (Lane Cooper's translation).

In *Hamlet: Father and Son,* Peter Alexander seeks to avoid the difficulties connected with applying Aristotelian theory to *Hamlet* by denying that the concept of *hamartía* significantly illuminates the play's meaning.[4] But this judgment ignores a highly significant strain of imagery in the play, imagery which suggests that Shakespeare was indeed concerned with some concept of *hamartía*. Since that imagery figures prominently in Hamlet's apology to Laertes, let us look first to it and to what the critics have had to say about it.

> Give me your pardon, sir. I have done you wrong,
> But pardon't, as you are a gentleman.
> This presence knows, and you must needs have heard,
> How I am punished with a sore distraction.
> What I have done
> That might your nature, honor, and exception
> Roughly awake, I here proclaim was madness.
> Was't Hamlet wronged Laertes? Never Hamlet.
> If Hamlet from himself be ta'en away,
> And when he's not himself does wrong Laertes,
> Then Hamlet does it not, Hamlet denies it.
> Who does it then? His madness. If't be so,
> Hamlet is of the faction that is wronged;
> His madness is poor Hamlet's enemy.
> Sir, in this audience,
> Let my disclaiming from a purposed evil
> Free me so far in your most generous thoughts
> That I have shot my arrow o'er the house
> And hurt my brother. (V, ii, 215–233)

Dr. Johnson regarded the excuse which Hamlet here offers as being unworthy of a hero: "I wish Hamlet had made some other defence; it is unsuitable to the character of a brave or a good man to shelter himself in falsehood." [5] A. C. Bradley counters by asking, *"What* other defence can we wish Hamlet to have made? I can think of none. He cannot tell the truth." [6] Among contemporary critics, Dover Wilson and Harry Levin defend the sincerity of Hamlet's apology. But Wilson says only that "to question the good faith of his request for pardon and of his plea of 'a sore distraction', as most critics have done, is to murder a beautiful effect." [7] Levin shows his misgivings about the meaningfulness of the apology he has described as reflecting a "touching sincerity" by characterizing it a few pages later as "disingenuous." [8] All four critics seem at least slightly uneasy when commenting upon the passage, and not one of them regards it as furnishing genuine insight into the crucial problems of the play. It is here, however, that the meaning of *Hamlet* comes closest to being explicit.

According to Liddell and Scott's *Greek-English Lexicon,* the primary meaning of *hamartáno,* the verb from which *hamartia* is derived, is "miss the mark, esp. of a spear thrown." (Other meanings include "fail of one's purpose, go wrong," "fail to do, neglect," and secondarily, "do wrong, err, sin.") Now the image with which Hamlet concludes his apology, "I have shot my arrow o'er the house/And hurt my brother," might seem less significant than it does if it were not one of a whole series of miss-the-mark images appearing throughout the play. Consider, for instance, the one in the player's speech about Pyrrhus's killing of Priam:

> His antique *sword,*
> Rebellious to his arm, lies where it falls,
> Repugnant to command. Unequal matched,
> Pyrrhus at Priam drives, *in rage strikes wide,*
> But with the whiff and wind of his fell sword
> Th' unnervèd father falls. Then senseless Ilium,
> Seeming to feel this blow, with flaming top
> Stoops to his base, and with a hideous crash
> Takes prisoner Pyrrhus' ear. For lo! his *sword,*
> Which was declining on the milky head
> Of reverend Priam, *seemed i' th' air to stick.*

So as a painted tyrant Pyrrhus stood,
And like a neutral to his will and matter
Did nothing. (II, ii, 457–470)

Pyrrhus's position here is exactly analogous to Hamlet's later in the play, in which case Denmark corresponds to Ilium and Claudius to Priam. In another, more general way, Pyrrhus's predicament parallels that of Claudius himself as he describes it in the prayer scene:

My stronger guilt defeats my strong intent,
And like a man to double business bound
I stand in pause where I shall first begin,
And both neglect. (III, iii, 40–43)

Claudius twice uses miss-the-mark images. He does so when he is planning what he will do in order that no one may blame him or Gertrude for Polonius's death. They will explain to their wisest friends what has happened—

[So, haply, slander]
Whose whisper o'er the world's diameter,
As level as the *cannon* to his blank
Transports his poisoned shot, *may miss our name*
And hit the woundless air. (IV, i, 40–44)

He does so again in explaining to Laertes why he has not punished Hamlet for killing Polonius: first, because he does not want to offend Gertrude; and second, because he does not dare to go against the general public, which holds Hamlet in high esteem.

. . . so that my *arrows*
Too slightly timbered for so loud a wind,
Would have reverted to my bow again,
And not where I had aimed them. (IV, vii, 21–24)

The significance of weapons and shooting dominates the last scene of the play. It is no more than metaphorical in the analogy with archery which Hamlet uses to end his apology; but it rises above mere metaphor when Hamlet, having changed his attitude toward the way he will seek revenge for his father, declares that "The readiness is all," and goes to meet his enemies on their own ground by accepting Laertes' challenge to a duel. Only then does he score "A *hit*, a very palpable hit" (V, ii, 270). And of course, Fortinbras ends the play by speaking of Hamlet as a soldier and issuing the command, "Go, bid the soldiers shoot."

Unless we simply ignore this wealth of related imagery, we cannot lightly dismiss the concept of *hamartia,* as Alexander would have us do. Actually, his method of dealing with the *hamartia* problem is like Grebanier's way of avoiding the "madness" problem. Both critics, because they see that all traditional solutions are inadequate, not only reject these solutions but declare that the problems themselves are spurious. But in doing so, they disregard some highly significant elements in the play. At this stage of *Hamlet* criticism, the essential problem may be stated as follows: (1) how to account, in nonpsychological terms, for what Hamlet calls his "madness"; (2) how to explain the use of *hamartia* imagery in *Hamlet* without getting into the difficulties that result from applying Aristotle's *Poetics* to the play; and (3) how to provide a single frame of reference that will not only account for the *hamartia* imagery and the "madness," but will explain the ghost's function and Hamlet's "delay." Fortunately, such a frame of reference does exist and was almost certainly familiar to Shakespeare himself.

In the seventh chapter of his letter to the Romans, St. Paul identifies himself with the insoluble problem which man faces under the Jewish law. He writes as follows:

> We know that the law is spiritual; but I am carnal, sold under sin. I do not understand my own actions. For I do not do what I want, but I do the very thing I hate. Now if I do what I do not want, I agree that the law is good. So then it is no longer I that do it, but sin which dwells within me. For I know that nothing good dwells within me, that is, in my flesh. I can will what is right, but I cannot do it. For I do not do the good I want, but the evil I do not want is what I do. Now if I do what I do not want, it is no longer I that do it, but sin [*hamartia*] which dwells within me.

So I find it to be a law that when I want to do right, evil lies close at hand. For I delight in the law of God, in my inmost self, but I see in my members another law at war with the law of my mind and making me captive to the law of sin which dwells in my members. Wretched man that I am! Who will deliver me from this body of death? (Rom. 7:14–24)

The first thing that we notice about the passage is that Paul's description of how sin dominates man under the Law exactly parallels Hamlet's excuse to Laertes for his own behavior. Hamlet says that he himself was not responsible for the injury Laertes has suffered; instead, the fault *residing in* Hamlet was responsible. In structure, the two accounts are identical—both are conditional statements—and both attribute error to something which is *within* the self but somehow distinct *from* it. Compare Hamlet's words with Paul's, ignoring for the moment the word "madness" in the first case, and the words "sin which dwells within me" in the second:

> If Hamlet from himself be ta'en away,
> And when he's not himself does wrong Laertes,
> Then Hamlet does it not, Hamlet denies it.
> Who does it then? His madness. (V, ii, 223–226)

> Now if I do what I do not want, it is no longer I that do it, but sin which dwells within me. (Rom. 7:20)

If we can accept for a moment the hypothesis that there is a connection between Hamlet's apology and Romans 7, we observe that since Paul's word for sin is the Hellenistic Greek word *hamartía*, Hamlet's "madness" and his *hamartía* (his "missing the mark," the "sin which dwells within him") must be one and the same thing. Here we have precisely what we need: a non-psychological explanation of the "madness," and a justification for the *hamartía* imagery without bringing in Aristotle. The implications of this point are very significant, because we see for the first time that what critics have ordinarily regarded as two separate problems is really only one. The commentators have said in effect, "Hamlet is burdened with two afflictions—one which *he* calls his 'madness,' and another which *we* call his 'tragic flaw.' " Why it has never occurred to anyone that these might be one and the same thing is not clear.

We notice too that some of Paul's attitudes as expressed in this passage are strikingly similar to the ones reflected in Hamlet's soliloquies. Paul's obvious distaste for "the flesh" suggests "O that this too too sullied flesh. . . ." Paul's "Wretched man that I am!" is not very different from "O, what a rogue and peasant slave am I!" And Paul's "I do not understand my own actions. . . . I can will what is right, but I cannot do it" is really very close to Hamlet's

> I do not know
> Why yet I live to say, 'This thing's to do,'
> Sith I have cause, and will, and strength, and means
> To do't. (IV, iv, 43–46)

These parallels indicate that the problem of Hamlet's "delay" is not a question of motivation in dramatic terms, indeed that it is not simply a literary question, but a theological one as well. If when one speaks of the "Hamlet problem," he means the question why Hamlet does not quickly take direct action which would "hit the mark," he could just as well call it the "St. Paul problem"—perhaps better so, since Paul articulated it long before Shakespeare did. The person who would ignore the whole issue by saying that if Hamlet did not delay, there would be no play, is really only saying in obvious fashion that if there were no problem, there could be no presentation of the problem. But such an assertion in no way argues that the problem itself is contrived or unreal.

Hamlet's "delay" comes about not because he consistently fails to act, but because his actions utterly miss the mark. If we apply Paul's words to Hamlet's situation, we may say that the "good he wants" is to redress the killing of his father; but the "evil he does not want" (the murder of Polonius and the "contriving against" his mother) is "what he does." And like Paul, the only explanation he can give is that it was not he that did it, but something ("madness," *hamartia*) "which dwelt within him."

Obviously, time passes while Hamlet misses the mark (kills Polonius instead of Claudius and exhorts his mother to repent) or waits for a better shot (spares the praying Claudius). Thus, the "delay," like the *hamartía,* is inseparable from the "madness." It is not, however, identical with it; it is simply the operation of the *hamartía* (or "madness") through time.

The stabbing of Polonius is an elaborate theatricalization or acting out of the *hamartía* image. It differs from the verbal instances of the image only in this: the other examples of "missing the mark" or "failing of one's purpose" come about through paralysis of the would-be agent (the player's speech and Claudius's prayer) or through unfavorable circumstances (Claudius's "arrows" and slander's "cannon"); but Hamlet's sword thrust is accurately aimed—it just happens to be aimed at the wrong target. "I took thee for thy better," says Hamlet when he discovers what he has done. The results are even more disastrous in this case than in the others. Instead of merely failing to produce the desired results, the agent apparently achieves his purpose, but *not* upon the desired victim. The "accidental" killing of Polonius is therefore a natural next step in Hamlet's accelerated but misguided campaign against Claudius.

Paul's analysis describes the dilemma of the man who would seek salvation through obedience to the Law. Man under the Law, according to Paul, seeks life as the reward for obedience, but his attempted obedience is actually sin, because by it he tries to establish his own righteousness rather than submit to God's (cf. Rom. 10:3). Comparing *Hamlet* again to the Pauline text, we observe that the same relation holds between Paul and the commandments of the Law as between Hamlet and the commands of the ghost. In the long passage quoted earlier, we find these words: "We know that the law is spiritual. . . ." The obvious way for a Renaissance dramatist to represent what is spiritual would be by means of a spirit, or ghost.

Associating the ghost's commands with spiritual Law may account for the appearance of the ghost, but not for the subtlety of its function in the play. This subtlety is achieved by the com-

plexity of its commands. After ordering Hamlet to avenge his
father's "foul and most unnatural murther," the ghost adds
these words of caution as further commands:

> But howsoever thou pursues this act,
> Taint not thy mind, nor let thy soul contrive
> Against thy mother aught. (I, v, 84–86)

Since Gertrude shares Claudius's guilt, Hamlet is thus commanded both to condemn and to pardon his mother, and in
doing so he almost inevitably "taints his mind." Returning now
to the apology in Act V, we see that because the audience has
heard everything spoken between Hamlet and the ghost, the
hero's apology to Laertes on the basis of "madness" constitutes,
as far as the audience is concerned, a symbolic admission by
Hamlet that he has disobeyed the ghost's command, "Taint not
thy mind." That is, Hamlet's "madness" (his *hamartia*) is (as
we predicted) the same thing as his disobedience, or, in Pauline
terms, his failure under the Law (*hamartia*, sin).

At least once the connection between Hamlet's madness and
his disobedience to the ghost is suggested in the play. After hearing the commands, Hamlet vows:

> And thy *commandment* all alone shall live
> Within the book and volume of my *brain*,
> Unmixed with baser matter. Yes, by heaven! (I, v, 102–104)

Then immediately after the closet scene, Gertrude speaks of
Hamlet as one

> O'er whom his very *madness*, like some ore
> Among a mineral of metals base,
> Shows itself pure. (IV, i, 25–27)

But if the ghost's commands are so closely identified with the
madness, is it not possible that the ghost is actually part of the
madness? May we not take seriously Gertrude's conclusion that
the ghost is "the very coinage of [Hamlet's] brain"? (III, iv, 138).
W. W. Greg thought so half a century ago when he asserted that
the ghost was merely a figment of Hamlet's imagination.[9] But

this view cannot be correct. In the first act Marcellus, Bernardo, and Horatio all testify to the objective existence of the ghost. Gertrude's inability to see the ghost during the closet scene is apparently the result of her guilt; her acceptance of Claudius as husband makes her incapable of acknowledging the imperative upon which Hamlet acts. In the parallel part of Romans 7, Paul upholds the objective goodness of the law:

> What then shall we say? That the law [ghost's command] is sin? [*hamartía*, "madness"]. By no means! Yet, if it had not been for the law [command], I should not have known sin ["madness"]. I should not have known what it is to covet if the law had not said, 'You shall not covet.' But sin, finding opportunity in the commandment, wrought in me all kinds of covetousness. Apart from the law sin lies dead. I was once alive apart from the law, but when the commandment came, sin revived and I died; the very commandment which promised life proved to be death to me. For sin, finding opportunity in the commandment, deceived me and by it killed me. So the law is holy, and the commandment is holy and just and good. (Rom. 7:7–12)

"It is an honest ghost," but "madness" causes Hamlet to "miss the mark" when he tries to fulfill its commands: "I have shot my arrow o'er the house/And hurt my brother."

We should consider whether it is likely on the basis of external evidence that Shakespeare knew the facts upon which this interpretation is based. At least two objections might be raised: one, that Shakespeare had "small *Latine,* and lesse *Greeke*" and would therefore probably not have known the root meaning of the word *hamartía;* and the other, that though he read the bible, he certainly did not read it in the Revised Standard Version. To the first of these we answer that he need have known only one word of Greek, the New Testament word for *sin,* and he is perhaps more likely to have known that than to have known any other. An American student who takes an undergraduate course in English bible is required to know that word and its original meaning ("miss the mark") whether or not he knows any other word of Greek. Shakespeare was not biblically illiterate.[10] Even the gravedigger asks in the midst of his puns, "What, art a heathen? How dost thou understand the Scripture?" (V, i, 33–34). As for the other objection, the essential wording of Romans 7 is the same in the Geneva Bible (1560) and the Bishops' Bible (1568) as in the Revised Standard Version.

If these observations are correct, then a good commentary on Romans 7 ought to illuminate the "Hamlet problem." The best such commentary that I have found is Rudolf Bultmann's "Romans 7 and the Anthropology of Paul" (1932), contained in *Existence and Faith,* a collection of Bultmann's shorter writings. He seems almost to be thinking of *Hamlet* as he writes near the end of his essay:

> Paul's whole conception becomes clear if, as is now possible, we ask what is to be understood by "sin," if it is something that is already present in man that can be awakened by the "law." The "law" encounters man as the claim of God, "Thou shouldst (not)!" i.e., it wants to take from man the disposition of his own existence. Therefore, sin is man's wanting to dispose of his existence, to raise claims for himself, to be like God. Inasmuch, then, as this "sin" brings "death," it becomes evident (1) that the man who wants to be himself loses himself; instead of the "I," "sin" becomes the subject (vs. 9); and (2) that being a self nevertheless belongs to man, for in losing himself he dies (vss. 9 f.); but also that his self is not realized when he himself tries to lay hold of it by disposing of his existence, but only when he surrenders himself to the claim of God and exists from him. This would be "life" for him; then he would exist in his *authenticity.* It is precisely through his willing to be himself that man fails to find the authenticity that he wills to achieve; and this is the deceit of sin (vs. 11). But just because the will to be authentic is preserved in the false will to be oneself, even if only disguisedly and distortedly, it is possible so to speak of the split in man's existence that the authentic I is set over against the factual one.
>
> For this reason, what is portrayed in vss. 7–13 is not "the psychological process of the emergence in man of individual sins" (Lietzmann), but rather *the process that is at the basis of existence under the law and that lies beyond subjectivity and psychic occurrences.* Because man is a self who is concerned with his authenticity and can find it (as that of a creature) only when he surrenders himself to the claim of God, there is the possibility of sin. Because from the begin-

ning the claim of God has to do with man's authentic existence, there is the possibility of misunderstanding: the man who is called to authenticity falsely wills to be himself.[11]

This exposition illuminates several things in *Hamlet*. It shows, for instance, that when Hamlet apologizes to Laertes, he is not "sheltering himself in falsehood," and that there is nothing "disingenuous" about the apology itself. There is, to be sure, an element of irony in the speech, but only because the characters who hear it know nothing of the ghost's command, "Taint not thy mind," and therefore understand the word "madness" in a literal sense rather than in the context of the relation between Hamlet and the ghost. Even so, this particular irony is no greater than the irony which permeates most of the play.

The Bultmann analysis also makes clear why A. C. Bradley was wrong to regard Hamlet's attitude toward the end of the play as "fatalistic" rather than religious in any significant sense. In Act V, scene ii, Hamlet is no longer capable of saying, "The time is out of joint. O cursèd spite/That ever I was born to set it right!" (I, v, 188–189). He ceases trying to "dispose of his existence," and only then is he able to achieve his purpose, which is to redress his father's murder. If this is "fatalism," then apparently both St. Paul and Bultmann are fatalists according to Bradley's definition. If Hamlet, who says explicitly that "The readiness is all," were merely "ready to leave his duty to some other power than his own," [12] in the sense that Bradley is talking about, then he certainly would not have accepted Laertes' challenge to a duel. He would have rejected the challenge and withdrawn to sulk in a corner. On the contrary, for the first time he responds to the opportunity which offers itself, trusting (also for the first time) that he will achieve his purpose. And by a supreme irony he (again for the first time) actually achieves that purpose.

The subject of *Hamlet* is action, and the use of weapons is the dominant metaphor. The play disposes of an entire arsenal—daggers and rapiers, foils and targets, axes and partisans, slings and arrows, brazen cannon and "murd'ring pieces," petars and mines all serve as vehicles for meaning. The passive man suffers "the slings and arrows of outrageous fortune," while the man who wills "to be" must "take arms against a sea of troubles." Even the person who wills "not to be" must make his quietus "with a bare bodkin." The ghost, "armed at point exactly, cap-a-pe," is the *spur* to action; when it returns to "whet [Hamlet's] almost blunted purpose," the hero exclaims, "His form and cause conjoined, preaching to stones,/Would make them capable" (cf. Luke 19:40). Yet the ghost itself is beyond the reach of human action, as Hamlet's friends discover when Marcellus strikes at it with his partisan: "For it is as the air invulnerable,/And our vain blows malicious mockery." Having verified the ghost's authenticity, Hamlet knows that to kill Claudius at prayer would be to miss the mark; he therefore restrains himself, saying "Up, sword, and know thou a more horrid hent." Attempting to obey the ghost's commands, he decides how he will deal with his mother: "I will speak daggers to her, but use none." He succeeds, for she responds to his reproof by saying, "These words like daggers enter in mine ears." Even the gravedigger tells us by means of an elaborate pun that biblical Adam was "the first that ever bore arms."

But the reason why the weapons metaphor works so perfectly is that the relation between aim and hit or miss corresponds exactly to the relation between intention and fulfillment in human action ("will and matter," "thoughts and ends"). In any really complex human situation it is almost inevitable that a man will "miss the mark"; hence the Pauline conception of *hamartia* and Hamlet's "madness" point to something basic in human experience. Hamlet's plea for pardon rests solely on his "disclaiming from a purposed evil." He cannot deny that he has missed the mark with disastrous consequences; he can only insist that the consequences of his actions were totally different from what he intended. Earlier in the play when Hamlet had asked Polonius to "see the players well bestowed," the old courtier had said that he would treat them "according to their desert." Hamlet's reply is to this effect: "God's bodkin, man, much better!

Use every man after his desert, and who shall scape whipping?
Use them after your own honor and dignity. The less they
deserve, the more merit is in your bounty" (II, ii, 516–519). In
like manner, Hamlet's apology in Act V appeals to the "honor
and dignity" of the man he has woefully offended, for the hero
knows at last that if he himself is treated "after his desert," he
will not "scape whipping." Hamlet is at this point so conscious
of his own "bad marksmanship" that when he pays tribute to
that of Laertes, the latter thinks that Hamlet is mocking him.

> *Hamlet.*   Give us the foils. Come on.
> *Laertes.*   Come, one for me.
> *Hamlet.*   I'll be your foil, Laertes. In mine ignorance
>   Your skill shall, like a star i' th' darkest night,
>   Stick fiery off indeed.
> *Laertes.*   You mock me, sir.
> *Hamlet.*   No, by this hand. (V, ii, 243–247)

The irony that permeates the play is evident here, because just as
those who had heard Hamlet's apology knew nothing of the
ghost's command, "Taint not thy mind," so Hamlet in compli-
menting Laertes on his swordsmanship knows nothing of his opponent's treacherous intention (the envenomed weapon).

Once we have seen that the "madness" and the *hamartía* are
the same thing and that the *hamartía* is Pauline rather than
Aristotelian, our main problem has to do with the fact that the
meaning of the word "madness" obviously does not remain the
same throughout the play. In this matter, "We must speak by
the card, or equivocation will undo us." When Hamlet uses the
phrase "antic disposition" at the end of Act I, he does not yet
know what form his machinations will take. The evidence upon
which Polonius bases his "madness for love" theory (Hamlet's
appearance to Ophelia in her closet) is pure hearsay, and it must
be borne in mind that its source is Ophelia. At any rate, Hamlet
soon knows that others regard him as "mad," for he tells Rosencrantz and Guildenstern that the king and queen are deceived
and that he is "but mad north-north-west" (II, ii, 369). Hamlet
brings up the subject of "madness" himself during the closet

scene, and he furnishes a synonym in the same sentence. He
shows Gertrude the pictures of his father and Claudius, and asks:

> . . . what judgment
> Would step from this to this? Sense sure you have,
> Else could you not have motion, but sure that sense
> Is apoplexed, for *madness* would not err,
> Nor sense to *ecstasy* was ne'er so thralled
> But it reserved some quantity of choice
> To serve in such a difference. What devil was't
> That thus hath cozened you at hoodman-blind? (III, iv, 71–78)

When the ghost reappears, Gertrude concludes that Hamlet is
"mad." (Both she and Hamlet use "ecstasy" and "madness" interchangeably at this point.) But Hamlet rejects the charge, and
linking the ideas of "trespass" and "madness," he replies:

> Lay not that flattering unction to your soul,
> That not *your trespass* but *my madness* speaks. (III, iv, 146–147) 1

In the first of these speeches Hamlet insists that "madness
would not err" in achieving its purpose, whereas in the apology
he designates "madness" as the source of error. The difference
is confusing at first, but there is a verbal connection between
the apology and the closet scene which helps to clarify matters.
In the apology Hamlet says:

> This presence knows, and you must needs have heard,
> How *I am punished with* a sore distraction. (V, ii, 217–218)

Shortly before leaving his mother's closet, Hamlet had spoken to
her very solemnly of Polonius's death:

> For this same lord,
> I do repent; but heaven hath pleased it so,
> To *punish me with this, and this with me,*
> That I must be their scourge and minister.
> I will bestow him and will answer well
> The death I gave him. (III, iv, 173–178)

These words illustrate very well Bultmann's definition of sin,
which is man's wanting "to raise claims for himself, to be like

God." Hamlet talks in this scene and the next two as if murdering a faithful but foolish courtier were all in a day's work for God's instrument among men.

The difference between the two meanings of the word *madness* in these two scenes is clear. In the closet scene, Hamlet uses *madness* as a synonym for *ecstasy* and denies that he is mad, lamenting at the same time that he is "punished with" the responsibility of being heaven's "scourge and minister." In the apology, he says that he is "punished with a sore distraction" and calls that distraction—madness. When did the change of attitude take place? Presumably during his "exile," but the audience sees the meaning of the word begin to change (under several layers of irony) when Hamlet quarrels with Laertes at the grave of Ophelia, the only mad person in the play.

> *Laertes.* The devil take thy soul!
>   [Grapples with him.]
> *Hamlet.* Thou pray'st not well.
>   I prithee take thy fingers from my throat,
>   For, though I am not splenitive and rash,
>   *Yet have I in me something dangerous,*
>   Which let thy wisdom fear. (V, i, 245–250)

Claudius then tries to pacify Laertes by saying, "O, he is mad, Laertes," and Gertrude concurs in that judgment: "This is mere madness;/And thus a while the fit will work on him." Here the king and queen are still using the word to mean *ecstasy,* but for the first time it becomes associated significantly in the audience's mind with whatever Hamlet is referring to when he says, "Yet have I in me something dangerous." This "something dangerous" is the "sore distraction" which Hamlet calls "madness" in the apology.

But if Hamlet's "flaw" is anything so commonplace as the Pauline conception of sin, are not the other characters in the play afflicted by it as much as he is? Indeed they are. This is why, for instance, Gertrude and Claudius delay just as much in repenting their misdeeds as Hamlet does in achieving his revenge. When Hamlet tells his mother that her "sense is apoplexed," he is diagnosing both her difficulty and his own. Gertrude speaks four lines in an aside which might serve very well as an epigraph for the play:

> To my sick soul (as *sin's* true nature is)
> Each toy seems prologue to some great *amiss*.
> So full of artless jealousy is guilt
> It spills itself in fearing to be spilt. (IV, v, 17–20)

This commonplaceness is the reason too why Aristotle's statement about "the least tragic possibility" does not apply to *Hamlet*. Though Hamlet does not do Claudius a deadly injury during the prayer scene, it cannot be said that Claudius does not suffer. Claudius, in love with the fruits of his own misdeed ("my crown, mine own ambition, and my queen"), cannot repent and he suffers no less intensely than does the Ancient Mariner before the albatross falls from his neck.

Laertes parallels, or rather parodies, Hamlet's situation, though on a much lower level, from the first act, when both receive "commandments" which they cannot finally obey. Polonius serves as "ghost" to Laertes: "And these few precepts in thy memory/ Look thou character" (I, iii, 58–59). Laertes cannot in the long run be "true to his own self," and is therefore false to Hamlet in Act V. Laertes is closer to Hamlet's position than either Claudius or Gertrude is because his task, like Hamlet's, is revenge rather than repentance; but he, like Claudius, is guilty of treachery. Only Hamlet among the male characters can honestly disclaim "a purposed evil," and this is perhaps what makes him worthy to be the hero.

The commonplaceness of human sin is also the root of the play's pervading irony. One may even say that much of the irony in *Hamlet* stems from speeches or actions that "miss the mark" in a way that becomes apparent only later in the play. Thus Claudius can use rich poetry to console Hamlet for his father's "natural" death when Claudius himself is guilty of the murder. For the same reason Polonius can, Godlike, give sage advice to his son because we do not yet know that Polonius himself needs the advice more urgently than anyone else. From his position on the battlement, Hamlet can discourse with Olympian detachment on the "vicious mole of nature" in his fellow man to which he begins to fall victim that same night. Because we are no less subject to the "flaw" than are the dramatic characters, these and other speeches do not seem ironic when we first hear them; but they become so in the context of the whole play. *Hamlet* is our Mousetrap; we have the same relation to the hero as Gertrude does to the queen in the play within a play. We study *Hamlet* very soberly and then conclude with unintended irony, "The gentleman doth delay too much, methinks."

The strictly literary questions raised by *Hamlet* are not unanswerable. The theological questions are satisfactorily treated in Romans 7, though the more speculative questions which have long puzzled critics (e.g., why Hamlet—or man—is the way he is) admit of no answers in this life. As Polonius says, to expostulate "Why day is day, night night, and time is time,/Were nothing but to waste night, day, and time." To put the matter another way, *Hamlet* holds an almost perfect mirror up to nature; if we limit ourselves to questions about the mirror itself, there is no particular difficulty. But if we attempt to explain the meaning and purpose of everything reflected in that mirror, we soon become lost in speculation, not about the mirror, but about the "nature" which it reflects. The question why Hamlet is what he is implies that he might well have been quite different from what he is. St. Paul does not admit this possibility for man; neither does he attempt a speculative explanation of man's situation. Instead, he describes that situation in its stark reality, holding out the possibility of an ultimate resolution. Surely it is enough to take at face value Hamlet's statement on the purpose of playing, "whose end, both at the first and now, was and is, to hold, as 'twere, the mirror up to nature, to show virtue her own feature, scorn her own image, and the very age and body of the time his form and pressure." If we refuse to take that statement seriously as the point of view which underlies the play, we find ourselves unconsciously adopting a position closely related to the one which Hamlet savagely ridicules when Polonius asks him what he is reading: "Slanders, sir, for the satirical rogue says

here that old men have grey beards, that their faces are wrinkled.
. . . All which, sir, though I most powerfully and potently believe, yet I hold it not honesty to have it thus set down, for you
yourself, sir, should be as old as I am if, like a crab, you could go
backward."

IV

King Lear and the Corinthian Letters

*If I speak in the tongues of men
and of angels, but have not love,
. . . I am nothing. If I give away all I have,
and if I deliver my body to be burned,
but have not love, I gain nothing.*

I CORINTHIANS 13:1–3

᷄ᴥ Bᴏᴛʜ as a literary work and as a commentary on human behavior, *King Lear* is a subtler play than either *Hamlet* or *Macbeth*. Though Hamlet's dilemma is insoluble from a purely human point of view, the dilemma itself is not difficult to specify; and Macbeth's problem has never seemed particularly obscure to commentators and critics. Many readers, however, have considerable difficulty articulating with any degree of confidence exactly what *King Lear* is all about. The bantering tone of the opening speeches gives very little indication of the suffering that is to follow; and the conception of fate, which is prominent in some other Shakespearean tragedies, is not intrusive at the beginning of this one. No murder is represented as taking place either before the play begins, as in *Hamlet,* or within the first two acts, as in *Macbeth*. The scene opens on the clearly illuminated and obviously peaceful court of a British king who feels no threat to his power other than that of old age. We cannot help wondering, therefore, what the source of tragic action really is in *King Lear*.

The phrase *filial ingratitude* is inadequate as a statement of the play's theme if for no other reason than this: it totally disregards the play's emphasis upon the difference between *claiming* to love and actually *loving*. Lear doles out rewards to his daughters in the first scene not according to their love for him, but according to their willingness to *verbalize* about love. The basic irony of *King Lear* resides in this disparity between what people *say* and what they *do*, between the feelings which they profess and the ones which govern their behavior. Shakespeare explores this discrepancy all through the play and stresses it again at the end, when Edgar puts it into the form of an explicit moral: "The weight of this sad time we must obey,/Speak what we feel, not what we ought to say." Try as we may, we cannot make these lines mean filial ingratitude without completely distorting them. That final speech says nothing about ingratitude; it is a simple plea for sincerity of expression.

Moreover, the contention that *King Lear* deals primarily with filial ingratitude ignores the wording of the dispute in the first scene, which hinges upon each daughter's protestation of *love* for her father, not her statement of gratitude. Because Goneril and Regan both realize that any reference to gratitude on their part would tend to reveal their awareness that these declarations of love are being bought and paid for, they scrupulously avoid any such suggestion. Only Cordelia says that she loves "according to her bond"; and this is precisely what her father does *not* want to hear. The word *ingratitude* and its synonyms do not appear until later in the play, and they do so then only as Lear's explanation of Goneril and Regan's failure to love their "old kind father" as they *ought* to do. In this respect, Lear's ingratitude idea is exactly parallel to Polonius's madness-for-love theory about Hamlet: it is an attempt by one dramatic character to account for the unacceptable behavior of certain other characters, in the only terms that he can understand. And to regard that explanation as being accurate and satisfactory in *King Lear* is to assume that the protagonist himself is untouched by the irony that permeates everything else in the play. From a common-sense point of view, it does not seem likely that this would be the case in a Shakespearean drama.

Because critics have not been able to determine the play's real subject, they are equally uncertain about its general tone and the attitude toward life which it finally embodies. In the Introduction to his edition of *King Lear,* Alfred Harbage summarizes this aspect of the problem.

> The question now most frequently debated is whether the play is Christian and affirmative in spirit, or pagan and pessimistic. No work of art could endure the tugs of such a debate without being somewhat torn. "Pessimistic," like "optimistic," is a small word for a small thing, and *King Lear* is not small. It is sad, as all tragedies are sad. It is religious, as all great tragedies are religious. The exclusion of specific Christian reference, more consistent than in any other Shakespearean play of non-Christian setting, is in harmony with its Old Testament atmosphere ("when Joas ruled in Juda"), but it may reflect nothing more than evasion, in the printed text, of a recent Parliamentary ruling, which in effect labelled *God* in stage speech as blasphemy, *gods* as mere classical allusion. Although the play is rather inclusively than exclusively Christian, which can scarcely be deemed a fault, it shows obvious signs of its genesis in a Christian culture.[1]

The question as to "whether the play is Christian and affirmative in spirit, or pagan and pessimistic" may indeed provide a focus for determining the fundamental meaning of the play. In order to make such a determination, however, we must limit our attention to the actual words of the text, rather than conjecture about its teasingly elusive "spirit."

Sound critical method as applied to any important literary work is not the only thing that dictates careful attention to the words of the play. *King Lear* is clearly a special case, as A. C. Bradley indicates when he says that "while it would be going too far to suggest that he was employing conscious symbolism or allegory in *King Lear,* it does appear to disclose a mode of imagination not so very far removed from the mode with which, we must remember, Shakespeare was perfectly familiar in Morality plays and in the *Fairy Queen.*" [2] Bradley acknowledges that "the improbabilities in *King Lear* surely far surpass those of the other great tragedies in number and in grossness," [3] and he feels called upon to defend at least two scenes against the charge of absurdity—the famous first scene, and the one which represents

Gloucester's "leap." Of the former he says that "to imagination the story is not at all incredible. It is merely strange, like so many of the stories on which our romantic dramas are based." And of the latter he says that it "is not, if properly acted, in the least absurd on the stage." [4] Thus Bradley shifts his ground, saying at one moment that the play undoubtedly contains a great many gross improbabilities and at another moment that the grossest of these improbabilities is not really so improbable after all. But in order to be consistent, we must either defend the action represented in *King Lear* as realistic and therefore not absurd in any significant sense, or else we must take seriously the play's affinity with the morality plays or the *Fairy Queen* and account for the "absurdities" on some coherent literary basis external to the play itself. Anyone who has read Tolstoy's devastating attack upon the play[5] will hesitate to choose the first alternative; and yet, no one has ever thoroughly and convincingly explored the second.

Exhaustive research has shown that Shakespeare seldom invented a plot—he almost always borrowed one from earlier plays or stories—but strangely, it has often been assumed that the insights he conveyed by those plots were distinctly his own. According to Kenneth Muir, in *King Lear* "Shakespeare goes back to a pre-Christian world and builds up from the nature of man himself, and not from revealed religion, those same moral and religious ideas that were being undermined." [6] This view saves the poet from being labelled a theologian merely by labelling him a philosopher; it still implies that what we sometimes call "Shakespeare's conception of man" somehow emerged spontaneously from the poet's marvelously comprehensive mind. But why should we assume that a literary man who did not even bother to invent his own plots agonized over "the nature of man himself" in order to come up with "those same moral and religious ideas that were being undermined"? It is a much simpler hypothesis to suppose that he appropriated his conception of human nature in the same fashion that he borrowed his plots—and more reasonable too, since he added nothing to the moral and religious ideas that were already current. It seems perfectly obvious that William Shakespeare was neither a theologian nor a philosopher; he was a master of language; that is to say, he was a poet. He created a garment of language for ideas that were not his own; and we will be in a better position to evaluate his contribution if we accurately identify the ideas and conceptions with which he started than if we confuse what he created with what he took from somewhere else.

Most editors of *King Lear,* attending carefully to what Roland Frye calls the "pre-Christian and explicitly pagan" setting of the play,[7] identify only one reference to St. Paul's Corinthian letters, and that one is quite insignificant: "To say 'ay' and 'no' to everything that I said! 'Ay' and 'no' too was no good divinity" (IV, vi, 98–100; cf. II Cor. 1:18). It is in the Corinthian letters, however, that all the important evidence for a Christian interpretation of *King Lear* lies. New Testament scholars face exactly the same problem with these letters that Shakespearean commentators face with *King Lear,* that of reducing their contents to any satisfactory unity,[8] and it is hardly coincidental that the highly varied content of *King Lear* corresponds at many points to the equally diversified content of the Corinthian letters. St. Paul sets forth with great clarity most of the problems which vex the interpreters of *King Lear,* and he is very specific about their solutions.

If we undertake to answer the question about *King Lear* as to "whether the play is Christian and affirmative in spirit, or pagan and pessimistic," we find that the question itself requires analysis. In its present form it leads inevitably to generalizations based on assumptions that may or may not be implied by the play itself. Only when the question is broken down into its component parts can we proceed toward answers that rest solidly upon literary evidence. The more limited questions, contained within the larger one, may be stated as follows: (1) What is the fundamental subject of *King Lear?* (2) Is there, from a literary viewpoint, anything genuinely and specifically Christian about Shakespeare's treatment of that subject? And (3) may that treatment be adequately described as either affirmative or pessimistic? The first question may be answered rather quickly; the second will require the examination of considerable evidence; and what we learn in exploring the first two will help to provide an answer for the third.

The subject of *King Lear* is love—love between king and subject, father and daughter, father and son, father-in-law and son-in-law, brother and brother, sister and sister, husband and wife, man and mistress, gentleman and servant, lady and servant. In short, the subject is love in all human relationships; and most of these relationships are represented by parallel examples in order to show them at both their best and their worst. Generally speaking, the relation between persons in *King Lear* is best when the two parties regard each other as fellow human beings, with mutual rights and responsibilities; it is worst when either or both parties take advantage of the relationship to satisfy some selfish purpose. We are not allowed to forget during the play that such relationships are always reciprocal and that in the long run the flatterer is not much guiltier than the person who requires flattery. In one sense Lear is an "innocent," he certainly wishes "no harm" to anyone, but through the attitude which he reveals in the first scene he does immeasurable harm. As we see by the initial demand that he makes upon his daughters, he craves the love of other people; and as we see by his treatment of Cordelia, he himself does not know how to love.

The words *love* and *loved* occur thirty times in the first scene; and their synonyms are almost uncountable from the first line of Act I: "I thought the King had more affected the Duke of Albany than Cornwall." This first scene contains a negative definition of love by the king who takes Cordelia for his bride: "Love's not love/When it is mingled with regards that stands/Aloof from th' entire point" (I, i, 238–240); and this definition bears a striking resemblance to a statement in Sonnet 116, "Love is not love/Which alters when it alteration finds." (That sonnet concludes with the words, "If this be error, and upon me proved,/I never writ, nor no man ever loved.") Lear in this scene makes the division of his kingdom depend upon his daughters' protestations of love; and strangely Cordelia, who loves most, says least. Conversely, Goneril and Regan, who love least, say most. Their declarations are models of what Cordelia calls "that glib and oily art/To speak and purpose not" (I, i, 224–225), set pieces mouthed by actresses who do not understand the play in which they are acting. They are without honor and therefore do not behave as if they understood that "to plainness honor's bound/When majesty falls to folly" (I, i, 148–149). Obviously, flattery and love are not the same thing at all, however eagerly we may mistake the one for the other.

Though the play is chiefly concerned with love, *King Lear* is neither "romantic" nor sentimental. Sexual love, which the topic inevitably suggests to the reader or viewer, is not treated very charitably in the play. The opening speeches deal at some length with pure carnality; we learn from them that Edmund is illegitimate and that "there was good sport at his making." In the light of the whole play it is neither surprising nor ironic that the fruit of this encounter between Gloucester and his mistress is a consummate villain. Another point at which sexual relationships come into prominence involves the rivalry of Goneril and Regan for the affections of this same Edmund. The only marriage in *King Lear* which is represented as being successful and therefore presumably happy, is that of Cordelia to the King of France; and the sexual overtones of that relationship are conspicuous by their absence. These features of the play seem to imply that just as there is no necessary connection between claiming to love and actually loving, there is none between the sex relation and the love relation either. Lust, like flattery, is only the counterfeit of love. Gloucester has a predilection for the one, Lear for the other.

If the subject of *King Lear* is love, our next question is whether or not, from a purely literary point of view, the treatment of that subject may be said to be genuinely and specifically Christian. The great Christian text on love is, of course, the thirteenth chapter of First Corinthians. Let us look at that chapter again carefully, for the special purpose of finding out whether it throws any real light on what has often been called "Shakespeare's greatest achievement."

If I speak in the tongues of men and of angels, but have not love, I am a noisy gong or a clanging cymbal. And if I have prophetic powers, and understand all mysteries and all knowledge, and if I have all faith, so as to remove mountains, but have not love, I am nothing. If I give away all I have, and if I deliver my body to be burned, but have not love, I gain nothing.

Love is patient and kind; love is not jealous or boastful; it is not arrogant or rude. Love does not insist on its own way; it is not irritable or resentful; it does not rejoice at wrong, but rejoices in the right. Love bears all things, believes all things, hopes all things, endures all things.

Love never ends; as for prophecy, it will pass away; as for tongues, they will cease; as for knowledge, it will pass away. For our knowledge is imperfect and our prophecy is imperfect; but when the perfect comes, the imperfect will pass away. When I was a child, I spoke like a child, I thought like a child, I reasoned like a child; when I became a man, I gave up childish ways. For now we see in a mirror dimly, but then face to face. Now I know in part; then I shall understand fully, even as I have been fully understood. So faith, hope, love abide, these three; but the greatest of these is love. (I Cor. 13:1–13)

We notice first that the words which St. Paul uses to describe what love *is* accurately characterize Cordelia, whereas the words he uses to define what love is *not* fit Goneril and Regan perfectly. Cordelia is "patient and kind"; she "does not insist on her own way"; she "does not rejoice at wrong, but rejoices in the right." She "bears all things, believes all things, hopes all things, endures all things." Goneril and Regan, on the other hand, are "jealous," and they vie with each other in "boasting" of their love; they are "arrogant and rude." They "insist on their own way"; they are "irritable and resentful"; they often "rejoice at wrong," but almost never do they "rejoice in the right."

As we explore the parallel further, we begin to see that this passage in First Corinthians clarifies the relation between elements in *King Lear* that might otherwise seem arbitrary and unconnected—or even "absurd." Take, for instance, these three. First, Mark Van Doren, unconsciously contradicting Tolstoy's assertion that Shakespeare's characters "all talk alike," [9] suggests that "Lear and Gloucester do not sound alike. The first is a great poet; . . . the second is a plain man. . . . As Lear rises on the wings of metaphor Gloucester lowers his voice to a mumble." [10] Secondly, Lear stubbornly and arbitrarily carves up his kingdom and gives it away. Thirdly, there is much insistence on the word *nothing* in the play, as when the Fool tells Lear very bluntly, "I am a fool, thou art nothing" (I, iv, 184–185). In the light of First Corinthians 13, these three elements fall together quite naturally: though Lear "speaks in the tongues of men and of angels," and though he "gives away all he has," still he has not love and consequently, he is "nothing."

It would be difficult to overestimate the importance of this chapter as a source of imagery, humor, and symbolic action in *King Lear*. The king, however unconsciously he may do so, even "delivers his body to be burned"; for he says to Cordelia, "Thou art a soul in bliss; but I am bound/Upon a wheel of fire, that mine own tears/Do scald like molten lead" (IV, vii, 46–48). (Gloucester, who suffers more than anyone else in the play except for Lear himself, likewise "delivers his body to be burned"; when he appears at the hovel carrying a torch, the Fool exclaims, "Look, here comes a walking fire," III, iv, 107.) The Fool follows St. Paul in minimizing the significance of "prophecy" when he introduces one of his moralizing rhymes with the words "I'll speak a prophecy ere I go" and concludes by explicitly turning his prediction into a joke: "This prophecy Merlin shall make, for I live before his time" (III, ii, 79–80, 95–96).[11] And faithful Edgar, who leads his blind old father, despondent and bent upon suicide, to the "extreme verge" of a "cliff" so that he may leap from it (IV, vi), apparently has "all faith, so as to remove mountains." Consequently, Gloucester is delivered as if by miracle from death and despair. He dies only later; and when he does, we are told, "His flawed heart . . . burst smilingly" (V, iii, 197–200). Thus, the whole incident of Gloucester's "leap," the most patently "absurd" thing in the play, takes on the character of a gigantic pun which is primarily dramatic rather than verbal.

For Lear himself, love is strictly a matter of cause and effect. Unless he can perceive some "cause in nature" for people's loving or hating, he simply cannot fathom their attitude. And whenever he encounters the cause without the effect or the effect without the cause, he is simply amazed. This is why he rails so much about ingratitude. As he wanders in the storm "ill-clad and buffeted and homeless" (I Cor. 4:11), he indicates why he does not "tax the elements with unkindness": "I never gave you kingdom, called you children;/You owe me no subscription" (III, ii, 17–18). Later he demands to know, "Is there any cause in nature that makes these hard hearts?" (III, vi, 75–76). And when Cordelia returns to him, he still insists upon cause and effect:

> *Lear.*   I know you do not love me; for your sisters
>   Have, as I do remember, done me wrong.
>   You have some cause, they have not.
> *Cordelia.*   No cause, no cause. (IV, vii, 73–75)

It is of course the essence of Christian love that it springs from no "cause in nature."

Lear's conception of love is most succinctly expressed early in the play when the disguised Kent "serves" the king by tripping and humiliating Oswald. Lear is pleased, and says to Kent, "I thank thee, fellow. Thou serv'st me, and I'll love thee" (I, iv, 83–84). The causal relation is not explicit in the grammar of Lear's sentence, but it is obviously implied—I'll love thee *because* thou serv'st me. Moments later, Lear concludes the episode as one might expect that he should: "Now, my friendly knave, I thank thee. There's earnest of thy service. [*Gives money*]" (I, iv, 88–89). Curiously, Lear's attitude is close to that of Oswald himself. In a later set-to, Kent and Oswald exchange these words:

> *Oswald.*   Prithee, if thou lov'st me, tell me.
> *Kent.*   I love thee not.
> *Oswald.*   Why then, I care not for thee. (II, ii, 5–7)

In this bit of dialogue, Oswald simply reiterates the substance of Lear's position in the first scene: If thou say'st not that thou lov'st me, why then there is no "cause in nature" why I should care for thee. But in his relation to Goneril, Oswald is no less faithful a servant than Kent is to Lear. It is a common love of evil that binds Oswald to his lady, but it *is* love. Edgar pronounces such a judgment at the time of Oswald's death: "A serviceable villain,/As duteous to the vices of thy mistress/As badness would desire" (IV, vi, 248–250). In this one respect, even Oswald, the despicable servant, comes closer to the love St. Paul describes than Lear does. (The implied comparison between Lear and Oswald on the matter of love apparently escaped Dr. Johnson, who said, "I know not well why Shakespeare gives to Oswald, who is a mere factor of wickedness, so much fidelity.")[12]

In his attitude toward Nature Lear is much closer to Edmund than to Cordelia. Not until the middle of the play does he call upon the storm to "Strike flat the thick rotundity o' th' world,/ Crack Nature's moulds, all germains spill at once,/That makes ingrateful man" (III, ii, 7–9). Before that, we have heard Edmund, in Act I, scene ii, pray with obvious sincerity, "Thou, Nature, art my goddess; to thy law/My services are bound" (I, ii, 1–2). And Lear, soon after that, invokes the wrath of the same deity upon Goneril; "Hear, Nature, hear; dear goddess, hear:/ Suspend thy purpose if thou didst intend/To make this creature fruitful" (I, iv, 266–268). Edmund's being the "natural" son of Gloucester becomes a means for expressing one of the most important paradoxes in *King Lear*. This "natural" son behaves in a most "unnatural" way to his father: he abuses and torments him in a way for which there is no "cause in nature." Legitimate Edgar, on the other hand, also behaves in an "unnatural" manner —there is no "cause in nature" why he should remain faithful to the father that has cursed him and put a price upon his head. The word *unnatural* thus comes to have a double meaning: *below* the level of nature (Goneril, Regan, Edmund), or, *above* that level (Cordelia, Edgar, Kent). Lear easily mistakes the one for the other, as when he calls Cordelia "a wretch whom nature is ashamed/Almost t' acknowledge hers" (I, i, 212–213). Gloucester and Lear are the "natural" figures in the play; all the other characters stand either above or below that level.

But Lear is magnificently inconsistent in his reliance upon Nature. When Regan tries to reduce the number of her father's retinue and asks why he needs even one retainer, Lear bursts forth passionately, "O reason not the need! Our basest beggars/ Are in the poorest thing superfluous./Allow not nature more than nature needs,/Man's life is cheap as beast's" (II, iv, 259–262). When it becomes a question of his own wants, then reason and nature are no longer appropriate standards of judgment. Lear is of course right in this speech, but the irony derives from the fact that in his relations with other people, he himself insists upon reason and nature, and thus, without realizing it, makes "man's life as cheap as beast's." During the storm scene, he reaps the consequences of this attitude, is himself reduced to the level of a beast, and therefore becomes mad. Out of that madness comes wisdom.

First Corinthians 1 through 4 comprehensively treats the paradoxical relation of wisdom and foolishness, just as First Corinthians 13 is the definitive statement on Christian love. To cite only one passage among many, "If any one among you thinks that he is wise in this age, let him become a fool that he may become wise. For the wisdom of this world is folly with God" (I Cor. 3:18–19). Robert Heilman has demonstrated in *This Great Stage* the extent to which Shakespeare exploits this theme in *King Lear*.[13] My purpose is to point out that the treatment of the play's major theme (love) and that of a secondary theme (wisdom and foolishness) apparently have a single source—the book of First Corinthians. One further point remains to be made in this connection, however; and that is the manner in which Shakespeare binds the two themes together. A single example will suffice. On different occasions Lear, in all his natural wisdom, tells both the Fool and Cordelia (whom he finally calls "my poor fool") that "Nothing will come of nothing" (I, i, 90) and that "Nothing can be made out of nothing" (I, iv, 126). Yet Lear, though he begins as "nothing" (I, iv, 185) because he "has not love," turns himself, through suffering, into "something"; by "becoming a fool" he makes himself capable of love. Thus paradoxically, in *King Lear* Shakespeare, by converting wisdom into foolishness, produces "something" (a man capable of love) out of "nothing" (one who "has not love").

On what grounds in the Corinthian letters may we assert that

Lear "has not love"? The demonstration is simple. We merely take three of the key words used to describe love in First Corinthians 13, *patient, kind,* and *endure,* and examine Shakespeare's use of them in *King Lear.* A. C. Bradley concluded his famous discussion of the play by saying that it "seems to preach to us from end to end, 'Thou must be patient,' 'Bear free and patient thoughts.' " [14] The word *kind* is particularly useful, since in Shakespeare *unkind* frequently involves the meaning of *unnatural* and thus becomes connected with another element of the play's meaning. Perhaps the most famous lines in the entire play are those spoken by Edgar in the last act, "Men must endure/Their going hence, even as their coming hither;/Ripeness is all." An examination of how Lear uses these three words and how the other characters apply them to him may then yield some insight into the structure and meaning of the play.[15]

When Lear curses Goneril, Albany interrupts the eloquent tirade by saying, "Pray, sir, be patient." But Lear continues, "Detested kite, thou liest . . ." (I, iv, 252–253). Later, when Goneril tries to reduce his retinue, Lear says, "I can be patient, I can stay with Regan,/I and my hundred knights" (II, iv, 225–226). Then in the speech which begins "O reason not the need!" he prays, "You heavens, give me that patience, patience I need" (II, iv, 266). During the storm, in words that echo Cordelia's at the beginning of the play, he says, "No, I will be the pattern of all patience;/I will say nothing" (III, ii, 37–38). At the mock trial, Kent asks Lear in a way that points up the irony of the play, "O pity! Sir, where is the patience now/That you so oft have boasted to retain?" (III, vi, 57–58). Even Gloucester learns the necessity of patience before Lear does. Just before he "leaps" upon the heath, he prays, "O you mighty gods!/This world I do renounce, and in your sights,/Shake patiently my great affliction off" (IV, vi, 34–36); and after the "leap" he vows, "Henceforth I'll bear/Affliction till it do cry out itself/'Enough, enough, and die,' " to which Edgar responds, "Bear free and patient thoughts" (IV, vi, 75–80). Ironically, it is after this that Lear, who still must learn the meaning of patience fully, tells Gloucester, "Thou must be patient. We came crying hither . . ." (IV, vi, 175).

The Fool introduces the subject of kindness when he tells of the foolish man who "in pure kindness to his horse, buttered his hay." Immediately thereafter, Lear passes the same judgment upon Goneril that the Fool had passed on him; he calls her "nothing" and links that term with "unkindness." "Beloved Regan,/Thy sister's naught. O Regan, she hath tied/Sharp-toothed unkindness, like a vulture, here." Regan responds, "I pray you, sir, take patience" (II, iv, 128–133). During the storm scene Lear tells the wind and rain, "I tax not you, you elements, with unkindness" (III, ii, 16), because after all he had never given them any reason to be grateful to him. On the heath he exclaims, "O Regan, Goneril,/Your old kind father, whose frank heart gave all—/O, that way madness lies; let me shun that" (III, iv, 19–21); and moments later in the hovel he cries, "Death, traitor; nothing could have subdued nature/To such a lowness but his unkind daughters" (III, iv, 68–69). When Gloucester does what he can to comfort the raging Lear, Kent comments upon Lear's "impatience" and associates the idea of kindness with the gods: "All the power of his wits have given way to his impatience. The gods reward your kindness" (III, vi, 4–5). And late in the play, Kent once more puts his finger on the irony of Lear's position:

> A sovereign shame so elbows him; *his own unkindness,*
> That stripped her from his benediction, turned her
> To foreign casualties, gave her dear rights
> To his dog-hearted daughters—these things sting
> His mind so venomously that burning shame
> Detains him from Cordelia. (IV, iii, 42–47)

When Kent had first invited Lear to enter the hovel, Lear hesitated, saying, "This tempest will not give me leave to ponder/On things would hurt me more, but I'll go in" (III, iv, 24–25); and one cannot help thinking that he rants about "his unkind daughters" in order to escape what "would hurt him more"—the thought of "his own unkindness" to Cordelia.

The third defining term is *endure.* Appropriately, it is first used (negatively, of course) by Goneril. Irritated by the behavior of Lear and his followers, she cries, "I'll not endure it./His knights grow riotous, and himself upbraids us/On every trifle" (I, iii, 5–7). Kent describes the storm as "too rough/For nature to endure" (III, iv, 2–3), but moments later when Lear characterizes himself as an "old kind father," the king insists, "I will endure" (III, iv, 18). Regan, competing with her sister for Edmund's "love," tells him, "I never shall endure her" (V, i, 15). Edgar gives the word its broadest application in the lines "Men must endure/Their going hence, even as their coming hither" (V, ii, 9–10); and at the end of the play Kent says of Lear, "The wonder is, he hath endured so long" (V, iii, 317). Thus ironically Lear, who has "ever but slenderly known himself" (I, i, 292–293), calls himself a "kind father," and insists, "I will be the pattern of all patience" and "I will endure." But Kent, who sees the king more clearly than Lear sees himself, always lays bare the real difficulty. At the crucial moment he asks, "where is the patience now/That you so oft have boasted to retain?" He understands that "a sovereign shame," the memory of "his own unkindness,/. . . Detains him from Cordelia." And after Lear is dead, Kent observes that "the wonder is, he hath endured so long."

Some critics have objected, on the basis of realism, to the fact that Lear and Gloucester remain blind so long to the virtues of Cordelia and Edgar. But if we use the Corinthian letters as the frame of reference for interpreting the play, the explanation is simple. We have indicated that both Gloucester and Lear are "natural" men, more interested in the counterfeit of love than in love itself; and according to St. Paul, "The natural man receiveth not the things of the Spirit of God: for they are foolishness unto him: neither can he know them, because they are spiritually discerned" (I Cor. 2:14, K.J.V.; the R.S.V. uses the words *unspiritual* and *natural* interchangeably. Incidentally, this passage immediately follows the one which Bottom comically misquotes in *A Midsummer Night's Dream*, IV, i, 218–221). As for Lear's progress through the action of the play, another of St. Paul's comments seems applicable: "That was not first which is spiritual, but that which is natural; and afterward that which is spiritual" (I Cor. 15:46, K.J.V.). Being a natural man, Lear is long unable to perceive Cordelia's love, which is one of "the things of the Spirit of God." Her behavior seems mere foolishness to him; and only after he has been refined and made spiritual by suffering, can he recognize those things which are "spiritually discerned." Because Cordelia's love is spiritual (and therefore "unnatural"), it long escapes his comprehension.

As for Cordelia herself, she seems almost to hover over the play rather than to appear in it. As we have already said, the words which St. Paul uses to describe Christian love characterize accurately both her speech and her behavior. When Kent asks the messenger from France how Cordelia had received the letters sent to her, that gentleman replies, "Patience and sorrow strove/ Who should express her goodliest" (IV, iii, 16–17). She cannot be accused of unkindness, and she "endures all things," even death. She does not speak "in the tongues of men and of angels" as Lear does; on the contrary, she prefers most of the time to "love, and be silent" (I, i, 62). Indeed, as A. C. Bradley indicated, Cordelia speaks "scarcely more than a hundred lines" in the whole play.[16] At times, others must take her part and say for her what she herself declines to say, as when Kent tells Lear, "To plainness honor's bound/When majesty falls to folly." Cordelia willingly "gives away all she has" (herself), but unlike Lear she makes no great show about doing it. The Fool calls Lear "nothing," and he in turn calls Goneril "naught"; but no one calls Cordelia nothing, though she is the first character to speak that word (I, i, 87).

Despite her obvious reticence, Bradley, who admired the characterization of Cordelia very much, found at least one of her speeches inappropriate and objectionable. The lines he thought troublesome were these:

> Why have my sisters husbands if they say
> They love you all? Haply, when I shall wed,
> That lord whose hand must take my plight shall carry
> Half my love with him, half my care and duty. (I, i, 99–102)

Bradley objects:

> But truth is not the only good in the world, nor is the obligation to
> tell truth the only obligation. The matter here was to keep it

inviolate, but also to preserve a father. And even if truth *were* the one and only obligation, to tell much less than truth is not to tell it. And Cordelia's speech not only tells much less than truth about her love, it actually perverts the truth when it implies that to give love to a husband is to take it from a father. There surely never was a more unhappy speech.[17]

The reason why Cordelia speaks as she does is easily explained, again by reference to First Corinthians. Paul, discussing the problems of marriage, observes that "the unmarried woman or girl is anxious about the affairs of the Lord, how to be consecrated in body and spirit; but the married woman is anxious about worldly affairs, how to please her husband" (I Cor. 7:34). Cordelia is merely suggesting that by remaining single, she is able to devote herself entirely to "the Lord" (in this case, Lear), whereas her sisters must devote time and attention to other matters, including "how to please their husbands."

Cordelia's death has also presented a problem for some critics. But the objections to her death are purely moral ones; most of them may be reduced to the contention that she does not deserve to die. Kenneth Muir answers these objections intelligently: "Of those critics who complain that she died guiltless we can only enquire if they would rather she had died guilty." [18] They would probably respond in words like these: "By no means; but she ought not to die at all in the play." This, however, is tantamount to saying the play should imply that she "lives happily ever after"; and this contention is surely as far removed from both tragedy and Pauline Christianity as it could possibly be. We are told that Cordelia "redeems nature from the general curse/Which twain have brought her too" (IV, vi, 202–203), and such redemption is not achieved without sacrifice. According to St. Paul, a human being is like a kernel of wheat in that it "does not come to life unless it dies" (I Cor. 15:36); and there is at least one symbolic resurrection in this final scene. Kent, recognized at last by Lear, asks the king, "Where is your servant Caius?" Lear replies:

> He's a good fellow, I can tell you that.
> He'll strike, and quickly too. He's dead and rotten.

Kent.   No, my good lord; I am the very man.
Lear.   I'll see that straight. (V, iii, 284–288)

The suggestion of resurrection and the possibility of redemption through suffering are unmistakably present in this scene, whether or not such implications are consistent with academic theories of tragedy.

Bradley admits something of the sort; but when he deals with the question, he sounds embarrassed and apologetic. He mentions the feelings of "bewilderment or dismay," and says that

> it may sound a wilful paradox to assert that the slightest element of reconciliation is mingled with them or succeeds them. Yet it seems to me indubitable that such an element is present, though difficult to make out with certainty what it is or whence it proceeds.
>
> The feeling I mean is the impression that the heroic being, though in one sense and outwardly he has failed, is yet in another sense superior to the world in which he appears; is, in some way which we do not seek to define, untouched by the doom that overtakes him; and is rather set free from life than deprived of it. Some such feeling as this . . . accompanies the more prominent tragic impressions, and, regarded alone, could hardly be called tragic. For it seems to imply (though we are probably quite unconscious of the implication) an idea which, if developed, would transform the tragic view of things. It implies that the tragic world, if taken as it is presented, with all its error, guilt, failure, woe and waste, is no final reality, but only a part of reality taken for the whole, and, when so taken, illusive; and that if we could see the whole, and the tragic facts in their true place in it, we should find them, not abolished, of course, but so transmuted that they had ceased to be strictly tragic,—find, perhaps, the suffering and death counting for little or nothing, the greatness of the soul for much or all, and the heroic spirit, in spite of failure, nearer to the heart of things than the smaller, more circumspect, and perhaps even 'better' beings who survived the catastrophe.
>
> And some such thought as this (which, to bring it clearly out, I have stated, and still state, in a form both exaggerated and much too explicit) is really present through the whole play.[19]

Bradley seems to be saying that at the end of *King Lear* he has the distinct impression that "Death is swallowed up in victory"

(I Cor. 15:54), but he is embarrassed to say so straight out because that conflicts with his theory of tragedy. Why he should automatically mistrust his own reaction to a great work of art rather than suspect that his tragic theory is inadequate, he does not explain.

The symbolic action in the play which has been singled out for perhaps more discussion than any other is Lear's "unbuttoning," his disrobing. Robert Heilman devotes a whole chapter of *This Great Stage* to what he calls "The Clothes Pattern," which he regards as being (among other things) an index of Lear's spiritual progress: "If we see the movement of Lear from well-accoutered king to half-clad fugitive, from putting off of cares to giving up of life, we also observe his progress from eyeless rage to seeing beneath the surfaces that deceived him." [20] The evidence Heilman presents is certainly enough to convince almost anyone that the imagery of clothing is a highly important vehicle for meaning in the play and that there is a fundamental ambiguity about that meaning. Again St. Paul provides the key to understanding the work:

For we know that if the earthly tent we live in is destroyed, we have a building from God, a house not made with hands, eternal in the heavens. Here indeed we groan, and long to put on our heavenly dwelling, so that by putting it on we may not be found *naked*. For while we are still in this tent, we sigh with anxiety; *not that we would be unclothed, but that we would be further clothed, so that what is mortal may be swallowed up by life.* (II Cor. 5:1–4)

Ultimately, even in *King Lear,* it is not merely clothes but "the flesh" which deceives us by concealing the reality beneath the surface of things. When Gloucester desires to kiss Lear's hand, the king replies, "Let me wipe it first; it smells of mortality" (IV, vi, 132).

The imagery of sight and blindness, to which Heilman devotes another long chapter, likewise has its counterpart in the Corinthian letters. The passage just quoted continues in this fashion: "So we are always of good courage; we know that while we are at home in the body we are away from the Lord, for *we walk by faith, not by sight"* (II Cor. 5:6–7). Paul, like Shakespeare after him, uses the imagery of cloth to illustrate the relationship between sight and blindness, between faith and the lack of it. With the unbelievers, "a veil lies over their minds; but when a man turns to the Lord the veil is removed" (II Cor. 3:15–16). Moreover, Paul anticipates the speeches of Cordelia, Kent, and Edgar in which they urge sincerity and directness as the only way of confronting blindness:

> We have renounced disgraceful, underhanded ways; we refuse to practice cunning or to tamper with God's word, but *by the open statement of the truth we would commend ourselves to every man's conscience in the sight of God.* And even if our gospel is *veiled,* it is veiled only to those who are perishing. In their case *the god of this world has blinded the minds of the unbelievers.* (II Cor. 4:2–4)

The sight–blindness paradox receives nearly as full a treatment in Second Corinthians as the foolishness–wisdom paradox does in First Corinthians; and together they elaborate the love theme, which is fully stated in First Corinthians 13.

At least one other aspect of the sight–blindness imagery deserves mention in connection with the Corinthian letters. The five senses are the subject of considerable wordplay in *King Lear,* sometimes facetious and sometimes painful or sinister. This wordplay begins in one of the Fool's riddles:

> *Fool.* Thou canst tell why one's nose stands i' th' middle on's face?
> *Lear.* No.
> *Fool.* Why, to keep one's eyes of either side's nose, that what a man cannot smell out he may spy into. (I, v, 16–20)

This suggestion reappears several times. The Fool picks it up again in the next act: "All that follow their noses are led by their eyes but blind men, and there's not a nose among twenty but can smell him that's stinking" (II, iv, 66–68). When Regan finishes the blinding of Gloucester, she orders a servant, "Go thrust him out at gates, and let him smell/His way to Dover" (III, vii, 93–94). And when the blinded Gloucester replies to one of Lear's questions, "I see it feelingly," Lear asks, "What, art mad?

A man may see how this world goes with no eyes. Look with thine ears" (IV, vi, 147–149). The eyes, as the source of tears, become associated with the play's main theme; and this connection becomes explicit when Gloucester speaks of the man "that will not see/Because he does not feel" (IV, i, 68–69). But still this confusing of the bodily organs seems fanciful and arbitrary. In First Corinthians, however, just before the great passage on love, St. Paul raises these questions:

> If the whole body were an eye, where would be the hearing? If the whole body were an ear, where would be the sense of smell? But as it is, God arranged the organs of the body, each one of them, as he chose. If all were a single organ, where would the body be? As it is, there are many parts, yet one body. (I Cor. 12:17–20)

Thus, the Fool not only ridicules prophecy, as we have already noted; he also makes light of knowledge by inquiring facetiously into matters which St. Paul takes for granted.

The "moral" of *King Lear,* for those readers whose attention to the play is not "mingled with regards that stands/Aloof from th' entire point," is perfectly clear. It tells us that if we would be men, we must "give up childish ways." We must be patient and kind; we must endure—in a word, we must love. For unless we do that, even a fool can see that we are nothing.

The evidence that Shakespeare's treatment in *King Lear* of his main subject (love) and his secondary subjects (wisdom and foolishness, sight and blindness) is derived from the Corinthian letters seems overwhelming; and the assertion that *King Lear* is "Christian only in [its] insistence on the radical imperfectibility of man" [21] appears to have its origin in completely inappropriate standards of judgment. Shakespeare seems to have molded the substance of the Corinthian letters to the form of the old *Leir* play and by this transformation to have produced something entirely new. Indeed, if we may regard *King Lear* as typical of his method, Shakespeare's fabled objectivity may be quite simply the product of his unwillingness to rely upon his own subjective experience except as he saw it mirrored in earlier literary texts.

But let us turn to our third question about *King Lear*; in the light of what has been said so far, can we claim that the treatment of the subject matter may be adequately described as either affirmative or pessimistic? Alfred Harbage, by pairing the terms as he does, implies that if the play could be shown to be *Christian* in its emphasis, then it would follow that it was also *affirmative* in spirit; and conversely, if it is *pagan* in emphasis, then it would also be *pessimistic*. I must confess that I see no grounds whatever for pairing the terms in this fashion. Nor do I mean to imply that the opposite pairing would be any more accurate. The term *affirmative,* if it applies to Christianity and therefore to *King Lear,* does so only by means of a gigantic irony or an extremely elusive paradox. And the term *pessimistic* is, as Harbage says, "a small word for a small thing."

Friedrich Nietzsche, who understood Christianity better than many Christians do and who despised it heartily, distinguished (in *The Genealogy of Morals*) between the "aristocratic ethic" and the "slave ethic." He identified Christianity, which has at its center the "debilitating narcotic power" of the "holy cross," with the latter, and "triumphant self-affirmation" with the former.[22] Nietzsche was at least partly right—St. Paul always speaks of himself as a "servant" or "slave" of Christ, whereas descendants of the Goethe-Nietzsche tradition of "triumphant self-affirmation" prefer to think of themselves as "masters." The affirmation which may rightly be associated with Christianity, and therefore with *King Lear,* is actually a *double negation,* which yields an indirect and ambiguous "affirmation."

The categories which Nietzsche supplies make possible a description of Lear himself. Throughout the first scene, Lear "affirms himself" in magnificently aristocratic fashion. What could be more regal than this pronouncement?

> Of all these bounds, even from this line to this,
> With shadowy forests and with champains riched,
> With plenteous rivers and wide-skirted meads,
> We make thee lady. (I, i, 63–66)

Lear insists upon the relation of lord and vassal, with himself of course as lord of all; but the whole point of the play is that this will never do. Lear's insistence upon a feudal structure in society is a denial of the brotherhood of man; and in order to escape the consequences of this attitude, he must deny his denial, as he does in the "Poor naked wretches" speech:

> O, I have ta'en
> Too little care of this! Take physic, pomp;
> Expose thyself to feel what wretches feel,
> That thou mayst shake the superflux to them
> And show the heavens more just. (III, iv, 32–36)

And Gloucester reinforces the necessity of this double denial in a speech which echoes the one just quoted:

> That I am wretched
> Makes thee the happier. Heavens, deal so still!
> Let the superfluous and lust-dieted man,
> That slaves your ordinance, that will not see
> Because he does not feel, feel your pow'r quickly;
> And each man have enough. (IV, i, 65–71)

Both of these speeches set forth the social implications of love (charity), and their content is simply a paraphrase of a passage in the second Corinthian letter:

> For you know the grace of our Lord Jesus Christ, that though he was rich, yet for your sake he became poor, so that by his poverty you might become rich. . . . I do not mean that others should be eased and you burdened, but that as a matter of equality your abundance at the present time should supply their want, so that their abundance may supply your want, that there may be equality. (II Cor. 8:9–14)

It is, as we would expect, only in the second half of the play that Gloucester and Lear are able to achieve these insights.

Ironically, when Lear "triumphantly affirms himself" by bestowing such royal gifts, he simultaneously denies his own identity. The king who gives away his kingdom, with however royal a gesture, soon finds himself ruler of no kingdom at all.

And the father who voluntarily makes himself dependent on his children, by that act plunges himself into a second childhood. (Cordelia's term for Lear, "this child-changèd father" [IV, vii, 17], means both "father changed by his children" and "father changed into a child." Edgar's exclamation, "He childed as I fatherèd" [III, vi, 108], has a similar double meaning.) When Lear discovers this irony, he says something which is even more heavily charged with irony than the first scene had been: "Thou shalt find/That I'll resume the shape which thou dost think/I have cast off for ever" (I, iv, 299–301). He finally does "resume the shape" of king and father, but only after suffering in a way that he does not imagine when he speaks those lines.

One must therefore be very circumspect about applying the word *affirmative* either to *King Lear* in particular or to Christianity in general. And much the same is true of the adjective *pessimistic*. The conception of grace is almost all that keeps Christianity from being the most pessimistic view imaginable. The notion that a human being is like a kernel of wheat in that it "does not come to life unless it dies" stems from a rather grim view of natural life. But the same process of redemption through suffering, the same suggestion that "Death is swallowed up in victory" characterizes both, and makes the words *pessimistic* and *optimistic* seem feeble indeed when applied either to the play or to the religious texts on which it is based.

The difficulties of interpreting *King Lear* tend to evaporate when the correct frame of reference is used. Those who find the New Testament incomprehensible will also find *King Lear* puzzling and ambiguous; and they will have great difficulty reconciling the implications of the play with any theory of tragedy that depends heavily upon Aristotelian concepts. As Alfred Harbage says, *King Lear* is "religious, as all great tragedies are religious." Because Aristotle's insights are purely moral, they cannot penetrate religious meaning—they are inadequate even for the analysis of Greek tragedy; and when we misguidedly apply them to Shakespeare, we are left marveling at how completely Shakespearean drama eludes our attempt to analyze it. We cannot dissect a frog with a tomahawk, at least not in such a way as to discover anything significant about the anatomy of the frog. By the same token, we will never gain much insight into the structure and meaning of Shakespearean tragedy through examining it by means of the categories which Aristotle provides in his *Poetics.* Shakespeare probably did not know Aristotle, but it seems reasonable to assume that he did know the bible.

V

Macbeth Divided Against Himself

*"Every kingdom divided against itself
is laid waste, and house falls upon house.
And if Satan also is divided against himself,
how will his kingdom stand?"*
LUKE 11:17–18

⧽ THE Porter scene in *Macbeth* has been a source of
concern or even embarrassment to almost everyone that has
written about the play. Few critics will agree with Coleridge,
who attributed every word the Porter speaks, except for one sentence, to "some other hand" than Shakespeare's;[1] but a good
many commentators seem willing to allow the drunken servant's
lines to pass as comic relief, with no suggestion at all as to why
he should speak those particular words at that point in the play.
Even De Quincey's brilliant essay, "On the Knocking at the Gate
in 'Macbeth,'" says nothing whatever about the Porter himself;[2]
and until recently the best attempts to justify the Porter's "low
soliloquy" have depended at least as heavily upon the fact that
there are similar scenes in the other tragedies, as upon any demonstration that *this* scene is appropriate to *Macbeth*. A. C. Bradley suspected that the Porter was there for some serious purpose,
and he was quite certain that Shakespeare "despised the ground-
lings if they laughed."[3] Bradley, when all is said and done,
merely dilutes and combines the views of Coleridge and De
Quincey; he admits the possibility (though he sees no evidence
to support it) that someone other than Shakespeare may have
written the *words* of the passage; but, he maintains, "that anyone

except the author of the scene of Duncan's murder *conceived* the passage is incredible."

Only within the past few decades has any serious effort been made to interpret the Porter's speeches and to show their relation to the rest of the play. Kenneth Muir, in his Introduction to the Arden *Macbeth,* makes what is probably the best contribution. Elaborating on the suggestion of Hales, he associates the Porter with "the traditional figure of the miracle plays, the porter of hell-gate, who was expected to make jests, but who was something more than a jester." [4] He points out that the reference to treason in the Porter's speech "looks back to the executed Thane of Cawdor; . . . and it looks forward to the dialogue between Lady Macduff and her son, and to the long testing of Macduff by Malcolm." [5] He shows too that the emphasis upon "equivocation" is not merely a topical allusion to Father Garnet's involvement in the Gunpowder Plot, but that it becomes the clue to one of the play's major themes. Moreover, Muir demonstrates that the speech on "drink and lechery" points up the "contrast between *desire* and *act* [that] is repeated several times in the course of the play," and that this speech reflects "one of the predominant characteristics of the general style of the play—it consists of multitudinous antitheses." [6] These points are well taken, and they should certainly remove any doubts as to the Porter's authenticity.

But the passage is far richer than Kenneth Muir indicates. We should heed the final words of the scene's first speech, "I pray you remember the porter." For this minor character does more than open the gate upon which Macduff is knocking; he carries the key to the whole play. His speeches have three distinct levels of significance: first, a level of topical reference and broad humor, whose meaning is entirely independent of the play itself; secondly, a level of biblical reference and allusion, which reveals the source of the play's dominant motifs and images; and thirdly, a level of structural relationships, which reflect in miniature the pattern of the entire work. Scholarship and criticism have explored the first, probably as fully as the present state of historical knowledge will permit. Kenneth Muir and others have explicated portions of the third. But the second has remained if not entirely concealed, at least consistently ignored. We shall examine the three levels in order, summarizing the first briefly, exposing the second as fully and clearly as possible, and expanding the third in the light of the other two.

The dialogue which involves the Porter is short enough (37 lines) that it may be reproduced in its entirety; and since the meaning is closely packed, depending as it often does upon puns, we should have the speeches before us.

Enter a Porter. Knocking within.

Porter.   Here's a knocking indeed! If a man were porter of hell gate, he should have old turning the key. (*Knock.*) Knock, knock, knock. Who's there, i' th' name of Belzebub? Here's a farmer that hanged himself on th' expectation of plenty. Come in time! Have napkins enow about you; here you'll sweat for't. (*Knock.*) Knock, knock. Who's there, in th' other devil's name? Faith, here's an equivocator, that could swear in both the scales against either scale; who committed treason enough for God's sake, yet could not equivocate to heaven. O come in, equivocator. (*Knock.*) Knock, knock, knock. Who's there? Faith, here's an English tailor come hither for stealing out of a French hose. Come in, tailor. Here you may roast your goose. (*Knock.*) Knock, knock. Never at quiet! What are you? —But this place is too cold for hell. I'll devil-porter it no further. I had thought to have let in some of all professions that go the primrose way to th' everlasting bonfire. (*Knock.*) Anon, anon! [*Opens the way.*] I pray you remember the porter.

Enter Macduff and Lennox.

Macduff.   Was it so late, friend, ere you went to bed,
That you do lie so late?
Porter.   Faith, sir, we were carousing till the second cock; and drink, sir, is a great provoker of three things.
Macduff.   What three things does drink especially provoke?
Porter.   Marry, sir, nose-painting, sleep, and urine. Lechery, sir, it provokes, and unprovokes: it provokes the desire, but it takes away the performance. Therefore much drink may be said to

be an equivocator with lechery: it makes him, and it mars
him; it sets him on, and it takes him off; it persuades him, and
disheartens him; makes him stand to, and not stand to; in
conclusion, equivocates him in a sleep, and, giving him the
lie, leaves him.

Macduff. I believe drink gave thee the lie last night.

Porter. That it did, sir, i' the very throat on me, but I requited
him for his lie; and, I think, being too strong for him, though
he took up my legs sometime, yet I made a shift to cast him.
(II, iii, 1–37)

On the first level, the broad humor of the passage resides in the
apparently random profanity (the reference to Beelzebub and "th'
other devil"), the elaboration upon the sexual impotence produced by excessive drinking ("Lechery, sir, it provokes, and unprovokes . . ."), and the well-worn jokes about farmers who
hoard their crops in an effort to make huge profits when the
harvest is bad, and about tailors who steal pieces of cloth from
unsuspecting clients. G. B. Harrison reminds us that in Ben
Jonson's *Every Man Out of His Humor* "Sordido the farmer believes from the weather forecast in his almanac that the harvest
will fail. When his hopes of profiteering are disappointed he
hangs himself, but is cut down by his neighbors. When he revives,
he abuses them for cutting and not untying the rope." [7] The
tailor is related to the lechery motif ("Here you may roast your
goose"); and both he and the farmer are presumably among those
who "go the primrose way to th' everlasting bonfire."

The word *nose-painting* presents a problem even on the surface
level. In the glossary of *Shakespeare's Bawdy*, Eric Partridge defines it as "lechery; (excessive) copulation"; and he also says that
"the remainder of the Porter's speech makes it clear that lechery,
not the nose-reddening that results from over-drinking, is primarily meant, though there may be a pun." [8] But if this definition
is correct, then the Porter contradicts himself immediately—he
names *nose-painting* as one of the three things which "drink especially provokes"; and then he says, "Lechery, sir, it provokes,
and unprovokes," as if to make a distinction between *nose-painting* and *lechery*. Moreover, the other two things which "drink

especially provokes" (sleep and urine) are obviously short-term effects of intoxication, whereas the "nose-reddening" Partridge refers to results only from a long career of drinking; it is usually taken to be a sign of alcoholism. In view of these two facts, it seems more likely that nose-painting means quite literally *painting one's nose*, that is, primping or making mouths in a glass, manifestations of the human vanity which finds freer expression during intoxication than at any other time. Such a definition involves no contradiction with what the Porter then says about lechery; and it makes nose-painting consistent with sleep and urine as immediate, temporary effects of drinking. As we shall see later, this definition also fits into a significant pattern of imagery that runs through the rest of the play.

The main topical reference is of course to the doctrine of equivocation, propounded by the Jesuits and used by Father Garnet (who also went by the name of Farmer) to evade responsibility for the Gunpowder Plot. According to Kenneth Muir, "The words 'yet could not equivocate to heaven' imply that the speech was written after Garnet's death by hanging" on May 3rd, 1606.[9] Garnet claimed that in certain cases one might equivocate under oath without being guilty of perjury; that is, such equivocation was permissible "if just necessity so require." To Protestant Englishmen the doctrine was naturally abhorrent; and the Porter clearly reveals such an attitude when he uses the word *equivocate* to represent the relationship between drunkenness and lechery. However repugnant the doctrine may have been from a religious point of view, it was extremely useful to Shakespeare, since *equivocate* also means *lie* and *equivoque* means *pun*. The Porter's lines are full of puns—he and Macduff even pun several times upon the word *lie* at the end of their conversation.

The second level of significance in the Porter's speeches rests upon biblical reference and allusion. Before examining those references, however, we should call attention to a point that is frequently ignored: Shakespeare repeatedly associates Macbeth with Satan, cautiously at first, then more and more explicitly as the play proceeds. In a soliloquy, Macbeth regrets seeing his "eternal jewel/Given to the common enemy of man" (III, i, 68–69); and when Banquo's ghost appears, Macbeth asserts that he himself is a man, "and a bold one, that dare look on that/Which might appal the devil" (III, iv, 59–60). During the long conversation between Macduff and Malcolm, Macduff cries, "Not in the legions/Of horrid hell can come a devil more damned/In evils to top Macbeth" (IV, iii, 55–57). The most explicit association of all comes in the last act, when Young Siward confronts Macbeth and tries to kill him:

> *Young Siward.* What is thy name?
> *Macbeth.* Thou'lt be afraid to hear it.
> *Young Siward.* No, though thou call'st thyself a hotter name
>   Than any is in hell.
> *Macbeth.* My name's Macbeth.
> *Young Siward.* The devil himself could not pronounce a title
>   More hateful to mine ear.
> *Macbeth.* No, nor more fearful. (V, vii, 5–9)

For reasons that will become clear later, the name *Satan* never appears in *Macbeth*; even the Porter avoids mentioning it when he calls out, "Who's there, in th' other devil's name?"

Shakespeare also uses, as we would expect, subtler and more poetic ways of associating Macbeth with the Prince of Darkness. Shortly before the statement of Macduff which is quoted above, Malcolm, who refuses to become cynical about all men simply because Macbeth has shown himself to be evil, has said, "Angels are bright still though the brightest fell" (IV, iii, 22). Now the only passage in the New Testament which identifies Satan as a "fallen light" occurs in the tenth chapter of Luke: "And he said to them, '*I saw Satan fall like lightning from heaven.* Behold, I have given you authority to *tread upon serpents and scorpions,* and over all the power of *the enemy*; and nothing shall hurt you'" (Luke 10:18–19). These lines are particularly arresting, because they make one wonder if they might also be the source of several other things in the play, such as Lady Macbeth's exhortation to her husband, "Look like th' innocent flower,/But *be the serpent* under't" (I, v, 63–64) and Macbeth's own exclamation, "O, *full of scorpions is my mind,* dear wife!" (III, ii, 36). The possibility of such a connection seems more likely when we recall

that Malcolm looks forward, in this same conversation with Macduff, to the time "When I shall *tread upon the tyrant's head*"
(IV, iii, 45). (The word *serpent* is fairly frequent in Shakespeare;
but *scorpion* occurs only two other times in all of the plays.)

It is possible of course that these correspondences are accidental, but they at least suggest a hypothesis which is worth testing. Cleanth Brooks takes passing notice of "the view emphasized
by some critics (notably Coleridge and Bradley) of the likeness
between Macbeth and Milton's Satan in grandeur and sublim-
ity." [10] And Kenneth Muir, in a footnote designed to summarize
the biblical references in *Macbeth*, observes in connection with
the porter scene that "*Luke* xi mentions Beelzebub three times,
and also knocking." [11] Since the passage which Muir points to
comes only twenty-odd verses after the reference we have tenta-
tively identified, let us juxtapose the porter scene and these two
or three chapters in Luke in order to find out whether the latter
may not have been the matrix for the imagery and symbolism in
Macbeth. We shall depart from the porter scene whenever the
material in Luke leads us to another part of the play.

Luke 11 opens with one version of the Lord's prayer and continues with the parable about a man who goes to his friend's
house at midnight to ask for three loaves of bread. But the friend
refuses, calling from within that "the door is now shut" and that
he and his children are all in bed. Jesus asserts that "though he
will not get up and give him anything because he is his friend,
yet because of his importunity he will rise and give him whatever
he needs. . . . Knock, and it will be opened to you" (Luke
11:5–9). The paragraph ends with another reference to serpents
and scorpions (vss. 11–12), and the chapter continues:

Now he was casting out a demon that was dumb; when the demon
had gone out, the dumb man spoke, and the people marveled. But
some of them said, "He casts out demons by Beelzebub, the prince of
demons"; while others, to test him, sought from him a sign from
heaven. But he, knowing their thoughts, said to them, "Every kingdom divided against itself is laid waste, and house falls upon house.
And if Satan also is divided against himself, how will his kingdom
stand?" (vss. 14–18)

The most direct statement of this theme in *Macbeth* comes in the middle of the first act. Reflecting on what the witches have revealed to him, Macbeth says:

> *My thought,* whose murder yet is but fantastical,
> *Shakes so my single state of man that function*
> *Is smothered in surmise* and nothing is
> But what is not. (I, iii, 139–142)

In both the Geneva and the Bishops' Bibles, *single* is the word used to describe a condition of soundness or integrity—"The light of the bodie is the eye: therfore when thyne eye is single, then is thy whole bodie lyght" (Luke 11:34, Geneva Bible).

Now if Macbeth is linked with the Prince of Darkness (as he certainly is in the course of the play), and if Satan's being "divided against himself" would inevitably cause his kingdom, like Macbeth's, to fall (as the gospels assert that it would), then it should come as no surprise that "multitudinous antitheses" are (as Kenneth Muir rightly observes) "one of the predominant characteristics of the general style of the play." A. C. Bradley, who was more interested in psychological analysis of characters than in technical analysis of style, reaches essentially the same conclusion by a different method: Macbeth's "conscious or reflective mind, that is, moves chiefly among considerations of outward success and failure, while his inner being is convulsed by conscience." [12] Because Shakespeare is a consistent writer, the two observations are equally just.

There is, to be sure, a fundamental ambiguity about Macbeth's identification with Satan: the Scottish tyrant both *is* and *is not* the Prince of Darkness. Lady Macbeth, after reading her husband's letter, describes his character accurately:

> Glamis thou art, and Cawdor, and shalt be
> What thou art promised. Yet do I fear thy nature.
> It is too full o' th' milk of human kindness
> To catch the nearest way. Thou wouldst be great,
> Art not without ambition, but without
> The illness should attend it. What thou wouldst highly,
> That wouldst thou holily; wouldst not play false,
> And yet wouldst wrongly win. (I, v, 13–20)

In a word, Macbeth lacks Satan's consistency as a partisan of evil. It is the point of Christ's deductive argument in the passage just quoted from Luke that Satan's kingdom *does stand*, that he is *not* divided against himself, and therefore, that it is *not* by Beelzebub's power that Christ casts out demons. Macbeth would be the devil but for the fact that his nature is "too full of the milk of human kindness." He is, paradoxically, the being that Christ describes in hypothetical language—Satan divided against himself. It is for *this* reason (not simply because he is evil) that Macbeth's kingdom cannot stand.

The next paragraph in Luke 11 is extremely interesting in the context of *Macbeth*, particularly the matter of Banquo's ghost and the "show of eight kings." During the banquet scene Macbeth dispels the spirit of the murdered Banquo with these words:

> Take any shape but that, and my firm nerves
> Shall never tremble. Or be alive again
> And *dare me to the desert* with thy sword.
> If trembling I inhabit then, protest me
> The baby of a girl. Hence, horrible shadow!
> Unreal mock'ry, hence! [*Exit Ghost*] (III, iv, 102–107)

The ghost returns three scenes later, bringing with it the spirits of eight kings, which represent the various Stuart monarchs, James I being the ninth of that dynasty. Macbeth, who is greatly disturbed by the first appearance of Banquo's ghost, is nearly undone by the "show of eight kings"—"Let this pernicious hour/ Stand aye accursèd in the calendar!" (IV, i, 133–134). We turn now to the next paragraph in Luke:

> "When the unclean spirit has gone out of a man, he passes *through waterless places* seeking rest; and finding none he says, 'I will return to my house from which I came.' And when he comes he finds it swept and put in order. *Then he goes and brings seven other spirits more* evil than himself, and they enter and dwell there; *and the last state of that man becomes worse than the first.*" (Luke 11:24–26)

The ghost of Banquo is "unclean" and the other spirits are "more evil" than the first only of course from Macbeth's point of view—he kills his comrade in an effort to destroy the line of kings that

are to descend from him, and the "other spirits" therefore un-
nerve Macbeth far more than does the solitary ghost of Banquo.

In any extended discussion of the Porter's lines the question
naturally arises, what connection is there, if any, between the
biblical references and the emphasis upon sexuality? As we shall
see later, this question is absolutely central to the meaning of the
play. For the moment, however, we shall limit our attention to
one aspect of the matter—the repeated allusions to breast-feeding.
In an article called "Image and Symbol in 'Macbeth,'" contained
in Volume 19 of the *Shakespeare Survey*, Kenneth Muir writes,
"Whatever the origin of the images in *Macbeth* relating to breast-
feeding, Shakespeare uses them for a very dramatic purpose." [13]
We need not wonder about their origin; the next two verses in
Luke are these:

> As he said this, a woman in the crowd raised her voice and said to
> him, "Blessed is the womb that bore you, and the breasts that you
> sucked!" But he said, "Blessed rather are those who hear the word
> of God and keep it!" (Luke 11:27-28)

We recall Lady Macbeth's words, "Come to my woman's breasts/
And take my milk for gall," and her later speech,

> I have given suck, and know
> How tender 'tis to love the babe that milks me:
> I would, while it was smiling in my face,
> Have plucked my nipple from his boneless gums
> And dashed the brains out, had I so sworn as you
> Have done to this. (I, vii, 54-59)

When she finishes her tirade, Macbeth exclaims, "Bring forth
men-children only;/For thy undaunted mettle should compose/
Nothing but males." The emphasis upon procreation, and in
Macbeth's case the *failure* to procreate, is extremely important in
the play. It extends even to the birds: Banquo refers to the
"pendent bed and procreant cradle" of the "temple-haunting
martlet" (I, vi, 3-10). These two verses in Luke provide the most
satisfactory way of resolving the apparent contradiction between
"Lady Macbeth's children" and Macbeth's being without an heir.

Shakespeare's bible imagery and his Holinshed plot simply failed to coincide at this point.

Almost every commentator on *Macbeth* has observed that the three dominant symbols in the play are darkness, blood, and water: the darkness is of course both internal and external; the blood represents the guilt of murder; and the water is the "purifying agent" which fails to purify. But apparently no one has pointed out that these three symbols, used in combination, come directly from the same chapter in Luke which "mentions Beelzebub three times, and also knocking." All three of the symbols figure importantly in the last twenty-two verses of that chapter; and the purpose which they serve in that context is closely related to their function in *Macbeth*. The darkness which is both internal and external comes first:

> "No one after lighting a lamp puts it in a cellar or under a bushel, but on a stand, that those who enter may see the light. Your eye is the lamp of your body; *when your eye is sound, your whole body is full of light; but when it is not sound, your body is full of darkness.* Therefore be careful lest the light in you be darkness." (Luke 11:33–35)

The passage continues with the story of the man who showed surprise that Jesus did not wash his hands before sitting down to eat:

> While he was speaking, a Pharisee asked him to dine with him; so he went in and sat at table. The Pharisee was astonished to see that he did not first wash before dinner. And the Lord said to him, *"Now you Pharisees cleanse the outside of the cup and of the dish, but inside you are full of extortion and wickedness.* You fools! Did not he who made the outside make the inside also? But give for alms those things which are within; and behold, everything is clean for you." (Luke 11:37–41)

The blood-red "gilt of murder" comes third in Luke:

> "Therefore also the Wisdom of God said, 'I will send them prophets and apostles, some of whom they will kill and persecute,' that *the blood of all the prophets,* shed from the foundation of the world, may be required of this generation, *from the blood of Abel to the*

blood of Zechariah, who perished between the altar and the sanctuary. Yes, I tell you, it shall be required of this generation. Woe to
you lawyers! for you have taken away the key of knowledge; you
did not enter yourselves, and you hindered those who were enter-
ing." (Luke 11:49–52)

This last quotation, with its mention of Zechariah, who "perished between the altar and the sanctuary," helps explain why
Macduff employs the metaphor he does in announcing Duncan's
death:

> *Macduff.*   Confusion now hath made his masterpiece:
>   Most sacrilegious murder hath broke ope
>   The Lord's anointed temple and stole thence
>   The life o' th' building!
> *Macbeth.*   What is't you say? the life?
> *Lennox.*   Mean you his Majesty? (II, iii, 62–66)

It also suggests, with its harsh attitude toward hypocritical "interpreters of the Law" (Geneva Bible), that lawyers are among
those whom the Porter has in mind when he says that he "had
thought to have let in some of all professions that go the primrose way to th' everlasting bonfire."

In the twelfth chapter of Luke we come to a story which reminds us of the Porter's reference to the farmer who lost his life
"on th' expectation of plenty":

And he told them a parable, saying, *"The land of a rich man brought
forth plentifully;* and he thought to himself, 'What shall I do, for
I have nowhere to store my crops?' And he said, 'I will do this: I
will pull down my barns, and build larger ones; and there I will
store all my grain and my goods. And I will say to my soul, Soul,
you have ample goods laid up for many years; take your ease, eat,
drink, and be merry.' But God said to him, *'Fool! This night your
soul is required of you;* and the things you have prepared, whose
will they be?' So is he who lays up treasure for himself, and is not
rich toward God." (Luke 12:16–21)

The next three verses juxtapose three more symbols that are
prominent in *Macbeth*—eating (the banquet scene), clothes (the

ill-fitting garments), and birds (sparrows, ravens, martlets, owls, and many others):

> And he said to his disciples, "Therefore I tell you, do not be anxious about your life, *what you shall eat,* nor about your body, *what you shall put on.* For life is more than food, and the body more than clothing. *Consider the ravens:* they neither sow nor reap, they have neither storehouse nor barn, and yet God feeds them. Of how much more value are you than the birds!" (Luke 12:22–24)

This reference to ravens echoes a motif which appears earlier in the same chapter:

> "Are not five sparrows sold for two pennies? And not one of them is forgotten before God. Why, even the hairs of your head are all numbered. Fear not; you are of more value than many sparrows." (Luke 12:6–7)

As we think of *Macbeth,* these references to ravens and sparrows recall another statement that appears just after the words "I saw Satan fall like lightning from heaven," which we quoted earlier: "I thank thee, Father, Lord of heaven and earth, that thou hast hidden these things from the wise and understanding and *revealed them to babes*" (Luke 10:21). When we combine the two passages, we have the essential elements of the beautiful dialogue between Lady Macduff and her son. That conversation begins:

> *Wife.*   Sirrah, your father's dead;
>   And what will you do now? How will you live?
> *Son.*   As birds do, mother.
> *Wife.*   What, with worms and flies?
> *Son.*   With what I get, I mean; and so do they.
>
> *Wife.*   How wilt thou do for a father?
> *Son.*   Nay, how will you do for a husband?
> *Wife.*   Why, I can buy me twenty at any market.
> *Son.*   Then you'll buy 'em to sell again.
> *Wife.*   Thou speak'st with all thy wit; and yet, i' faith,
>   With wit enough for thee. (IV, ii, 30–43)

But the most important connection between *Macbeth* and Luke remains that of the divided-self theme and its accompanying imagery. We see it perhaps most clearly when we juxtapose Macbeth's speeches with the three knocking parables in Luke (11:5–13; 12:35–48; 13:22–30). The hero sees himself at one and the same time as the "steward" who is responsible for Duncan's safety and as the "thief" who breaks into the house and "steals thence the life of the building."

> *Macbeth.* He's here in double trust:
> First, as I am his kinsman and his subject,
> Strong both against the deed; then, as his host,
> *Who should against his murderer shut the door,*
> *Not bear the knife myself.* (I, vii, 12–16)

Macbeth is not a morality play representing the career of a man who does wrong and is then punished as he deserves. It is instead a tragedy which portrays a great man divided against himself, whose kingdom, therefore, cannot stand.

The third level of significance in the Porter's speeches is the one involving structural relationships; and it is here that we encounter a problem, or at least an apparent inconsistency. On the one hand, what the Porter says points up and binds together some of the play's important motifs—as Kenneth Muir indicates, the remark about "treason" recalls "the executed Thane of Cawdor; . . . and it looks forward to the dialogue between Lady Macduff and her son, and to the long testing of Macduff by Malcolm." Similarly, the emphasis upon "equivocation" is a commentary upon the role of the witches. Near the end of the play Macbeth begins to "doubt th' equivocation of the fiend,/That lies like truth" (V, v, 43–44); and moments later he exclaims against the "juggling fiends" that "palter with us in a double sense,/That keep the word of promise to our ear/And break it to our hope" (V, viii, 20–22). In both cases the Porter alerts us to recurrent themes. But on the other hand, the over-all tone of the Porter's lines seems entirely different from that of the rest of the play. In *Shakespeare's Bawdy*, Eric Partridge compares Shakespeare's works with each other on the basis of their bawdiness and indicates that "the Tragedies, despite the comparative innocuousness of *Macbeth*, are, as a class, the most indelicate." He then singles out each play for separate comment, stating flatly that "*Macbeth* is the 'purest' of the Tragedies and, except for the Porter Scene, pure by any criterion." [14] (The word *purest* in this context does not mean most consistently tragic, but rather least bawdy.) Our problem is this: how can the Porter's words be both "the key to the whole play" (as we have been assuming), and, at the same time, the only "impure" part of an otherwise "pure" work? Surely one of these conclusions is at least partly in error. Either there is an important way in which the Porter does not serve as a reliable guide to the entire play, or else the rest of *Macbeth* is not quite so "pure" as Partridge seems to think.

Let us examine the possibility that perhaps *Macbeth* is not so different from the other tragedies on this score, and that we should "remember the porter" even when he uses "improper" language and discusses the sexual impotence that results from excessive drinking. If we follow this procedure, making use of Partridge's own glossary (which he compiled from the "less pure" Shakespearean dramas), we begin to notice some interesting things. For instance, near the beginning of the play, while Macbeth is still very much a man and is not yet in any sense "divided against himself," Ross refers to him as "Bellona's bridegroom, lapped in proof" (I, ii, 54). The footnotes in most editions explain that Bellona is the goddess of war and that *lapped in proof* means clad in proven armor. That this is the surface meaning no one will deny. But we notice in Partridge that "for Shakespeare, the word *lap* seems to have always borne a sexual connotation." [15] This case is apparently no exception, since the word in question immediately follows the word *bridegroom*. Considered in this light, the words *in proof* also take on another meaning, and the whole phrase turns out to mean husband to the goddess of war— he had so proven himself in her lap. When we look again at the rest of the speech in which this phrase appears, we see that it fairly bristles with terms that figure prominently elsewhere in Partridge's glossary, and still more that take on a sexual meaning from the context.

> Norway himself, with terrible numbers,
> Assisted by that most *disloyal* traitor
> The Thane of Cawdor, began a dismal *conflict,*
> Till that Bellona's *bridegroom, lapped in proof,*
> Confronted him with self-comparisons,
> *Point* against *point* rebellious, arm 'gainst arm,
> *Curbing his lavish spirit:* and to conclude,
> The victory *fell on us.* (I, ii, 51–58)

Later in this act, Macbeth concludes the soliloquy which first reveals that he is beginning to be "divided against himself" with these words:

> I have no *spur*
> To *prick* the sides of my intent, but only
> *Vaulting ambition,* which *o'erleaps* itself
> And *falls on th' other*—
>   *Enter Lady [Macbeth].* (I, vii, 25–28)

Clearly, Macbeth's "horsemanship" is not what it used to be. Only about thirty lines earlier, Duncan, who had tried unsuccessfully to keep pace with Macbeth as they rode toward the latter's castle, had said,

> We coursed him at the heels and had a purpose
> To be his purveyor; but he *rides* well,
> And his *great love, sharp* as his *spur,* hath holp him
> To his home before us. (I, vi, 21–24)

Once we are alerted to the double meaning of these passages, we begin to see the significance of Lady Macbeth's constantly urging her husband to "be a man," of Macbeth's being without an heir, and of his despair over the fact that his rival Banquo is to be the "father of kings." The whole play takes on a different cast, including such familiar speeches as this one: "But screw your courage to the sticking place/And we'll not fail" (I, vii, 60–61). Lady Macbeth now begins to sound desperate as well as shrewish. But this conclusion presents another problem—if the "bawdy element" is so significant in *Macbeth,* how does it happen that Partridge completely missed it? There are three principal reasons. First, this material is more closely related to the play's main theme (Macbeth's division against himself) than is the case in the other plays. It never springs from an obviously humorous intention except in the Porter's lines; consequently, in the rest of the play it goes unnoticed. Secondly, after the first few scenes, it consistently represents sexual failure rather than sexual prowess, whereas most of "Shakespeare's bawdy" is associated with the latter. Thirdly, the two principal characters are joined in wedlock—most of the sexual innuendoes in Shakespeare occur in the conversation of men among themselves (as in *Henry V,* III, vii), in that of women among themselves (as in *Much Ado About Nothing,* III, iv), or between a man and a woman not married to each other (as in *All's Well That Ends Well,* I, i). That is to say, the "bawdy stuff" is used in a different way and for a different purpose in *Macbeth* than it is in the other plays. (It is for similar reasons that the most significant biblical material in Shakespeare has remained almost entirely concealed. When the bible is reflected in occasional verbal flourishes or pious reflections, it can be identified without much difficulty; but when the biblical fiber is woven directly into the fabric of the play, it escapes notice for a long time.)

Partridge indicates in his glossary that *horsemanship* (which apparently involves a pun on *whoresmanship*) is the source of a good many terms that carry a double meaning in Shakespeare, including *ride, rider, leap, mount,* and *vault.* We recall that Macbeth uses a participial form of this last word in one of the speeches already quoted. Admitting the possibility of double meaning in this case, we find that his phrase "vaulting ambition" means two quite different things depending on whether we emphasize the first word or the second. Vaulting *ambition* means lust for power; but *vaulting* ambition means desire to vault, or, to use the Porter's term, *lechery.* In other words, even the most "improper" language of the Porter is pure metaphor. But obviously, a part of that metaphor remains to be interpreted. We have established *lechery* as the equivalent of Macbeth's lust for power; and we have shown that Macbeth finally understands that the witches have been equivocating with him, "paltering with him in a double sense."

What then is the significance of *drink* in the Porter's speech and action? We immediately recall Lady Macbeth's speech near the end of the first act, when she upbraids her husband for his failure of spirit:

> Was the hope *drunk*
> Wherein you dressed yourself? Hath it *slept* since?
> And wakes it now to look so green and pale
> At what it did so freely? From this time
> Such I account thy *love*. Art thou afeard
> To be the same in thine own *act* and valor
> As thou art in *desire?* (I, vii, 35–41)

Here the last term of the metaphor falls into place, and another of the Porter's symbolic words begins to be clear, *sleep*, one of the things which "drink especially provokes." The source of Macbeth's "drunken hope" is the witches; and when we turn to the first scene in which he encounters the "weird sisters," we find Banquo asking,

> Were such things here as we do speak about?
> Or have we eaten on the insane root
> That takes the reason prisoner? (I, iii, 83–85)

The intoxication here alluded to is more profound than that produced by alcohol—it is of the psychedelic variety. Banquo accurately describes the effect of the witches' prediction, seriously taken: "That, trusted home,/Might yet *enkindle* you unto the crown,/Besides the Thane of Cawdor" (I, iii, 120–122). Thus, the Porter's term *drink* designates what for the common man produces an *enkindled imagination,* just as the term *lechery* establishes a commonplace equivalent for Macbeth's *lust for power.*

We are now in a position to interpret the whole metaphor, "Therefore much drink may be said to be an equivocator with lechery." It means quite simply: The witches' prediction, which enkindles Macbeth's imagination, may be said to "palter" with his lust for power. The Porter continues, "It *makes* him, and it *mars* him. . . ." When we return to the speeches near the end of the first act in which Lady Macbeth upbraids her husband, we find her saying:

> When you durst do it, then you were *a man;*
> And to be more than what you were, you would
> Be so much *more the man.* Nor time nor place
> Did then adhere, and yet you would *make* both.
> They have *made* themselves, and that their fitness now
> Does *unmake you.* I have given suck, and know
> How tender 'tis to love the babe that milks me . . . (I, vii, 49–55)

In short, the entire metaphor provides an objective correlative for Macbeth's division against himself. Sexual impotence becomes the prototype of the "contrast between *desire* and *act* [that] is repeated several times in the course of the play"; and *Macbeth's* imagery of impotence corresponds to the *hamartia* motif in *Hamlet.* But the two kinds of imagery are by no means interchangeable. The moral difference between the two heroes makes it appropriate that Macbeth's "fault" should be peculiar to him as an individual, whereas Hamlet's "fault" is something which all "flesh is heir to." Macbeth murders in cold blood and with malice aforethought; Hamlet murders by accident, as it were.

That the metaphor of impotence dictates a large part of the play's vocabulary is easily demonstrated. One more example from the first act will perhaps suffice. In the speech that Lady Macbeth pronounces after receiving her husband's letter, she says:

> Hie thee hither,
> That I may pour my spirits in thine ear
> And chastise with the valor of my tongue
> All that impedes thee from the golden round
> Which fate and metaphysical aid doth seem
> To have thee crowned withal. (I, v, 23–28)

Because it is associated with the word *pour,* *spirits* takes on the meaning of *drink* (alcoholic spirits); that is, Lady Macbeth will inflame her husband's imagination simply by talking to him. The next line goes beyond mere talk, however—*valor* (properly spelled *valour*) probably involves a pun on *velure* (cf. *The Taming of the Shrew*, III, ii, 63); and according to Partridge's *Dictionary of Slang* (1938 ed.) *velvet* has long been a slang word for *tongue*. (It appears, with that meaning, in one or two very old and very earthy idioms.) Since *tongue* is the next significant word in this line, the pun seems almost certain. The rest of the passage is too "greasy" (as Partridge would say) to explicate fully. In this connection we may note A. C. Bradley's comment on Lady Macbeth's chaste character:

> Perhaps it may be well to add that there is not the faintest trace in the play of the idea occasionally met with, and to some extent embodied in Madame Bernhardt's impersonation of Lady Macbeth, that her hold upon her husband lay in seductive attractions deliberately exercised. Shakespeare was not unskilled or squeamish in indicating such ideas.[16]

We should also note that Shakespeare was not unskilled in "Masking the business from the common eye/For sundry weighty reasons." As a matter of fact, the first part of the sentence just quoted is as follows: "And thence it is/That I to your assistance do make love . . ." (III, i, 123–126).

We turn now to the "three things which drink especially provokes"—nose-painting, sleep, and urine. As we have already indicated, it is not adequate even on the surface level to equate *nose-painting* (painting one's nose) with *lechery*, as Partridge does. The terms *primping* and *making mouths in a glass* fit the immediate context better. But the "nose-painting" which Macbeth's inflamed imagination provokes is of a much more sinister kind. Only moments before the Porter's entrance, Macbeth has accomplished Duncan's murder. Angered by her husband's impotence of spirit, Lady Macbeth cries,

> Infirm of purpose!
> Give me the daggers. The sleeping and the dead
> Are but as pictures. 'Tis the eye of childhood
> That fears a *painted* devil. If he do bleed,
> I'll *gild the faces* of the grooms withal,
> For it must seem their *guilt*. (II, ii, 51–56)

She finds later of course that some of the "paint" sticks to her hands and simply will not wash off. Macduff also makes it abundantly clear in the final scene that Macbeth himself is in for some "nose-painting":

> Then yield thee, coward,
> And live to be the show and gaze o' th' time.
> We'll have thee, as our rarer monsters are,
> *Painted upon a pole,* and underwrit
> 'Here may you see the tyrant.' (V, viii, 23–27)

The "sleep" which Macbeth's "drink" provokes is no less ghastly than the "nose-painting." While preparing himself to commit the murder, Macbeth tells a servant, "Go bid thy mistress, when my drink is ready,/She strike upon the bell" (II, i, 31–32). Later, he reflects upon his deed with quiet horror:

> Better be with the dead,
> Whom we, to gain our peace, have sent to peace,
> Than on the torture of the mind to lie
> In restless ecstasy. Duncan is in his grave;
> After life's fitful fever *he sleeps well.*
> Treason has done his worst. (III, ii, 19–24)

The sleep motif is not all that recalls the Porter—treason is here, and so is the overtone of sexuality ("to lie/In restless ecstasy"). Because of the obvious connection between sleep and sexuality, drink in one sense equivocates with sleep no less than with lechery. The impotent man lies restless not simply through lechery, but through frustration as well. " 'Glamis hath murdered sleep, and therefore Cawdor/Shall sleep no more' " (II, ii, 41–42). The hero has immersed himself in guilt without really achieving his purpose, which is to revel in the unalloyed pleasure of being king. Once the object of his "lecherous" desire is at his disposal, the impotent Macbeth, now totally divided against himself, is incapable of enjoying it. As Lady Macbeth says, "Naught's had, all's spent,/Where our desire is got without content" (III, ii, 4–5). She of course suffers in the same manner; when the doctor observes her in the sleep-walking scene, he exclaims, "A great perturbation in nature, to receive at once the benefit of sleep and do the effects of watching!" (V, i, 9–10). Applied metaphorically to Macbeth, this statement means that by becoming king he receives the benefit of Duncan's "sleep" (death), and yet he "does the effects of watching"; that is, he must be constantly on guard against detection and overthrow. He must conceal and deceive; hence, he "*lies*/In restless ecstasy."

The third thing which "drink especially provokes" (urine) reappears by way of a pun in the last words the Porter speaks, "I made a shift to cast him." Dover Wilson was perhaps the first to explain the pun on *cast* as meaning both throw (in wrestling) and vomit.[17] But in the notes to his edition, Kenneth Muir associates these lines with Macbeth's speech in Act V, "If thou couldst, doctor, *cast/The water* of my land, find her disease,/And purge it to a sound and pristine health,/I would applaud thee" (V, iii, 50–53), and suggests that *cast* may, in the Porter's speech, mean simply " 'emit,' not necessarily through the *mouth*." [18] Other commentators have indicated that there is also a good deal of punning on *stealing* and *staling*, on words connected with the discomfort that accompanies venereal disease (*goose roasting, bonefire*), and the like. But I think that Kenneth Muir is right, and that the chief metaphoric value of the word *urine* in the Porter's speech comes through the pun on *cast*. And the wrestling term reinforces one meaning of the words *give the lie to*, since the wrestler who throws or casts his opponent thereby gives him the lie.

Let us return now for a moment to a passage in Luke, one which immediately follows the question about Satan's being divided against himself and the repeated references to Beelzebub. There we read this sentence: "When a strong man, fully armed, guards his own palace, his goods are in peace; but when one stronger than he assails him and overcomes him, he takes away his armor in which he trusted, and divides his spoil" (Luke 11:21–22). The Porter, according to his own testimony, was able to recover when "drink gave him the lie": "but I requited him for his lie; and, I think, *being too strong for him*, though he took up my legs sometime, yet I made a shift to cast him." At the end of the play, Macbeth is less fortunate than the Porter. Besieged in his own castle, Macbeth repeatedly calls for his armor (V, iii, 33, 36). The first time that anyone "gives him the lie," Macbeth "makes a shift to cast him."

> *Young Siward.*   Thou liest, abhorrèd tyrant! With my sword
>   I'll prove the lie thou speak'st
>   *Fight, and Young Siward slain.* (V, vii, 10–11)

But the second time, it is the witches themselves who "give the lie" to Macbeth—when Macduff reveals that he "was from his mother's womb/Untimely ripped," Macbeth knows that the end is near. It is only then that "one stronger than he assails him and overcomes him." (The "stronger one" in Luke is Christ himself.)

One suspects that a careful and thorough examination of *Macbeth* in the light of the porter scene and these two or three chapters in Luke would yield insight into both the genesis and the meaning of a great many other things in the play. Such an examination would unfortunately require more pages than the play itself occupies; and when that happens (as it often does in Shakespeare criticism), we begin unconsciously to attach more value to the explanations than to the works which they purport to explain. But as members of an intelligent and responsive audience, we should avoid "clapping for all the wrong reasons." The most remarkable thing about Shakespeare's imagination is not, as some people seem to think, that he created things *ex nihilo,* but that he was able to borrow all that he needed from earlier literary sources and stitch it together in such a way that the seams are almost invisible. Echoing Milton's praise of Spenser, we may call Shakespeare "a better teacher than Scotus or Aquinas," but what he teaches us has to do primarily with the nature of the literary imagination and the power of language, once they are fused with really valuable substance.

The combination of biblical theme and symbol with sexual metaphor in *Macbeth* should not, after all, be particularly surprising. We may say this not only because there is, quite apart from literature, a significant connection between authentic religion and genuine sexuality (Rom. 1:24–27), but also because among Shakespeare's works we have a parallel case in *Measure for Measure,* which was written only two or three years before *Macbeth.* Stanley Edgar Hyman, who categorically denies that the four greatest tragedies have anything to do with Christianity, is perfectly willing to admit that "Shakespeare may be Christian in *Measure for Measure.*" [19] And at the same time, Eric Partridge regards *Measure for Measure* as being one of Shakespeare's two "most sexual, most bawdy plays." [20] The religious and the sexual elements are so perfectly blended in *Macbeth* and so ingeniously woven into the fabric of the play that as long as one of them remained hidden "from the common eye," the other did so too. Conversely, the discovery and explication of either element almost inevitably draws our attention to the other, provided that we remain open-minded and attentive to the text. Surely the time has come when we should abandon the idea that any interpretation of Shakespeare which takes seriously the poet's indebtedness to the English bible must somehow spring from the critic's peculiar bias. In literary criticism, as in most other matters, nothing is quite so prejudicial as prejudice, even when it is against what appears to be prejudice.

VI

The Novel as a Tragic Mode

*Perhaps we ought to define what a
novel is before starting. This will
not take a second. M. Abel Che-
valley has, in his brilliant little
manual, provided a definition, and
if a French critic cannot define the
English novel, who can? It is, he
says, "a fiction in prose of a certain
extent" (une fiction en prose d'une
certaine étendue). That is quite
good enough for us, and we may
perhaps go so far as to add that the
extent should not be less than
50,000 words.*

E. M. FORSTER, *Aspects of the Novel*

◆§ IF we derive our notion of tragedy from the paradigms rather than simply borrowing it from an academic formula
such as Aristotle's, we are confronted by the fact that the universally accepted paradigms come to an end in the mid or late
seventeenth century with the work of Corneille and Racine, or
even earlier in the same period with the great Shakespearean
tragedies. There are partisans who would argue that certain
dramatists after the seventeenth century have produced works
that stand as perfectly good examples of tragedy; but the very
necessity of their arguing the point demonstrates that these
works cannot be taken as "universally accepted paradigms." The
problem which this situation presents is not theoretical but his-

torical. If we ask "Why have plays written after the seventeenth century failed to gain wide acceptance as tragedy?" our answer will be little more than conjecture. But on the other hand, if we ask "What happened to the tragic mode in literature after the seventeenth century?" we must examine works of literature other than plays before reaching a conclusion. The theoretical question rests on the assumption that tragedy is indissolubly wedded to the theater and that if new tragedies are no longer produced upon the stage, then tragedy itself ceases to be written. The historical question reflects no such assumption. It allows for the possibility that tragedy, which quite obviously has not ceased to interest audiences or to exercise the minds of writers, may have found its way into another literary genre at that point in history.

What remains relatively constant in the tragic paradigms is not after all the form but the content. Otherwise, there would be very little significance to Freud's statement in *Totem and Taboo*, "The hero of the tragedy had to suffer; this is to-day still the essential content of a tragedy." When we take a comparative look at the works of Sophocles, Euripides, Shakespeare, and Racine, the tremendous differences of form are what we find most arresting. Euripides' plots, vastly different from those of Sophocles, are distressing to many who admire the older poet greatly, though Aristotle insisted that Euripides, as far as his endings were concerned, was "the most tragic of the poets." It is common knowledge that people who learned while very young to admire the plays of either Shakespeare or Racine often have difficulty acquiring a taste for the other poet later in life. But in spite of the differences, all of these tragedies, when they are read or seen with equal interest and sympathy, produce a remarkably similar effect.

One phenomenon stands out and demands immediate attention when we turn to the historical question about the tragic mode in literature after the seventeenth century, and that is the rise of the novel in the first half of the eighteenth. Though the impulse from which prose fiction originally sprang was probably more closely related to comic drama than to tragic, and though most novels involve what Walter Allen calls an "intermingling of tragedy and comedy," [1] the novel has always been so flexible that it could lend itself to any kind of content. This fact is abundantly clear either when we survey the history of the novel or when we attempt to "define" it as a literary genre or type. In the Introduction to *Three Greek Romances,* Moses Hadas associates the earliest prose tales with comedy: "Only the comic poets could freely invent persons and events, and the closest affinity of prose fiction, which is the latest literary invention of the Greeks, is with New Comedy." [2] And Henry Fielding, one of the first great English novelists, set forth his conception of the novel as a "comic epic poem in prose." [3] Nevertheless, *Clarissa, Moby Dick*, and *Anna Karenina* are novels just as surely as *Tom Jones, Pride and Prejudice*, and *Ulysses* are. In the matter of definition, we cannot go any further than E. M. Forster does in *Aspects of the Novel* without excluding some works that are unquestionably novels. There is certainly nothing, then, in either the history or the "definition" of the novel which shows it to be unfit as a medium for expressing tragic meaning.

The rise of the novel is not only the most striking but also the most significant development of modern literary history. Lionel Trilling justly describes that significance in *The Liberal Imagination*:

> For our time the most effective agent of the moral imagination has been the novel of the last two hundred years. It was never, either aesthetically or morally, a perfect form and its faults and failures can be quickly enumerated. But its greatness and its practical usefulness lay in its unremitting work of involving the reader himself in the moral life, inviting him to put his own motives under examination, suggesting that reality is not as his conventional education has led him to see it. It taught us, as no other genre ever did, the extent of human variety and the value of this variety. It was the literary form to which the emotions of understanding and forgiveness were indigenous, as if by definition of the form itself.[4]

The word *form* is apparently used here for lack of a better one, since the novel as a literary kind or mode is not one form, but a multitude of forms. Be that as it may, what Trilling says is undeniably true; and, as far as we can tell from our vantage point in time, the literary genre of both the Periclean and Elizabethan ages about which one might most reasonably make parallel statements would, of course, be tragedy. This certainly does not mean that the novel is, by its very nature, tragic; but it does mean that the novel, whatever else it may also do, functions in relation to our age as tragic drama did in relation to the greatest periods of Greek and English history—by involving the members of its audience in the moral life, by inviting them to put their own motives under examination, by suggesting that reality is not as their conventional education had led them to see it. Moreover, understanding and forgiveness are no less indigenous to tragic drama than to the novel. Indeed, one of tragedy's obvious characteristics is that it usually represents understanding and forgiveness as coming, unfortunately, "too late."

Among post-Renaissance writers, one stands out from the rest as a possible successor to Shakespeare as the great practitioner of Christian tragedy—Fyodor Dostoevsky. Though he neither wrote plays nor derived his most important conceptions from the Pauline tradition, his attitude toward human suffering shows him to be in a direct line of descent from Aeschylus, whose chorus asserts that "Justice so moves that those only learn/who suffer"; and his vision of the world is demonstrably Christian. We are fortunate in Dostoevsky's case, as we are not in Shakespeare's, to have the writer's own explicit statements about his work—the letters, journals, and especially the notebooks are full of Dostoevsky's comments upon the novels. We read this passage, for instance, in *The Notebooks for Crime and Punishment*:

THE IDEA OF THE NOVEL

1

The Orthodox point of view; what Orthodoxy consists of.

There is no happiness in comfort; happiness is bought with suffering.

Man is not born for happiness. Man earns his happiness, and always by suffering. There's no injustice here, because the knowledge of life and consciousness (that is, that which is felt immediately with your body and spirit, that is, through the whole vital process of life) is acquired by experience *pro and contra,* which one must take upon one's self. (By suffering, such is the law of our planet, but this immediate awareness, felt with the life process, is such a great joy that one gladly pays with years of suffering for it.)[5]

This insistence upon the intimate connection between Orthodox Christianity and the tragic vision is at the heart of Dostoevsky's greatest novels.

As we have already indicated, St. John's writings are central to Eastern Orthodoxy in the same way that St. Paul's are central to Western Christianity. Dostoevsky's use of John as a chief literary source therefore corresponds exactly to Shakespeare's use of Paul. And just as the advent of Christianity between the time of Sophocles and that of Shakespeare changed the complexion of tragedy, so the rise of the novel between the time of Shakespeare and that of Dostoevsky changed its form. Thus, the history of great tragic literature, though interrupted for long periods of time, is continuous—always grounded in religious thought and feeling, it has moved from the pre-Christian dramatic works of Aeschylus, Sophocles, and Euripides, to the plays of Shakespeare which are permeated with Pauline thought, and then to the novels of Dostoevsky in which the Johannine influence is perfectly clear. In a sense, this is the "great tradition" of tragic writing in the Western world; and the two decisive influences upon that tradition have been the advent of Christianity, with its two mainstreams of development, and the rise of prose fiction as the dominant literary mode within the past two centuries.

Surprisingly, the main difficulty in discussing the novel as a Christian-tragic mode centers in its "Christian" rather than in its "tragic" aspect. Some critics refer quite casually to *Moby Dick* and *The Brothers Karamazov* as tragic novels, but take great pains to show that these same works are not genuinely Christian. In "Psychoanalysis and the Climate of Tragedy," for instance, Stanley Edgar Hyman has this to say: "Where tragic possibility is reintroduced in Christian history it is invariably repudiated as heresy, the Manichaean belief that the issue has not yet been finally settled, denying Incarnation its victory, or the Pelagian repudiation of Original Sin, obviating divine Atonement." [6] He speaks briefly of Shakespeare as being "only nominally Christian," and goes on to make this statement:

> The great tragic novels like *Karamazov* and *Moby-Dick* are similarly Manichaean and Pelagian, with Jesus appearing in person in the first to hear from the Grand Inquisitor the failure of his Incarnation, and Ahab in the second striking through the mask of the Christian Atonement, and finding his own sacrificial atonement, a Pelagian man-god, in the consubstantial mystery of immolation with the great whale.[7]

In the case of both novels, Hyman's judgment reflects what happens when the reader disregards the larger context and assumes that the actions and utterances of one or more characters are exempt from the irony which permeates the rest of the work.

In the first place, it would be extremely difficult to establish that Captain Ahab achieves any atonement at all, much less "his own sacrificial atonement, a Pelagian man-god, in the consubstantial mystery of immolation with the great whale." He seeks nothing but revenge, and he fails even in that. The difference between atonement, which involves satisfactory reparation and reconciliation, and revenge, which is simply vindictive retaliation, is not particularly subtle; and one does not succeed in the former merely by failing spectacularly at the latter. Revenge and atonement are alike only in that both are attempts to redress an earlier offense or injury. What starts out as a desire for revenge may finally lead to atonement—this is what happens in *Hamlet*—but only if the person who initially seeks revenge undergoes a change of attitude before the final confrontation takes place. This change of attitude is very marked (though frequently misunderstood) in *Hamlet*; in *Moby Dick* it is never forthcoming, though Ahab occasionally hesitates and reflects upon his undertaking.

Ishmael, the narrator of *Moby Dick*, is much given to philosophizing not only about the events of the story, but also about human life in general. In one such reflection he furnishes part of the evidence for thinking that original sin, far from being repudiated in the Pelagian manner, is taken very seriously in the context of *Moby Dick* as the one basic fact of life. We should bear in mind that the other principal tenet of Pelagianism, besides the repudiation of original sin, is the assertion that man has perfect freedom of the will. This second point is a corollary of the first, since the doctrine of original sin is the traditional explanation of what Martin Luther called "the bondage of the will." In the chapter called "The Mat-Maker," Ishmael sets forth his thoughts as he and Queequeg work together at a small loom.

> This warp seemed necessity; and here, thought I, with my own hand I ply my own shuttle and weave my own destiny into these unalterable threads. Meantime, Queequeg's impulsive, indifferent sword, sometimes hitting the woof slantingly, or crookedly, or strongly, or weakly, as the case might be; and by this difference in the concluding blow producing a corresponding contrast in the final aspect of the completed fabric; this savage's sword, thought I, thus finally shapes and fashions both warp and woof; this easy, indifferent sword must be chance—aye, chance, free will, and necessity—no wise incompatible—all interweavingly working together. The straight warp of necessity, not to be swerved from its ultimate course—its every alternating vibration, indeed, only tending to that; free will still free to ply her shuttle between given threads; and chance, though restrained in its play within the right lines of necessity, and sideways in its motions directed by free will, though thus prescribed to by both, chance by turns rules either, and has the last featuring blow at events. (Modern Library Edition, p. 214)

By no stretch of the imagination can this passage, spoken by the narrator about human life in general, be taken as supporting the Pelagian contention that man has "perfect freedom of the will," a doctrine which follows necessarily (in the Pelagian framework) from the denial of original sin.

If it is objected that Ishmael, as narrator, corresponds in some sense to the chorus in Greek tragedy and therefore represents a conservative viewpoint, we may cite other, equally "conservative" passages in which closely related attitudes find expression. We read, for instance, in Father Mapple's sermon about Jonah:

> As sinful men, it is a lesson to us all, because it is a story of the sin, hard-heartedness, suddenly awakened fears, the swift punishment, repentance, prayers, and finally the deliverance and joy of Jonah.

As with all sinners among men, the sin of this son of Amittai was in his wilful disobedience of the command of God—never mind now what that command was, or how conveyed—which he found a hard command. But all the things that God would have us do are hard for us to do—remember that—and hence, he oftener commands us than endeavors to persuade. And if we obey God, we must disobey ourselves; and it is in this disobeying ourselves, wherein the hardness of obeying God consists. (p. 41)

The same point of view is echoed in Fleece's sermon to the sharks:

Your woraciousness, fellow-critters, I don't blame ye so much for; dat is natur, and can't be helped; but to gobern dat wicked natur, dat is de pint. You is sharks, sartin; but if you gobern de shark in you, why den you be angel; for all angel is not'ing more dan de shark well goberned. (p. 295)

Stubb, Fleece's only human auditor, responds to the tirade by exclaiming, "Well done, old Fleece! . . . that's Christianity; go on." It is true, of course, that the narrator and these other characters are subject to interpretation within the context just as Ahab himself is; but when we hear a perfectly intelligible point of view echoed repeatedly within a novel, from several different quarters, we begin to suspect that it has a direct connection with the attitude which underlies the whole work and unifies it.

The split within the human psyche that Mapple and Fleece refer to is identical with the one which St. Paul analyzes fully in Romans 7. It is the warfare between "the law of God" and "the law of sin which dwells in my members." The "wilful disobedience" of Jonah, as represented by Mapple, is in a direct line of descent from what Milton called "man's first disobedience"; and the uneven battle between shark and angel is a beautiful image of man's condition as heir to the fall. Moreover, Ahab himself is represented as being split in this same way—conscious of the warfare going on within himself, but powerless to do anything about it. And exactly as with *Hamlet*, the "law of sin which dwells in Ahab's members" is called "madness."

Now, in his heart, Ahab had some glimpse of this, namely: all my means are sane, my motive and my object mad. Yet without power

to kill, or change, or shun the fact; he likewise knew that to mankind he did long dissemble; in some sort, did still. But that thing of
his dissembling was only subject to his perceptibility, not to his will
determinate. Nevertheless, so well did he succeed in that dissembling,
that when with ivory leg he stepped ashore at last, no Nantucketer
thought him otherwise than but naturally grieved, and that to the
quick, with the terrible casualty which had overtaken him. (p. 185)

Indeed, if any suspected Ahab of madness, they could but say as
Polonius did of Hamlet, "Though this be madness, yet there is
method in't" (II, ii, 203–204). Hamlet's desire for reconciliation
leads him finally to apologize for his "madness"; Ahab does nothing of the kind. The claim that Ahab achieves "his own sacrificial
atonement" has, therefore, very little support in the novel itself.

Hyman's remarks about *The Brothers Karamazov* have a more
direct bearing upon our inquiry than do his comments about
Moby Dick. The most obvious reason for suggesting that the
Dostoevsky novel might reflect a type of Manicheanism arises
from the imagery of the book. Manichean doctrine represents the
split in the human spirit as just one example of the eternal conflict between the Kingdom of Light and the Kingdom of Darkness. Johannine imagery, which Dostoevsky takes over without
much change, portrays Christ as the light of the world and sin as
darkness. As far as we know, these two strains of imagery are not
connected historically; and their implications within the two con-
texts are quite different. Manicheanism, for example, regards the
conflict as eternal and therefore absolutely incapable of resolution. Johannine thought, on the other hand, represents Christ
(the light of the world) as ultimately victorious. I cite again two
passages in the Dostoevsky novels already quoted, one in which
Myshkin exclaims "Our Christ whom we have kept and they have
never known must shine forth and vanquish the West" (*The
Idiot*, p. 519), and another in which Father Zossima urges his
hearers, "Doubt not the power of the heavenly light. . . . Your
light will not die even when you are dead. The righteous man departs, but his light remains" (*The Brothers Karamazov*, p. 386).

This similarity of imagery, which would be confusing to a
reader who did not recognize the Johannine character of Dosto-

evsky's thought, is not, however, the basis for Hyman's assertion that *The Brothers Karamazov* is essentially Manichean. Rather, he regards the Inquisitor's harangue as evidence that Dostoevsky rejected the incarnation, at least within the framework of this novel. But the Inquisitor chapter is thoroughly biblical in tone and feeling. It represents dramatically what Benoit calls "the great struggle between Jesus and the Prince of this world"; and Christ's silence in the face of the Inquisitor's charges is consistent with the New Testament account: "But when he was accused by the chief priests and elders, he made no answer. Then Pilate said to him, 'Do you not hear how many things they testify against you?' But he gave him no answer, not even to a single charge; so that the governor wondered greatly" (Matt. 27:12–14; cf. Mark 14:60 and Luke 23:9. These passages are usually taken as fulfilling the prophecy contained in Isaiah 53:7). Persons in the biblical narrative who were eager to condemn Christ no doubt considered his silence as proof that the charges were irrefutable; but it is obvious from the rest of their story that the gospel narrators themselves did not take this attitude. Similarly, readers who find in the Grand Inquisitor an articulate spokesman for their own point of view (as D. H. Lawrence did) will regard Christ's magnificently symbolic act of kissing the old cardinal as an expression of acquiescence. But one must ignore almost everything else in the novel to assert that as a work of art it effectively "denies Incarnation its victory."

Dostoevsky himself was quite explicit in the matter. Referring to contemporary atheists, for whose intellectual abilities he had no great respect, Dostoevsky said in his notebook that "those thickheads never dreamt of so powerful a negation of God as that embodied in the Inquisitor and in the preceding chapter, *to which the entire novel serves as an answer*." [8] And the affirmative power of the whole novel which "serves as an answer" is even greater than the negative power of the two chapters in question. Indeed, *The Brothers Karamazov* testifies more brilliantly than perhaps any other work of literature to the "victory of the incarnation." The logic of human experience, faithfully and fully represented in the book, is what renders meaningful Alyosha's final declaration to the boys—"Certainly we shall all rise again." This is what makes *The Brothers Karamazov* a Christian novel; and the fact that such a declaration can be made meaningfully only by one who recognizes that "we are all responsible for all" is what makes it a tragic novel. If anyone really believes that we are all responsible for all, then he must submit himself to tragic experience and accept suffering voluntarily though perhaps reluctantly. He does so not out of any desire to suffer or even out of any indifference to suffering, but because the acceptance of his responsibility makes it necessary for him to do so.

Perhaps the best way to discover how there can be any continuity between the plays of Shakespeare and the novels of Dostoevsky is to examine the implications of statements by two excellent writers on the novel, E. M. Forster and E. K. Brown. We shall focus our attention on what Forster says about *pattern, rhythm,* and *prophecy* in *Aspects of the Novel,*[9] and upon Brown's continuation of the same discussion in *Rhythm in the Novel.*[10] These statements provide a good point of departure not only because both critics are concerned to discover what lies "at the core of the novel," but also because Forster reinforces what he says about the novel by contrasting it with the drama. By such a procedure we can, I hope, gain some insight into the reasons why a critic like Arthur Sewell, in *Character and Society in Shakespeare,* can raise the question apropos of the final scenes of *King Lear,* "Does not the play look forward to Dostoievsky, rather than back to Seneca?"[11] The question may be rhetorical, and certainly Sewell does not provide any full answer; but still it draws our attention to something fundamental which the two writers have in common.

There is an interesting and revealing pattern within the examples and analogies which Forster and Brown use to express their views on the novel. In discussing the disadvantages of "a rigid pattern," Forster takes as his chief example Henry James's *Ambassadors.* He allows that in this case "beauty has arrived," and rounds out his sentence with a most damaging qualification —"but in too tyrannous a guise." He argues that when pattern dominates everything, the results may be satisfactory in the drama, but not in the novel.

In plays—the plays of Racine, for instance—she [beauty] may be justified because beauty can be a great empress on the stage, and reconcile us to the loss of the men we know. But in the novel, her tyranny as it grows powerful grows petty, and generates regrets. . . . To put it in other words, the novel is not capable of as much artistic development as the drama: its humanity or the grossness of its material hinder it (use whichever phrase you like). To most readers of fiction the sensation from a pattern is not intense enough to justify the sacrifices that made it, and their verdict is "Beautifully done, but not worth doing." [12]

Significantly, the dramatist named is not Shakespeare, whom the French do not hesitate to call romantic, but Racine, the master of French neoclassical tragedy; and it does not seem to occur to Forster that the judgment "Beautifully done, but not worth doing," which he apparently makes upon Henry James, is identical with the one passed by many readers upon a novelist that Forster admires very much—Jane Austen. ("How Jane Austen can write!" he exclaims while praising her novels in another chapter of the book.) Similarly, when he draws an analogy from music to illustrate what he says about rhythm, he refers not to Mozart, but to Beethoven. And Brown confirms our suspicion when he reports that Forster admits being "especially fond of Wagner." He quotes the older critic as saying, "With Wagner I always knew where I was—he ordained that one phrase should recall the ring, another the sword, another the blameless fool, and so on." [13]

Brown's own book repeats, with variations, the conception of novelistic rhythm which he borrows from Forster, a conception which emphasizes "repetition with variation" as being central to the novel. Brown elaborates this view in the chapter called "Expanding Symbols"; and he draws his main example from Forster's novel *Howards End*. He shows convincingly that the continually expanding symbol of vegetation comes to be "linked with everything that stands out against Wilcoxism"; and it finally includes "the wisps of hay, the bunch of weeds, the trickling grass, the grass on the Six Hills, the bumper crop of hay," a "beautiful but unproductive vine," and "a centenarian wych-elm." He shows too that these associations accumulate in the novel until "response to the hay" in *Howards End* becomes "an index to value in a character." [14] There can be little doubt that what he says is true, and it certainly enriches our understanding of Forster's method; but is must also be clear that this approach to fiction yields most when brought to bear upon late nineteenth- and twentieth-century novels, which we usually regard as being products of that gorgeous flowering of romanticism, the symbolist movement.

Another form of the "repetition with variation" which he considers essential to the novel, and which therefore might help to distinguish it from the drama, has to do with the relationship of all the characters to a single pervasive problem. "At the core of the novel," says Brown, "one finds not similar people confronted with dissimilar problems, not dissimilar people solving the same problem, but similar people confronted by the same problem." [15] He makes this statement in the midst of a series of comments upon Aldous Huxley's *Point Counter Point*; but the assertion directly contradicts what Huxley's novelist character, Philip Quarles, is quoted as saying within that same story. I therefore conclude that Brown, when he speaks of "the core of the novel," is referring not merely to this one book of Aldous Huxley's, but to the novel as a genre. This emphasis upon "similar people confronted by the same problem," together with others in *Rhythm in the Novel*, is consistent with Forster's point of view in *Aspects of the Novel*. We should recognize, however, that it would be difficult to find better examples of this characteristic in literature than we have in Shakespeare's tragedies.

Forster and Brown articulate a conception of the novel as an essentially *romantic* mode, which Forster explicitly contrasts with the drama as represented by the plays of Racine. There is a great deal of truth to this view; most novels do sprawl out in a way that is utterly foreign to the dramatic method of a French neoclassical playwright. But when we look at *Hamlet, King Lear,* and *Macbeth,* we cannot say that "their humanity or the grossness of their material" prevents them from reaching a very high degree of "artistic development." And when we consider Jane Austen's *Emma,* we cannot accurately say that its "rigid pattern" produces a sensation that is "not intense enough to justify the sacrifices that made it." In other words, we cannot accept reciprocal generalizations about the novel on the one hand and the drama on the other that leave both Shakespeare and Jane Austen in a kind of literary no-man's-land. It is precisely "their humanity and the grossness of their material" which make the plays of Shakespeare unpalatable to tastes formed by a study of Racinien tragedy; and it is precisely her "rigid patterns" and her high degree of "artistic development" that make Jane Austen's novels seem tame and dull to some readers who grew up on Melville and Faulkner. Conceptions which imply, when carried to their final conclusion, that Shakespeare was really a novelist who wrote plays and that Jane Austen was really a dramatist who wrote novels are simply inadequate.

But we must document our contention that *Emma* is constructed according to a "rigid pattern" and that *Hamlet,* for instance, has "at its core, similar people confronted by the same problem." Forster, though he condemns *The Ambassadors* as sacrificing too much in order to achieve the beauty of its pattern, has nothing but praise for *Emma*; and E. K. Brown, though he may argue that the novel characteristically represents people who have much in common with each other all struggling to solve a single problem, would surely not have denied that Shakespeare was a dramatist *par excellence.* Our only concern will be to show that there is something inconsistent about condemning one novel, as a novel, for possessing a feature that is present to an even higher degree in another work which the same critic regards as a masterpiece of fiction. We shall also be concerned to show that it is not very useful to find a distinguishing feature of the novel as a genre in a characteristic which emerges just as clearly in the great Shakespearean tragedies as it does in any work of prose fiction. Let us turn then, first to a consideration of the pattern in Jane Austen's *Emma,* which is obviously comic rather than tragic, and afterward to *Hamlet,* as a work which represents "similar people confronted by the same problem."

. . . .

To say that *Emma* is a book about marriage is like saying that *Moby Dick* is about the whaling industry or that *Anna Karenina* is about the Russian aristocracy. The statement is true but not at all helpful. Marriage does, however, provide an ideal framework for what happens in the novel. Holding herself aloof from the closest of human ties, Emma presumes to dispose of the lives of other people by playing the role of matchmaker. In the first third of the novel, she repeatedly declares that she will never marry. As she tells Harriet, her young protégée, "I never have been in love; it is not my way, or my nature; and I do not think I ever shall. And, without love, I am sure I should be a fool to change such a situation as mine" (R. W. Chapman edition, Oxford University Press, p. 84). Her later acceptance of the married state indicates her newly acquired willingness to participate in life on an equal footing with another human being. Only after she has become "more acquainted with herself" (p. 423) than she is when the story opens is she willing or even able to marry. This gradual achievement of self-knowledge at the cost of humiliating though comically represented experience is the real subject of *Emma*.

Self-knowledge is extremely difficult to come by; and the particular value of *Emma* as a novel lies in the fidelity with which it represents that complicated process. The book shows two complete cycles and part of a third through which the heroine must pass on her way to happiness. The second is longer and more complex than the first because Emma, having acquired a little self-knowledge from her experience with Harriet and Mr. Elton, is more circumspect in her behavior after that. But the second cycle is in all essentials similar to the first one. Both consist of the following steps: (1) Emma's perception of the situation in which she finds herself; (2) the formulation of her intention; (3) her action, designed to realize that intention; (4) the consequences of that action; and (5) her reaction to the consequences. These five steps lead her to a changed perception of the situation in which she finds herself, which is the beginning of a new cycle. The first cycle is completed within the first eighteen chapters of the book (i.e., Volume I), and our comprehension of the work as a whole depends upon how carefully we attend to what happens in this first part.

Of the five steps in each cycle, the first is the most difficult to analyze since it involves two simultaneous and interdependent matters, Emma's present state of self-knowledge and her interpretation of those things which are external to herself. We may define her self-knowledge at any given point as her conception of the relation between herself and what she professes to regard as the highest good. Throughout the novel, this "highest good" remains constant for Emma; it is, very simply, marriage. In the first chapter, her father tries to get her to promise that she will make no more matches, and she replies, "I promise you to make none for myself, papa; but I must, indeed, for other people. It is the greatest amusement in the world!" (p. 12). And in chapter 13 of Volume III, just before Mr. Knightley declares himself to Emma, she tells him that she has some news for him. When he asks, "Of what nature?" she replies, "Oh! the best nature in the world—a wedding" (p. 425). In both cases (and for that matter in all others) she obviously regards a good match as the finest thing in the world; but she carefully excludes herself from participation in the highest good except as an arranger of other people's involvement with it. She thus sets herself up as an amateur providence and unwittingly lays herself open to the condemnation which she herself later makes of Frank Churchill: "What has it been but a system of hypocrisy and deceit,— espionage, and treachery?—To come among us with professions of openness and simplicity; and such a league in secret to judge us all!" (p. 399).

E. M. Forster is perhaps right when he complains that "nearly all novels are feeble at the end," and observes that "if it was not for death and marriage, I do not know how the average novelist would conclude." [16] But the marriages that we have at the end of *Emma* constitute a perfect symbolic conclusion for an almost flawless novel—not only because marriage is the chief metaphor of the book, but because two of the weddings (Harriet's to Robert Martin and Jane Fairfax's to Frank Churchill) erase in superbly comic fashion the consequences of Emma's earlier blunders, and the third (Emma's to Mr. Knightley) represents the fulfillment of Emma's sensible intention to participate whole-heartedly in what she has taken all along to be the highest good in human experience. Her own marriage is therefore the third step of the third cycle in the elaborate but beautifully executed pattern of the novel, the contemplation of which may certainly *not* be said to create in us a sensation that is "not intense enough to justify the sacrifices that made it."

In short, we cannot accurately distinguish between the novel and the drama by asserting that the kind of pattern which we find in the plays of Racine is bound to be unsatisfactory when transposed to the realm of the novel. The pattern in *Emma* is every bit as "rigid" as anything in Racine; and *Emma* is surely one of the greatest of English novels. There is a closer affinity between the novels of Jane Austen and the plays of Racine than between the work of either of those writers and the greatest tragedies of Shakespeare, despite the fact that Jane Austen is an English writer and Racine is a dramatist. What they share is their devotion to the "austere" discipline of neoclassic art, while Shakespeare is, at least by French standards, wildly "romantic." *Aspects of the Novel,* published forty years ago, is still perhaps the best introduction we have to the art of prose fiction; but when Forster suggests that the novel inevitably breaks down when "its humanity or the grossness of its material" is brought within the confines of a delicately constructed pattern, we must hesitate, on the evidence of *Emma,* to accept his generalization, especially when the converse of that statement is so obviously not true. We know from the example of Shakespeare that beauty does not need the "rigid patterns" of a Racine in order to be "a great empress on the stage."

If we decline to accept Forster's generalization about pattern in the novel as opposed to the drama, we should also hesitate to place much weight on Brown's contention that "at the core of the novel one finds . . . similar people confronted by the same problem," not because the statement is untrue, but because its usefulness as a generalization about the novel is restricted by our finding exactly the same thing at the core of Shakespearean tragedy. The most obvious example of this characteristic in Shakespeare is the tendency of several different characters in one play to say essentially the same thing upon different occasions. We need not concur in Tolstoy's judgment that Shakespeare's characters "all talk alike" in order to observe this feature. Even A. C. Bradley apparently grants the point when he says of *Macbeth*, "I doubt if any other great play of Shakespeare's contains so many speeches which a student of the play, if they were quoted to him, would be puzzled to assign to the speakers." [17] Nor is this "repetition with variation" limited to "twin characters," such as Rosencrantz and Guildenstern or Goneril and Regan. It often permeates the whole play. Indeed, one might go so far as to claim that much of the "point" resides in this echoing of one character by another.

As we have seen, the central problem in *Hamlet* is action. It is, however, action of a special kind—that which is necessary in order to expiate murder. The action required of a particular character takes either of two forms, revenge or repentance, depending upon whether or not the person in question actually committed the murder; and in either case the action is tremendously difficult to take because it requires the person either to stand in judgment upon his fellow human beings and therefore "play God," or else to confess his own guilt and to stand condemned in his own eyes and the world's. Either way, "conscience does make cowards of us all." In *Hamlet,* the character whose task is purely and simply repentance is Claudius, and the one whose task is purely and simply revenge is Laertes. Hamlet himself confronts both forms of the central problem, since he must both avenge the death of his father, in whose murder he had no part, *and* repent the murder of Polonius, for whose death he is undeniably responsible. Hamlet's relation to the central problem is therefore more complex than anyone else's, but otherwise it is no different from theirs.

Thus, it should not be surprising that these three characters echo each other, especially in soliloquies, prayers, and asides. Hamlet's exclamation to the ghost in Act I, "Haste me to know't, that I, with wings as swift/As meditation or the thoughts of love,/ May sweep to my revenge," is identical in mood and meaning with what Laertes says in Act IV, "I dare damnation. To this point I stand,/That both the worlds I give to negligence,/Let come what comes, only I'll be revenged/Most thoroughly for my father." Claudius's admission that "like a man to double business bound/I stand in pause where I shall first begin,/And both neglect" reveals that his own dilemma is similar to Hamlet's. And Gertrude's aside, "To my sick soul (as sin's true nature is)/ Each toy seems prologue to some great amiss," would be just as appropriate in either Claudius's prayer or one of Hamlet's soliloquies as it is in her speech, partly because it juxtaposes the two crucial words *sin* and *amiss,* which are "at the core" of the play's meaning, just as one of Hamlet's speeches juxtaposes the words *trespass* and *madness.*

The list of parallels might be extended indefinitely, but the examples already cited are sufficient to show that at the core of Shakespearean tragedy, no less than "at the core of the novel," we find "similar people confronted by the same problem." Moreover, it would not be difficult to demonstrate that Shakespeare is at least as skillful as any novelist in the use of "expanding symbols," another form of the "repetition with variation" which Brown takes to be a distinguishing feature of the novel. Even Forster's term "prophecy," which he defines as being "in our sense . . . a tone of voice," [18] is not very helpful. Since he claims that it resides finally in the novelist's tone of voice, this characteristic ought to be the special property of fiction—it implies the presence of a narrator, a device which is not available to the playwright. But he takes Dostoevsky as his chief example of the prophetic novelist; and surely Vyacheslav Ivanov is right when he describes the "novel-tragedies" of Dostoevsky by saying that "in sharp contrast to the over-excited tone of the conversations, the style of the narrative is businesslike and sober, reminiscent of a court of law." [19] The tone of which Forster speaks is not so much the tone of a narrator's voice as it is the tone of a whole work; and this tone pervades the Shakespearean tragedies in the same sense that it pervades the Dostoevsky novels.[20] The "prophetic tone" which Forster describes, or the lack of it, may be a valid basis for distinguishing (as to relative merit) between novels; but it is not something which will serve to differentiate one particular novel from all plays.

But Forster and Brown were only seeking to say something significant about prose fiction, not to provide clear and rigid lines of demarcation between literary genres. The impossibility of our using their statements for such a purpose demonstrates, however, that it is probably even more hazardous to generalize about the novel than to do so about tragedy. How futile, then, must be the effort to generalize about the "novel-tragedy"! We shall therefore continue our inquiry using the same practical method that we brought to bear on particular dramatic works and on the gospel narratives. Instead of theorizing about what a "novel-tragedy" would have to be if such a thing existed, we shall examine three more works which seem, at least on their surface, to enunciate for our times the tragic meaning of life in somewhat the same fashion that the plays of Sophocles and Shakespeare did for theirs.

The novels of Dostoevsky will qualify as tragedies in so far as they demonstrate that the suffering they portray is *necessary* in the sense that we described earlier; and they will qualify as Christian works in so far as the thought structure, language, and imagery which went into their making is derived from the New Testament. If it is true that Dostoevsky shows us, perhaps more convincingly than any other modern writer, that "those only learn who suffer," we shall have at least a partial answer to our question, "What happened to the tragic mode in literature after the seventeenth century?" And if it is true that Dostoevsky's vision is authentically Christian, we shall be able to resolve some of the more difficult questions about his world view. Dostoevsky, no less than Shakespeare, makes it possible for readers to find in his work whatever they happen to be looking for; but like the great English dramatist he molds his works skillfully and gives them a coherence which can only mystify the reader who is willing to settle for anything less than the whole vision that informs these novels and makes them genuinely significant.

VII

Raskolnikov and the Resurrection of Lazarus

The fourth chapter of the fourth part—when Raskolnikov goes to Sonya and she reads the Gospel to him—greatly embarrassed the scrupulous editors of* The Russian Messenger *and they refused to print it. . . .

When sending the corrected chapter to his editors, the writer implored: "And now I* most earnestly *entreat you:* for the sake of Christ *let everything stand as it is now."

K. MOCHULSKY, *Dostoevsky: His Life and Work*

THE obvious importance of the Lazarus story in *Crime and Punishment* has led some critics to recognize that it may be there as a guide to the meaning of Raskolnikov's own story; but in the final analysis they have rejected this possibility, preferring to emphasize that the hero "remains essentially unrepentant to the end." Philip Rahv goes so far as to say that Dostoevsky, "as a number of critics have noted, appears to have been incapable of carrying out his declared intention to depict the renewal of life on Christian foundations." [1] Leo Shestov, whom Rahv quotes at length, seems entirely certain of the answer to his own question: "As a professed teacher of humanity, was not Dostoevsky in duty bound to let us in on the secret of the new reality and fresh possibilities that opened up to Raskolnikov?" [2] And even Konstantin Mochulsky, who represents Dostoevsky as "the great Christian writer," makes this bitter comment upon *Crime and Punishment*: "The novel ends with a vague anticipation of the hero's 'renewal.' It is promised, but it is not shown. We know Raskolnikov too well to believe this 'pious lie.' " [3] To put the matter briefly, we are told that the main character's regeneration is not really a significant consideration as far as the interpretation of the novel is concerned. In this respect, Rahv articulates the view of a good many commentators: "We, as critical readers, cannot overmuch concern ourselves with such intimations of ultimate reconcilement and salvation. Our proper concern is with the present story, with the story as written." [4]

But "the present story, the story as written" corresponds in both its outline and its conclusion to the record of Lazarus's death and ressurection, which Sonia reads aloud to Raskolnikov near the center of the novel; and the objections of critics to the epilogue of *Crime and Punishment* apply at least as well to the Lazarus story itself as to the novel which is based upon it. The biblical account also ends with the bare statement, "And he that was dead came forth"—Sonia reads only one more verse and says, "That is all about the raising of Lazarus" (p. 322). Are we to conclude therefore that the bible is "unable to depict the renewal of life on Christian foundations"? Should we reject the conclusion of this story because it fails to "let us in on the secret of the new reality and fresh possibilities that opened up" to the resurrected Lazarus? And is it not true that we know *too little* about Lazarus ever to believe this "pious lie" about his return from the dead?

If we answer these questions affirmatively, as Rahv, Shestov, and Mochulsky seem to imply that we should, we must realize that we are not making sound interpretive comment upon "the present story, the story as written"; we are simply rejecting the story's conclusion as a bit of literary foolishness. And it is obvious in the biblical account, if not in Dostoevsky's novel, that the conclusion is absolutely essential to the story as a whole. The point of the Lazarus story is not that a man, about whom we know almost nothing else, dies and apparently begins to rot, but that such a man is brought back to life by means that the narrator (John) is careful to represent fully. Likewise, the meaning of *Crime and Punishment* resides not in the sophomoric theories of a young man who uses "principle" to justify murdering his fellow human beings, but in the fact that even a man who is almost totally alienated from human life may at last be made "dimly conscious of the fundamental falsity in himself and his convictions" (p. 526), and thus be started back on his way to a place among the living.

The essential character of Dostoevsky's religious thought is revealed in his preoccupation with death and resurrection. In Dostoevsky, as in the bible, both terms have a symbolic as well as a literal meaning; and the paradigm is of course the crucifixion and exaltation of Christ. (In the gospel of John, the crucifixion itself is the "lifting up" of Jesus—see for instance John 12:31–33, which forms part of the chapter immediately following the Lazarus story and which comes only a few verses after the lines which become the epigraph for *The Brothers Karamazov*.) Perhaps because he did not aspire to equality with Christ, Dostoevsky became fascinated by two other resurrection stories, those of the twelve-year-old girl in Mark 5:21–43 and of Lazarus in John 11. Apparently, Christ's own death and resurrection were not so directly the basis for Dostoevsky's personal hope and belief as these other two stories were, since Christ after all was *worthy* to be brought back from the dead; but there is no indication in the New Testament that these two figures were anything but sinners like ourselves.

In *The Notebooks for Crime and Punishment* there is a passage dealing with Sonia which makes some of these associations explicit:

> She sacrificed herself for the family. Lord. Even in the most august sacrifice, there is ugliness [and vileness]. Fate humbles the humbled to the point that even in their noblest sacrifice there is disgrace and ugliness!

Memories appear:
Why when his mother was reading the Bible—Talifa kumi.[5]

These final words (spelled in English *Talitha cumi*) are from
Mark 5:41: "Taking her by the hand he said to her, 'Talitha
cumi'; which means, 'Little girl, I say to you, arise.'" Despite,
or paradoxically *because of,* the "disgrace and ugliness" of Sonia's
humiliation, she is represented as *arising* in *Crime and Punishment.* This passage in Mark remained permanently impressed
upon Dostoevsky's mind, as we may see by the miracle Christ
performs at the beginning of the Grand Inquisitor chapter in
The Brothers Karamazov: "He looks with compassion, and His
lips once more softly pronounce, 'Maiden, arise!' and the maiden
arises" (*The Brothers Karamazov,* p. 296; Constance Garnett
seems here to be indebted to the wording of this passage in the
Geneva Bible, the only version, other than Tyndale's, which
translates *Talitha cumi* as "Maiden, . . . arise.") Moreover, Dostoevsky's habit of associating this incident with the Lazarus story
is borne out by one of Ippolit's seemingly unanswerable questions in *The Idiot*: "How can they be overcome when even He
did not conquer them, He who vanquished nature in His life-
time, who exclaimed, 'Maiden, arise!' and the maiden arose—
'Lazarus, come forth!' and the dead man came forth?" (*The
Idiot,* p. 389).

It simply will not do to ignore the regeneration of Raskolnikov
in our interpretation, not only because this regeneration completes the parallel with the Lazarus story, but because to ignore
it would also reduce the role of Sonia to virtual meaninglessness.
The problem of interpreting *Crime and Punishment* is at least
partly, then, the problem of comprehending the Lazarus story,
which is both symbolic and complex. Many parts of the novel
which by themselves might present difficulties of interpretation
are in fact counterparts of elements that are already contained
in the biblical account, and they fall into place quite easily when
they are seen in that light. Though Dostoevsky quotes most of
the essential words of the Lazarus story at the appropriate time,
he is a subtle writer, and he dramatizes their meaning within
his own story rather than explicating it by direct statement.

This being the case, we should look at a reliable commentary upon the gospel of John, such as C. H. Dodd's *Interpretation of the Fourth Gospel*,[6] and see to what extent it illuminates not only the biblical account of Lazarus but also the relationship between that account and Raskolnikov's story.

We observe first of all that the raising of Lazarus is distinctly Johannine in character; that is, it appears nowhere in the bible except in the gospel of John, and it reflects several of John's thematic and stylistic preoccupations. Sonia is apparently aware of this fact almost intuitively, as we can tell by what she says when Raskolnikov tries to find the passage in her New Testament: " 'You are not looking in the right place. . . . It's in the fourth gospel,' she whispered sternly, without looking at him" (p. 319). And perhaps the most obviously Johannine feature of the story is the reiteration of the word *believe*. (The Greek word here is *pisteúō*, which according to Dodd has two main meanings in John: to give credence to, to believe; and to have confidence in, to trust.) In the Lazarus story (John 11), it occurs nine times, and in Dostoevsky's version (Part IV, Chapter 4), it appears twelve times, seven in the quoted biblical material and five more in Sonia's own words.

This verbal feature is extremely prominent in Dostoevsky's first significant reference to the Lazarus story, which takes place during one of Raskolnikov's interviews with Porfiry. Here is the passage:

> "Each class has an equal right to exist. In fact, all have equal rights with me—and *vive la guerre éternelle*—till the New Jerusalem, of course!"
>
> "Then you believe in the New Jerusalem, do you?"
>
> "I do," Raskolnikov answered firmly; as he said these words and during the whole preceding tirade he kept his eyes on one spot on the carpet.
>
> "And . . . and do you believe in God? Excuse my curiosity."
>
> "I do," repeated Raskolnikov, raising his eyes to Porfiry.
>
> "And . . . do you believe in Lazarus' rising from the dead?"
>
> "I . . . I do. Why do you ask all this?"
>
> "You believe it literally?"
>
> "Literally."

"You don't say so. . . . I asked from curiosity. Excuse me. But let us go back to the question." (p. 256)

The following chapter opens with the words, "I don't believe it, I can't believe it" (p. 262). And in the chapter which follows Sonia's reading from John, Raskolnikov reveals his squeamishness about the word: " 'I believe you said yesterday you would like to question me.' . . . 'Why did I put in "I believe" ' passed through his mind in a flash. 'Why am I so uneasy at having put in that *"I believe"?*' came in a second flash" (p. 327). We should perhaps note in this connection that the objections of Rahv, Shestov, and Mochulsky to the novel's epilogue may be summarized in the words, "We don't believe it, we can't believe it."

Now Sonia is extremely sensitive to the words "I believe," and Dostoevsky underscores this point in her reading of the Lazarus story.

"Jesus said unto her, thy brother shall rise again.

Martha saith unto Him, I know that he shall rise again in the resurrection, at the last day.

Jesus said unto her, I am the resurrection and the life; he that believeth in Me though he were dead, yet shall he live.

And whosoever liveth and believeth in Me shall never die. Believeth thou this?

She saith unto Him,"

(And drawing a painful breath, Sonia read distinctly and forcibly as though she were making a public confession of faith.)

"Yea, Lord: I believe that Thou art the Christ, the Son of God Which should come into the world."

She stopped and looked up quickly at him, but controlling herself went on reading. Raskolnikov sat without moving, his elbows on the table and his eyes turned away. (pp. 320–321)

Here, we are very close to the heart of the matter, since it is clear that Lazarus's being brought back to life is directly connected with Martha's affirmative and truthful answer to the question "Do you believe . . . ?" As Dodd says,

There is no story of the Raising of Lazarus—or none that we can now recover—separable from the pregnant dialogues of Jesus with His disciples and with Martha. On the other hand, these dialogues could not stand by themselves. They need the situation in order to be intelligible, and they not only discuss high themes of Johannine theology, but also promote and explain the action of the narrative.[7]

In short, without Martha's declaration of belief, which Sonia repeats "as though she were making a public confession of faith," there is no raising of Lazarus in "the present story, the story as written." And conversely, this dialogue would be "unintelligible" without the resurrection narrative which follows it.

What this means as applied to *Crime and Punishment* is that Sonia corresponds to Martha in the biblical account; and it is possible for Raskolnikov to be regenerated or "resurrected" be-cause—and *only* because—Sonia believes and loves. (The word *love* is no less characteristically Johannine than *believe;* ac-cording to the analytical concordance it appears at least three times as often in John as in any of the other gospels.) Raskolni-kov himself is "dead," utterly unable to break the deterministic chains that bind him. Dostoevsky makes all this quite explicit, not only in the epilogue but in Part VI of the novel as well. The first time that Raskolnikov undertakes to confess his guilt "at the cross-roads," he fails because people jeer at him, and "the words 'I am a murderer,' which were perhaps on the point of dropping from his lips, died away" (p. 510). But the second time, he sees Sonia hiding herself near him; and "Raskolnikov at that moment felt and knew once for all that Sonia was with him for ever and would follow him to the ends of the earth" (p. 510). Similarly, when he goes to confess to the police, he comes back down the stairs, having lost his nerve. But again he sees Sonia and returns—"There, not far from the entrance, stood Sonia, pale and horror-stricken. . . . He stood still a minute, grinned and went back to the police office" (p. 514). And during his time in Siberia, the imprisonment itself does little or nothing to revive him; but the presence of Sonia makes all the difference: "On waking up he chanced to go to the window, and at once saw Sonia in the distance at the hospital gate. She seemed to be waiting for some one. Something stabbed him to the heart at that minute" (p. 529). It is in connection with these events that it may be truthfully said that "life stepped into the place of theory" for Raskolnikov (p. 531).

But if Sonia corresponds to Martha in the Lazarus story, why is she represented as a prostitute? John never suggests that either Mary or Martha was a "fallen woman." There is another facet of the Johannine account, however, to which this feature of Dostoevsky's novel does correspond. First let us consider the situation in Dostoevsky's version. Immediately after Sonia reads the Lazarus story, Raskolnikov indicates that he identifies himself with her primarily because she has prostituted herself; and he equates her status as a harlot with his own as a murderer. "Haven't you done the same?" he asks her. "You, too, have transgressed . . . have had the strength to transgress. You have laid hands on yourself, you have destroyed a life . . . *your own* (it's all the same!) . . . So we must go together on the same road! Let us go!" (p. 323). The basis for this identification is actual, not merely imagined by Raskolnikov. Sonia has, in reality, come face to face with death by becoming a prostitute; and his knowledge of this fact makes it possible for Raskolnikov to communicate with her, to break through an alienation from humanity that would otherwise be total. What he does *not* realize is that Sonia's transgression was a voluntary though reluctant act of submission, whereas his own was a self-willed act of defiance. That is, he identifies himself with her because he mistakenly thinks they are both *Uebermenschen,* when in fact they are both suffering human beings. Thus, the identification is prompted, on Raskolnikov's side, by one of his many intellectual errors; but it comes about none the less. And it could never have done so if Sonia, in her turn, had not encountered death.

When we turn to the eleventh chapter of John, we find that the Lazarus story includes, at its outset and at its end, accounts which Dodd describes as being for Christ himself "a summons to face death." In the first case (John 11:5–16), we learn that going to Bethany, where Lazarus lies ill or already dead, means returning to Judea, where "the Jews were but now seeking to stone" Jesus (John 11:8). The disciples are dismayed at first, but they finally consent to go: "Thomas, called the Twin, said to his fellow disciples, 'Let us also go, that we may die with him'" (John 11:16). Dodd regards this verse as "in some sort an equivalent for the Synoptic saying, 'If anyone wishes to come after me, he must take up his cross and follow me.'" And he makes this further statement:

> Thus the narrative before us is not only the story of dead Lazarus raised to life; it is also the story of Jesus going to face death in order to conquer death. In the previous episode we were told that the Good Shepherd comes to give life to His flock, and that in doing so He lays down His life for the sheep (x. 10–11). The episode we are now considering conforms exactly to that pattern.[8]

The second account (John 11:47–53) tells about a meeting of the Sanhedrin, which had been called because of disturbing reports about Christ's activities, including the raising of Lazarus. At this meeting it is decided that Jesus must die. Dodd says of the passage:

> We may therefore take it that the evangelist designed the Council-meeting as a pendant to the episode of Lazarus. Its essential purport is that Jesus is formally devoted to death by a vote of the competent authority. This is, in fact, the act by which, in its historical or "objective" aspect, the death of Christ is determined.[9]

According to Dodd, then, part of the meaning of the Lazarus story is that Christ's raising the dead man to life requires his own going forth to meet death.

In these terms, Sonia corresponds not only to Martha, who says in all honesty and sincerity, "I believe," but also to Christ himself, who goes to meet death that others may live. As Edward Wasiolek indicates in his Introduction to *The Notebooks,* "In the novel itself we can discern, for example, that Sonia is a counterpoise to Svidrigaylov, but the notebooks tell us explicitly that this was Dostoevsky's intention; we can discern that she is meant to be a Christlike creature, but in the notebooks she is explicitly tied to the image of Christ." [10] It may seem shocking at first to suggest that in the final version it is precisely her being a prostitute which helps to link her directly to Christ, but this is

in fact the case; and it is not difficult to see how such an association may have developed in Dostoevsky's imagination. The
Lazarus story, John 11, makes it clear that the journey to Bethany
necessitates returning to Judea, where, as the disciples remind
Christ, "the Jews were but now seeking to stone you." John 8,
just a few pages earlier, opens with the story of the woman taken
in adultery, whom Jesus saved from death at the hands of the
self-righteous by saying to them, "Let him who is without sin
among you be the first to throw a stone at her" (John 8:7). The
identification seems quite natural when we recall Dostoevsky's
preoccupation with the image of stones—Raskolnikov hides his
booty under a very large one, and the extremely moving final
scene of *The Brothers Karamazov* is entitled "The Speech at the
Stone," the occasion being the funeral of Ilusha, "the poor boy
at whom we once threw stones, do you remember, by the bridge?
and afterwards we all grew so fond of him" (pp. 937–938). The
woman taken in adultery who faced death by stoning is indeed
close to the one who willingly risked the same death by stoning
in order to raise Lazarus from the dead.

Similarly, Raskolnikov corresponds to Lazarus in his renewal
or regeneration, which, as Mochulsky says, "is promised, but it
is not shown." That is, the hero's "new life" is asserted but is
not traced in detail, exactly as in the biblical account. No
further correspondence between Raskolnikov and Lazarus is
possible, since the only other thing we know about Lazarus is
that he died, a fact which does not serve to distinguish him
from any other man. If we take these correspondences as being
essential to the meaning of *Crime and Punishment,* we begin to
discover exactly what it is that elevates this novel to the level of
tragedy when it might very easily have been no more than a
naturalistic story about an ultimately meaningless crime. That
it does rise to such a level has been attested by several Russian
critics: Chulkov asserts that Dostoevsky's novels are "in their
essence tragedies";[11] Mochulsky analyzes *Crime and Punishment*
as "a tragedy in five acts with a prologue and an epilogue";[12]
and Ivanov insists that the most obvious feature of Dostoevsky's
work is "the very close approximation of the novel-form to the

prototype of tragedy." [13] But Chulkov and Mochulsky are pre-occupied with matters of form, and Ivanov emphasizes metaphysical considerations. Not one of the three clearly recognizes *Crime and Punishment* as being *a Christian tragedy in the form of a novel.*

It is this fact, however, which sets Dostoevsky's work, beginning with *Crime and Punishment,* apart from that of his predecessors (and most of his successors) in the novel. Being a shrewd observer of human nature, including his own, he knew that human behavior is for the most part externally determined. But unlike the naturalists, with the first of whom he was approximately contemporary, he also knew that there were, or at least *could* be, moments of real freedom in human experience—freedom which is, to be sure, excruciatingly difficult to achieve. It is only within such a context that tragedy can come into being. It cannot exist when men are convinced, as they apparently were in the middle of the nineteenth century, that the conception of fate was a curious holdover from a prescientific age—tragedy cannot exist, that is, when men believe that they are perfectly free to solve whatever problems might beset them. Nor can it exist when, by some gigantic irony of history, men return to a belief in fatalism, dignified by the name *scientific determinism.* Tragedy emerges only when they are able to experience the tension that exists between fate and freedom, when men are modest enough to see that much of their own behavior is almost as predictable as that of white rats, and yet courageous enough to overcome that fact by accepting responsibility for each other in a way that nature does not compel them to do. Even white rats care for their young and protect their own nests, but the adult males of the species are incapable of accepting very much responsibility for each other—as indeed men are except upon rare occasions. It is these few occasions which provide the substance of literary tragedy.

Summarizing the over-all significance of the Lazarus story, C. H. Dodd makes this statement:

It seems clear therefore that ch. xi constitutes a single and complete episode. Its theme is resurrection. This theme is elaborated in the dialogue between Jesus and the sisters of the dead Lazarus, as well as in the significant narrative of the raising of the dead; and its essential setting is provided by the dialogue between Jesus and His disciples which declares His intention of going to death, and by the appended report of the Council-meeting, in which He is devoted to death. Thus the theme is not only resurrection, but resurrection by virtue of Christ's self-sacrifice. More exactly, the theme is Christ Himself manifested as Resurrection and Life by virtue of His self-sacrifice.[14]

The raising of Lazarus, then, symbolizes the efficacy of Christ's suffering and death. The story makes clear that Christ's self-sacrifice is necessary in order to redeem human life from the meaninglessness with which death constantly threatens it. There is no resurrection of Lazarus without the powerful presence of Christ; and Christ's power resides in his willingness to die upon the cross. To put the matter even more simply, *meaning*— or, in biblical terms, Life and Resurrection—is brought about only by those who are willing to undergo the kind of suffering which the creation of that meaning requires. "Whoever does not bear his own cross and come after me, cannot be my disciple." This conception of necessary suffering, which is central to the Lazarus story, is identical with what Freud regarded in *Totem and Taboo* as the *sine qua non* of tragedy: "The hero of the tragedy had to suffer; this is to-day still the essential content of a tragedy."

But Dostoevsky represents a great many kinds of suffering in *Crime and Punishment*; and if we regard the book as a work of art rather than as a pathological outpouring, we are pressed to some such conclusion as this: he was apparently seeking to distinguish the necessary suffering of Sonia, and of Raskolnikov in the very last pages of the novel, from the unnecessary and ultimately meaningless suffering of Marmeladov, Luzhin, Svidrigailov, and even Raskolnikov himself through much of the book. (The names of the women characters other than Sonia, and possibly Dounia in the final chapters, might also be included in this list; but an examination of these three very interesting male characters will be sufficient to establish the point.) Marmeladov, Luzhin, and Svidrigailov as fictional characters are basically embodiments of three facets of Raskolnikov's own character. More bluntly, each of them represents one particular variety of the hero's colossal egocentrism: Marmeladov is a caricature of Raskolnikov in his most self-abasing mood; Luzhin, in his most self-glorifying moments; and Svidrigailov, in his incorrigible tendency to be self-indulgent. The chief difference between the three secondary characters and Raskolnikov himself is that each of the three consciously revels in his own form of egotism, whereas Raskolnikov has so little self-knowledge that he wallows in all three forms without in the least realizing what he is doing. These three characters raise to the level of consciousness, as far as the reader is concerned, elements of the hero's personality which might otherwise escape our notice and therefore our understanding. They serve to give the reader more perspective on Raskolnikov than Raskolnikov has upon himself until the very end, when he begins to be made "dimly conscious of the fundamental falsity in himself and his convictions." Let us deal with the three in the order of their appearance.

In an article called "Crime for Punishment: The Tenor of Part I," W. D. Snodgrass establishes the many similarities and parallels between Marmeladov and Raskolnikov.[15] There is no need to repeat the evidence which Snodgrass accumulates; suffice it to say that Raskolnikov identifies himself with Marmeladov so completely that at the time of the latter's fatal accident, he takes charge of matters "as earnestly as if it had been his father" (p. 174). Whereas Marmeladov had found obvious satisfaction in calling himself "a useless worm" (p. 14) and "a pig" (p. 15), Raskolnikov must single out an even more insignificant and obnoxious creature as a symbol of himself—the louse. But when Marmeladov abases himself, he does so "at his own expense," so to speak; that is, he abases himself in relation to other human beings, he does not pretend to judge *their* position in the order of creation. Not so with Raskolnikov. When he abases himself, he must abase all the rest of humanity too: "I had not the right to take that path, because I am just such a louse as all the rest" (p. 407). His cynicism is so total that he can engage in the most abject self-abasement without in any way professing that he is inferior to the rest of humanity. This attitude enables him to "have his cake and eat it too"; he can get the sentimental benefit of self-denigration while preserving his enormous vanity intact. Even at the time of his declaration to Dounia that he is ready to go to Siberia, the narrator tells us that "he seemed to be glad to think that he was still proud" (p. 502).

Crime and Punishment is so much the story of one man that we tend to identify ourselves uncritically with Raskolnikov, even though he is a murderer. But in the case of Marmeladov, we cannot help seeing him from two points of view. As Snodgrass points out, "However much we want to weep for Marmeladov, still something in us wants to join the tavern loungers and jeer." [16] It strikes us as comic that the old drunkard finds "a positive con-so-lation" (p. 27) in being dragged about and berated by his wife. For all of his talk about suffering, we can see that most of the suffering which Marmeladov undergoes is patently unnecessary—it serves no purpose except to salve his egocentric need. In psychological terms, the poor man is unmistakably masochistic; and his presence in the novel helps to illuminate this facet of Raskolnikov's personality through most of the book. Dostoevsky was acutely aware of this strain in human nature: he has Porfiry say, "Do you know, Rodion Romanovitch, the force of the word 'suffering' among some of these people! It's not a question of suffering for some one's benefit, but simply, 'one must suffer' " (p. 441). Marmeladov, just by being there, enables us to recognize this strain in Raskolnikov for what it is.

Luzhin, who seems at first to be totally different from Marmeladov, is perhaps even more closely related to Raskolnikov than is the would-be civil servant who drinks that he "may suffer twice as much" (p. 16). Luzhin, the successful lawyer, is simply Marmeladov's opposite—he finds pleasure not in self-abasement, but in self-glorification. Marmeladov delights in humiliating himself gratuitously in front of others; Luzhin finds a similar satisfaction in humiliating others, just as gratuitously, in front of himself. His most characteristic action in the entire novel is his attempt (Part V, Chapter 3) to prove that Sonia is a thief, and thereby to humiliate her before a large group of people, including himself. As Raskolnikov explains at the end of that chapter, Luzhin is trying to discredit Sonia in order to reinstate himself with Dounia; and, as we know from an earlier chapter, he wants to possess Dounia so that he will be master of a situation in which "this creature would be slavishly grateful all her life for his heroic condescension, and would humble herself in the dust before him" (pp. 301–302).

Such behavior does not in the long run endear Luzhin to most readers of *Crime and Punishment*. Ernest Simmons articulates what is probably the attitude of many when he says, "If Dostoevsky has scorn for any of the characters in the novel, it is for Luzhin, the would-be suitor of Raskolnikov's sister."[17] To be sure, Luzhin is obnoxious; the term *sadist* applies to him at least as well as the term *masochist* does to Marmeladov, and sadists tend to be more offensive to other people than masochists do, since one can usually ignore the latter without much difficulty when they become tiresome. But the juxtaposition of Raskolnikov and Luzhin serves to show that we can hardly admire one of them and despise the other without being utterly inconsistent from an intellectual point of view. After all, the vain little lawyer wants only to lord it over one or two women, and he is willing to pay at least one of them for letting him do so. Raskolnikov, on the other hand, wants to be a superman and to lord it over the whole contemptible mass of mankind; and he does not really care if he kills one or two women—or "lice"—in the process, without paying either one of them anything for the privilege. Just as Raskolnikov outdoes Marmeladov in self-abasement, he outdoes Luzhin in self-glorification; and again the primary difference is that Luzhin knows what he is doing, while Raskolnikov thinks that he is grappling with some objective intellectual problem.

The parallelism between Luzhin and Raskolnikov is not difficult to show in the text of the novel. Besides the obvious facts that both are hypochondriacs and that both would take pleasure in the other's death (pp. 42, 352), the narrator shows in the first interview between the two men that there is a close correspondence between the older man's theory and the younger man's practice. Raskolnikov himself clarifies the only part of this relationship which the reader might otherwise overlook: "Why, carry out logically the theory you were advocating just now, and it follows that people may be killed" (p. 150). Luzhin, whose thinking is not nearly so grandiose as Raskolnikov's, immediately denies the charge: " 'There's a measure in all things,' Luzhin went on superciliously. 'Economic ideas are not an incitement to murder.' " But the point stands, regardless of Luzhin's denial. Even more revealing is a parallel between two widely separated passages in which each man reflects upon the failure of his experiment in mastering the fate of other people. After the rupture with Dounia, Luzhin castigates himself:

> "It was my mistake, too, not to have given them money," he thought, as he returned dejectedly to Lebeziatnikov's room, "and why on earth was I such a Jew? It was false economy! I meant to keep them without a penny so that they should turn to me as their providence, and look at them! Foo! . . . H'm! I've made a blunder." (p. 352)

Raskolnikov, even after going to prison, finds "no particularly terrible fault in his past, except a simple *blunder* which might happen to anyone" (p. 525). Both men use the word *blunder* to account for their predicaments, because their attitudes are precisely parallel.

Mochulsky cites this same passage (p. 526) in support of a very interesting conclusion. According to the Russian critic,

> In the words "My conscience is at peace," the final truth about Raskolnikov is suddenly revealed. He is in fact a superman. He has not been defeated; it is he who has conquered. He wanted to try out his strength and found that there were no limits to it. He wanted "to transgress" and he transgressed. He wanted to show that the moral law had no relevance for him, that he stood beyond the confines of good and evil, and now—his conscience is at peace. . . .

None of his adversaries is worthy of the strong individual; he has but one single enemy—fate. *Raskolnikov has been brought to destruction like a tragic hero in battle with blind Destiny.* But how could the author present this bold truth about the new man to the readers of Katkov's well-meaning journal in the 1860's? He had to cover it by throwing an innocent veil over it. He did this, however, hurriedly, carelessly, "just before the final curtain." While the hero is in the labor camp, just after recovering from his illness, he casts himself at Sonya's feet . . . and he begins to love: "Their sick and pale faces already shone with the dawn of a renewed future, *of a total resurrection into a new life.* They had been resurrected by love." . . . We know Raskolnikov too well to believe this "pious lie." [18]

But we cannot have it both ways. Either Luzhin, who remains smug no matter what disasters befall his projects, is also a superman, foiled by "blind Destiny" in his attempts to reduce Dounia to virtual slavery and to prove Sonia a common thief; or else Raskolnikov, the dead Lazarus, is still just as "dead," just as self-deceived when he utters the words "My conscience is at peace," as he ever had been. We should bear in mind that saying something is at peace or at rest is also a commonplace way of indicating that it is *dead*. Raskolnikov's conscience has been "dead" through the whole novel; otherwise he would not have committed the crime which furnishes half of the title. It is significant that Mochulsky, in his chapter on *Crime and Punishment,* gives only scant attention to Luzhin; he regards him primarily as an embodiment of the money motif. One suspects that Mochulsky is well-advised not to examine the characterization very fully, since any detailed analysis would obviously be fatal to his interpretation of the story.

Luzhin and Raskolnikov both suffer in their own way, of course; but we cannot overstress the fact that all of their agonizing, except for the hero's in the last few pages of the book, is completely unnecessary, and therefore untragic. As Porfiry says about this kind of thing, "It's not a question of suffering for someone's benefit, but simply 'one must suffer.'" When Luzhin gets up, the day after the break with Dounia, the narrator tells us that "the black snake of wounded vanity had been gnawing at his heart all night" (p. 351). Raskolnikov's total inability to distinguish between the two kinds of suffering is revealed in two passages that come close together near the end of Part VI. To his sister he exclaims, "They say it is necessary for me to suffer! What's the object of these senseless sufferings?" (p. 504). And when Sonia gives him a cross to wear: " 'It's the symbol of my taking up the cross,' he laughed. 'As though I had not suffered much till now!' " (p. 506). Between the two passages we are told of Sonia's fear that he will commit suicide, since "she knew his vanity, his pride and his lack of faith" (p. 505). Until he "takes up the cross," his sufferings are inflicted chiefly by "the black snake of wounded vanity"; after that, it becomes "a question of suffering for someone's benefit," as it had been for Sonia all along. It is precisely his "taking up the cross" and his response to the love of Sonia—in a word, his regeneration—that makes *Crime and Punishment* a tragic novel. Otherwise, it would simply recount the blundering machinations of another Luzhin, inflated to heroic proportions.

Svidrigailov is more obviously Raskolnikov's double than either Marmeladov or Luzhin is. Though he is well dressed and genteel, he epitomizes the hero's capacity for self-indulgence without considering the cost to anyone else. But again, the primary difference between the two characters is that Svidrigailov knows himself for what he is, while Raskolnikov indulges his wildest fancy and imagines that he is acting in accordance with some categorical imperative. Svidrigailov, for instance, is perfectly frank about his use of flattery as a means of seduction. He points out that a "vestal virgin might be seduced by flattery" (p. 461); and he describes his own success in using this method with "a lady who was devoted to her husband, her children, and her principles." Through the whole business, however, he is fully conscious that he is merely seducing the woman for his own pleasure; and he clearly recognizes the difference between flattery and truth:

> Nothing in the world is harder than speaking the truth and nothing easier than flattery. If there's the hundredth part of a false note in speaking the truth, it leads to a discord, and that leads to trouble.

> But if all, to the last note, is false in flattery, it is just as agreeable, and is heard not without satisfaction. It may be a coarse satisfaction, but still a satisfaction. And however coarse the flattery, at least half will be sure to seem true. That's so for all stages of development and classes of society. (p. 461)

Needless to say, Svidrigailov is amused when the self-deceived person upon whom he practices his skill is told even a tiny portion of the truth about herself: "And how angry she was with me when I explained to her at last that it was my sincere conviction that she was just as eager as I" (p. 462).

In short, Svidrigailov is a conscious cynic; Raskolnikov an unconscious one. The conversation just quoted ends in a way that parallels very closely Svidrigailov's story of the "virtuous" woman seduced by flattery—taken aback by his interlocutor's self-deceiving attitude, he tells Raskolnikov a bit of the truth about himself: " 'Well, if you come to that,' Svidrigailov answered, scrutinising Raskolnikov with some surprise, 'if you come to that, you are a thorough cynic yourself' " (p. 468). A few moments later he is even more explicit: "But if you are convinced that one mustn't listen at doors, but one may murder old women at one's pleasure, you'd better be off to America and make haste" (p. 470). When all is said and done, Svidrigailov is much more admirable than Raskolnikov, if for no other reason than this— he is in touch with at least a small portion of reality. Even his statement on vice serves to distinguish him from Raskolnikov, to the latter's disadvantage:

> In this vice at least there is something permanent, founded indeed upon nature and not dependent on fantasy, something present in the blood like an ever-burning ember, for ever setting one on fire and maybe, not to be quickly extinguished, even with years. You'll agree it's an occupation of a sort. (p. 456)

Whatever we may think of Svidrigailov, it is undeniably true that he finds meaning, at least for a time, in something which is "founded indeed upon nature"; whereas for Raskolnikov, up to the very last pages of the book, meaning is "dependent on fantasy." Svidrigailov, until he puts a bullet through his head, is at least a little bit alive; Raskolnikov, until he begins to be resurrected, is *dead* at the very center of his being.

These three characters, Marmeladov, Luzhin, and Svidrigailov, serve to illuminate the tomb which contains the body and spirit of Raskolnikov. There is no point in the Lazarus parallel, no significance in the hero's "regeneration," if we fail to understand that Raskolnikov's superman theory is merely a colossal instrument of self-deception, a fantasy into which he can retreat from reality. One would think that our experience with Nazi Germany would help us to realize this fact. But some critics have preferred to slough off the significance of the Lazarus story, to prop up the corpse of Raskolnikov for public view, and then to proclaim that the corpse really *is* a living superman. When this happens, we must throw in our lot with Porfiry, and ask with modesty and deference,

> How do you distinguish those extraordinary people from the ordinary ones? Are there signs at their birth? I feel there ought to be more exactitude, more external definition. Excuse the natural anxiety of a practical law-abiding citizen, but couldn't they adopt a special uniform, for instance, couldn't they wear something, be branded in some way? (pp. 256–257)

We must live in the hope that they will have the courtesy to wear a swastika armband or some other, equally obvious, sign of superiority.

Nowhere is the importance of the Lazarus story in *Crime and Punishment* more evident than in the conception of time that operates throughout the book. Critics have commented extensively upon this conception of time; but they have apparently assumed that it was original with Dostoevsky. Philip Rahv's comments reflect the attitude of most commentators:

> Actually, there is no real lapse of time in the story because we are virtually unaware of it apart from the tension of the rendered experience. Instead of time lapsing there is the concrete flow of duration contracting and expanding with the rhythm of the dramatic movement.

Least of all is it a chronological frame that time provides in this novel. As the Russian critic K. Mochulsky has so aptly remarked, its time is purely psychological, a function of human consciousness, in other words the very incarnation of Bergson's *durée réelle*. And it is only in Bergsonian terms that one can do it justice. Truly, Dostoevsky succeeds here in converting time into a kind of progress of Raskolnikov's mental state, which is not actually a state but a process of incessant change eating into the future and expanding with the duration it accumulates, like a snowball growing larger as it rolls upon itself, to use Bergson's original image.[19]

It may be true that Bergson is helpful in understanding the nature of time in *Crime and Punishment*; but the conception itself came to Dostoevsky from the Johannine writings in the New Testament. And the Lazarus story is John's most pointed symbolic representation of time.

C. H. Dodd explains the significance of the Lazarus story as combining or fusing elements belonging to the last judgment with those present in Christ's earthly ministry. But we should quote Dodd's own words:

> Now the resurrection to which v. 28–9 refers is the general resurrection 'on the last day' (cf. vi. 54); but the raising of Lazarus is set in contrast with the resurrection on the last day, to which Martha had pinned her faith. It seems we might put it this way: the evangelist has taken an event associated with the 'last day', and transplanted it into the historic ministry of Jesus, thus making of it a 'sign' of the *zōopoíēsis* which that ministry (when consummated) brought into effect. The implication is that the absoluteness and finality which pertain to the resurrection on the last day belong also to the *zōopoíēsis* which Christ has effected. We might go so far as to say that if it were possible for us to contemplate the resurrection on the last day as a *fait accompli*, it would still be, as is the Raising of Lazarus, no more than a *sēmeîon* of the truth that Christ is Himself both resurrection and life.[20]

This compression of time, this reduction of past and future into a single all-inclusive present, is (as we have already observed) characteristic of the Johannine writings as a whole. We should note in the Lazarus episode, for instance, that an event which is usually associated with the last day is fused with the earthly ministry of Jesus, and that the very raising of Lazarus is represented as being part of the efficacy of Christ's self-sacrifice, the most powerful example of which had not yet taken place at the time he calls Lazarus back from the dead. In other words, John represents, perhaps more clearly in the Lazarus story than anywhere else, events taking place with a kind of tremendous simultaneity in what Dodd calls "God's eternal To-day."

What we are examining is not merely a part of Dostoevsky's novelistic technique; it is the essence of his world view. In *The Notebooks,* Dostoevsky says of Raskolnikov that "his moral development begins from the crime itself." [21] Such an assertion is not simply the reflection of his desire to make the story more compact; it springs rather from his conviction that self-knowledge comes about only when one recognizes that his own activity, unless it is guided by belief in Christ, is essentially self-destructive in a way that leads to total meaninglessness. Hence, Raskolnikov's answer to his own question: "Did I murder the old woman? I murdered myself, not her! I crushed myself once for all, for ever" (p. 407). Because he has not, at this point, achieved any degree of faith or belief, this statement is a cry of despair; it is, nevertheless, the beginning of self-knowledge. Razumihin articulates more abstractly the point we are considering: "One can always forgive lying—lying is a delightful thing, for it leads to truth—what is offensive is that they lie and worship their own lying" (p. 134). Applied to Raskolnikov this means: murder can be forgiven; what is "offensive" about Raskolnikov, what makes him as dead as Lazarus, is that he murders and exalts that murder as the ritualistic act of a superman. In this sense, it is perfectly true that "his moral development begins from the crime itself."

In the Johannine view, from which Dostoevsky's most important conceptions are derived, truth is not something which can be abstracted from the suffering which is necessary to its creation; and it must therefore be continually *re*-created through *necessary* suffering. For John, Christ's crucifixion and his exaltation are one and the same thing: "I," says the Johannine Christ, "when I am lifted up from the earth, will draw all men to myself." The narrator then adds these words: "He said this to show by what death he was to die" (John 12:32–33). Critics who take satisfaction in proclaiming that Dostoevsky was entirely pre-occupied with sadistic and masochistic suffering miss the entire point of his work. He does indeed represent a great deal of it—witness Marmeladov, Luzhin, and Svidrigailov—but he does so precisely to distinguish it from the necessary suffering of Sonia and the regenerated Raskolnikov. The same Porfiry who observes that "some of these people" suffer simply because "one must suffer," has this to say:

> "I am convinced that you will decide 'to take your suffering.' You don't believe my words now, but you'll come to it of yourself. For suffering, Rodion Romanovitch, is a great thing. Never mind my having grown fat, I know all the same. Don't laugh at it, there's an idea in suffering, Nikolay is right. No, you won't run away, Rodion Romanovitch." (p. 447)

When we realize that truth has its source in error (Razumihin) and in suffering (Porfiry), then it becomes clear that Raskolnikov's "moral development begins from the crime itself"; and consequently time, as we ordinarily think of it, begins to evaporate.

There is one final consideration in connection with the Lazarus story and the regeneration of Raskolnikov; and that is the relationship between Dostoevsky himself as author and the material he presents in *Crime and Punishment*. We know that he destroyed a preliminary version of the novel, which had been written in the first person. According to Georgy Chulkov, it was evidently Dostoevsky's dissatisfaction with the first-person point of view which prompted him to do so.[22] "Much in the original version, however," continues Chulkov, "was considered by Dostoevsky to have been successful, and before he gave up the subjective narration, he transferred very skillfully the first person narration into an objective narration in the author's person." Moreover, he claims that "the drafts to *Crime and Punishment* are less rich in variants and less diverse" than the drafts of the other novels, and that "the personage of the hero himself was not subjected to significant changes, such as those in the drafts to

The Idiot." In other words, whatever difficulties Dostoevsky may have had with the technique of the novel in *Crime and Punishment,* he appears to have been sure, from the very beginning, of the highly complex psychology of the main character. Dostoevsky, we recall, is one of the few writers that Tolstoy approved of after having formulated his definition of art as an activity in which one man "hands on to others feelings he has lived through." [23] In evaluating the significance of Raskolnikov's regeneration then, we must finally confront this question: who wrote *Crime and Punishment,* with its sympathetic representation of Sonia and its emphasis upon the Lazarus story, if not the regenerated Raskolnikov, the resurrected Lazarus himself? The main character embodies an ideology which the author himself must once have found irresistibly attractive. As Dostoevsky says of Raskolnikov in *The Notebooks,* "Sonia and love broke him"; and in the Johannine world view, the "breaking" of a man, if he accepts it willingly though perhaps reluctantly, is simultaneous with his being "lifted up."

VIII

Myshkin's Apocalyptic Vision

And the angel which I saw stand upon the sea
and upon the earth lifted up his hand to heaven,
And sware by him that liveth for ever and ever . . .
that there should be time no longer.
REVELATION 10:5–6, K.J.V.

◆ In Part II of *The Idiot,* Aglaia Epanchin recites a
poem called "The Poor Knight," which comes from Pushkin's
short dramatic piece, "Scenes from the Times of Knighthood."
Several of the characters who are present at the reading understand that Aglaia's purpose is to represent Myshkin as the poor
knight, and to link him romantically with Nastasya Filippovna
Barashkov. She does this by substituting Nastasya's initials for
the letters A. M. D. inscribed in blood upon the poor knight's
shield.[1] But the poem characterizes Myshkin and his whole
career, from the first page of the book to the last, far more accurately than Aglaia or the reader can possibly realize at this
point in the story. At his first appearance Myshkin is described,
like the poor knight, as being "Pale of face with glance austere."
As the novel closes, Myshkin returns to Switzerland, his home
"In far distant country side"; when we last see him, he (again
like the poor knight) is "Silent, sad, bereft of reason"; and though
the author does not tell us so, we assume that "In his solitude he
died."

This poem, together with comments which the characters
make about it, serves to clarify the nature of Dostoevsky's problem in presenting Myshkin as "a positively good man." [2] Before
the poem is read, several of the characters discuss the "poor

knight," and one of them blames Adelaida, the Epanchin sister
who is proficient as an artist, for their not having known "long
ago who the 'poor knight' was." The girl responds:

"What have I done?" . . .
"You wouldn't draw his portrait, that's what you did! Aglaia
Ivanovna begged you then to draw the portrait of the 'poor knight,'
and described the whole subject of the picture. She made the subject
up herself, you remember. You wouldn't."
"But how could I draw it? According to the poem, that 'poor
knight'

> *'no more in sight of any*
> *Raised the visor from his face.'*

How could I draw the face then? What was I to draw—the visor?—
the anonymous hero?"
"I don't understand what you mean by the visor," said Madame
Epanchin angrily, though she was beginning to have a very clear idea
who was meant by the nickname (probably agreed upon long ago)
of the "poor knight." But what specially angered her was that Prince
Lyov Nikolayevitch was also disconcerted, and at last quite abashed
like a boy of ten.
"Well, will you put a stop to this foolishness or not? Will they
explain to me this 'poor knight'? Is it such an awful secret that one
can't approach it?" (pp. 234–235)

Moments later Prince S. describes the occasion upon which the
matter had first arisen: "Some of us laughed at the subject, others
declared that nothing could be better, but that to paint the
'poor knight' we must find a face for him. We began to go over
the faces of all our friends. Not one was suitable, and there
we left it" (p. 235). This dialogue reflects the problem which
Dostoevsky undertook to solve in writing *The Idiot*.

The problem is defined even more clearly in the poem itself.
We are told of the knight that

> *He had had a wondrous vision:*
> *Ne'er could feeble human art*
> *Gauge its deep mysterious meaning,*
> *It was graven on his heart.* (p. 238)

How is Dostoevsky to depict or even suggest, in a way that will be genuinely effective, the experience or "vision" which accounts for Myshkin's character if that vision is beyond the reach of "feeble human art"? When a man puts on "the whole armor of God," including the "helmet of salvation" and the "shield of faith," how can the artist portray him as an individual? How does he reveal the man *inside* the suit of armor? But Dostoevsky solves the problem admirably, and to discover the way in which he does so we must examine most of the book, including several passages which Murray Krieger, speaking for a good many critics, has called "inconsistencies and excursions in this difficult, often confusing and imperfect novel." [3]

Dostoevsky's method for rendering intelligible the vision that is graven on Myshkin's heart is to bring together several kinds of experience which, though they may be unfamiliar to the reader, can at least be made understandable in realistic terms. The first of these involves the agony, the intense emotions and perceptions, of a person as he suffers through the last moments before his execution; and the instrument for execution in *The Idiot* is not the firing squad or even the gallows, but the guillotine. This kind of experience is first represented in Part I, Chapter 2, when we have hardly had time to find out who Myshkin is; and yet, according to Romano Guardini, "It has been said that this episode was a superficial addition. Dostoevsky, in this interpretation, simply wanted to recount the feelings he himself had experienced in the terrible moment of expectation which precedes an execution." [4] But if this is so, then there is no point in Dostoevsky's insisting as he does upon the guillotine as the instrument of execution, except perhaps as a disguise for the circumstances of his own experience. Either these incidents are indeed irrelevant, in which case Dostoevsky blundered very badly in the first chapters of his story; or else he was trying, at the earliest possible moment, to associate his main character with certain kinds of emotion and certain special *images* which would make that character's behavior more understandable to the reader. The latter explanation seems more likely, and it begins to be supported when Myshkin reiterates the whole story of the execution he had witnessed to Madame Epanchin and her daughters in Chapter 5.

As we look at this second instance retrospectively from the discussion of "The Poor Knight," we begin to see a direct connection between Myshkin and the man who is about to be executed. After learning that Adelaida is a painter and being asked to suggest a subject for one of her pictures, Myshkin says that she should

> paint the face of the condemned man the moment before the blade falls, when he is still standing on the scaffold before he lies down on the plank."
>
> "The face? The face alone?" asked Adelaida. "That would be a strange subject. And what sort of picture would it make? . . . Can you tell me how you imagine it to yourself? How is one to draw the face? Is it to be only the face? What sort of face is it?"
>
> "It's practically the minute before death," Myshkin began with perfect readiness, . . . "that moment when he has just mounted the ladder and has just stepped on to the scaffold. Then he glanced in my direction. I looked at his face and I understood it all. . . . But how can one describe it? I wish, I do wish that you or some one would paint it. It would be best if it were you. I thought at the time that a picture of it would do good. You know one has to imagine everything that has been before—everything, everything." (p. 58)

The problem of "how to draw the face, how to describe it" is the same in the case of the "poor knight," who stands for Myshkin in the novel, and in that of the man about to be guillotined, because the emotions which the face must be made to reveal are very closely related. We are reminded of St. Paul's words, "For I think that God has exhibited us apostles as last of all, like men sentenced to death" (I Cor. 4:9).

Another instance of the riotous emotions which invade one's being in the moment before execution comes from Lebedyev, the half-serious, half-comic interpreter of the Apocalypse. His nephew ridicules him for including the Countess du Barry in his drunken prayers, and he defends himself to Myshkin:

> The way she died after such honours was that the hangman, Sampson, dragged this great lady, guiltless, to the guillotine for the di-

version of Parisian *poissardes,* and she was in such terror she didn't know what was happening to her. She saw he was bending her neck down under the knife and kicking her, while the people laughed, and she fell to screaming, *'Encore un moment, monsieur le bourreau, encore un moment!'* which means 'Wait one little minute, Mr. *bourreau,* only one!' And perhaps for the sake of that prayer God will forgive her; for one cannot imagine a greater *misère* for a human soul than that. Do you know the meaning of the word *misère?* Well that's what *misère* is. When I read about that countess's cry for 'one little minute,' I felt as though my heart had been pinched with a pair of tongs. (p. 186)

Lebedyev concludes his tirade by saying, "My prayer was this: 'Lord, give rest to the soul of that great sinner the Countess du Barry and all like her.' "

The features which these instances have in common are readily apparent. The victims are "great sinners"—their sins are literally "mortal": they are made to prostrate themselves, to "lie down on the plank"; they experience the greatest *misère* which a human being can suffer; they are certain that death will overtake them within moments; and they become excruciatingly aware that time is indescribably precious, that the moment constitutes everything. But that moment is fleeting; and even if the intended victim survives his ordeal, he is not able to retain the sense of urgency which the experience produces in him. Myshkin tells of one man he knew in Switzerland who had been led out to execution and then reprieved, minutes before he was scheduled to die. (This is another of the "irrelevant autobiographical incidents" which Dostoevsky has been accused of including for no good literary reason.) Madame Epanchin picks up the matter and asks Myshkin:

how did that friend who told you such horrors . . . he was reprieved, so he was presented with that 'eternity of life.' What did he do with that wealth afterwards? Did he live counting each moment?"

"Oh no, he told me himself. I asked him about that too. He didn't live like that at all; he wasted many, many minutes."

"Well, there you have it tried. So it seems it's impossible really to live 'counting each moment.' For some reason it's impossible."

"Yes, for some reason it is impossible," repeated Myshkin. "I thought so myself . . . and yet I somehow can't believe it . . ."

"Then you think you will live more wisely than any one?" said Aglaia.

"Yes, I have thought that too sometimes."

"And you think so still?"

"Yes . . . I think so still," answered Myshkin, looking at Aglaia with the same gentle and even timid smile; but he laughed again at once and looked gaily at her. (p. 56)

The moment of vision and urgency when one lives in the awareness that his death is both imminent and certain cannot be prolonged. "For some reason it is impossible," but that moment can be represented as *recurring* and thereby renewing its effect in a man's life. Hence, the second kind of experience that is associated with Myshkin in an effort to communicate the vision which is "graven on his heart"—his epilepsy.

In Part II, Chapter 5, the epileptic fit is described at considerable length. As Myshkin reflects upon his disease, he is troubled by the thought that it is after all an abnormality, a disorder, which takes a heavy toll upon his health and his sanity.

"What if it is disease?" he decided at last. "What does it matter that it is an abnormal intensity, if the result, if the minute of sensation, remembered and analysed afterwards in health, turns out to be the acme of harmony and beauty, and gives a feeling, unknown and undivined till then, of completeness, of proportion, of reconciliation, and of ecstatic devotional merging in the highest synthesis of life?" These vague expressions seemed to him very comprehensible, though too weak. That it really was "beauty and worship," that it really was the "highest synthesis of life" he could not doubt, and could not admit the possibility of doubt. It was not as though he saw abnormal and unreal visions of some sort at that moment, as from hashish, opium, or wine, destroying the reason and distorting the soul. He was quite capable of judging of that when the attack was over. These moments were only an extraordinary quickening of self-consciousness—if the condition was to be expressed in one word—and at the same time of the direct sensation of existence in the most intense degree. Since at that second, that is at the very last conscious moment before the fit, he had time to say to himself clearly and consciously, "Yes, for this moment one might give one's whole life!" then without doubt that moment was really worth the whole of life. . . . "At that moment," as he told Rogozhin one day in Moscow at the time when they used to meet there, "at that moment I seem somehow to understand the extraordinary saying that *there shall be no more time*. Probably," he added, smiling, "this is the very second which was not long enough for the water to be spilt out of Mahomet's pitcher, though the epileptic prophet had time to gaze at all the habitations of Allah." (pp. 214–215)

That "extraordinary saying" about time is later identified by Ippolit, who stands under sentence of death through disease, as being from the book of Revelation: "And do you remember, prince, who proclaimed that there will be 'no more time'? It was proclaimed by the great and mighty angel in the Apocalypse" (p. 365). The wording of the passage in the Revised Standard Version makes Dostoevsky's reference unintelligible, but the King James Version preserves the literal meaning of the Greek word *chrónos:*

And the angel which I saw stand upon the sea and upon the earth lifted up his hand to heaven, And sware by him that liveth for ever and ever, who created heaven, and the things that therein are, and the earth, and the things that therein are, and the sea, and the things which are therein, that there should be time no longer. (Rev. 10:5–6)

In the Revised Standard Version the final words are "that there should be no more delay," but the meaning, which has to do with the urgency of the present moment, remains the same.

The problem of linking these two kinds of experience in order to create the combined impression of finality, which goes with execution, and of recurrence, which goes with attacks of epilepsy, is admirably done. Obviously, Dostoevsky insists in both cases upon the significance of the moment, the paramount importance of time as it slips away. But far more effective is the highly dramatic scene in which Rogozhin assaults Myshkin with a knife, fully intending to kill him, and in so doing precipitates an epileptic fit. Here the emotions of the man about to be killed and the feelings of the epileptic are literally identified with each other. The description of the attack is carefully worded:

> Then suddenly something seemed torn asunder before him; his soul was flooded with intense *inner* light. The moment lasted perhaps half a second, yet he clearly and consciously remembered the beginning, the first sound of the fearful scream which broke of itself from his breast and which he could not have checked by any effort. Then his consciousness was instantly extinguished and complete darkness followed.
>
> It was an epileptic fit, the first he had had for a long time. It is well known that epileptic fits come on quite suddenly. At the moment the face is horribly distorted, especially the eyes. The whole body and the features of the face work with convulsive jerks and contortions. A terrible, indescribable scream that is unlike anything else breaks from the sufferer. In that scream everything human seems obliterated and it is impossible, or very difficult, for an observer to realize and admit that it is the man himself screaming. It seems indeed as though it were some one else screaming from within the man. That is how many people at least have described their impression. (p. 222)

The two kinds of experience are fused here not only by coincidence in time, but by imagery as well. The "intense *inner* light" (p. 222), the "gleams and flashes of the highest sensation of life and self-consciousness" (p. 214) which are associated with the epileptic fit recall the earlier description of the man led out to execution and then reprieved, who looks around during what he thinks are his last moments: "Not far off there was a church, and the gilt roof was glittering in the bright sunshine. He remembered that he stared very persistently at that roof and the light flashing from it; he could not tear himself away from the light. It seemed to him that those rays were his new nature and that in three minutes he would somehow melt into them" (p. 55). The epileptic scream brings to mind the footman's question, when Myshkin first describes the execution of a French criminal, "Do they scream?" (p. 19) and Madame du Barry's "screaming, *'Encore un moment . . .'* " (p. 186). And as Rogozhin flees after the assault, he avoids "the prostrate figure" of Myshkin, who thus resembles the criminals "laid on the plank" for execution (p. 60; cf. p. 58).

The epileptic fits qualify the complex of emotions generated by the execution scenes not only by suggesting that the moment is recurring rather than simply final, but also by making the experience wholly internal, rather than imposed from the outside. The flashing light which catches the eye and the imagination of the man being executed is entirely external, a reflection of the sun's rays upon the gilt roof of a church. But at the moment before an epileptic fit, the victim's soul is "flooded with intense *inner* light," and the emotions themselves are called "gleams and flashes." Similarly, when Madame du Barry screams, it is in protest against what is being done to her; but when the epileptic brings forth his "indescribable scream," it is "as though it were some one else screaming from within the man." And whereas the criminal is made to "lie down on the plank" in order to suffer execution, the victim of "the falling sickness" falls of his own inner weakness. This combination of the two kinds of experience suggests then that Myshkin apprehends such a moment as both final and recurring; what he feels is as compelling as anything imposed from the outside, yet it is wholly internal; and, like the criminal, he stands under judgment for his wrongdoing, while at the same time he exults in a vision which is "the acme of harmony and beauty, . . . a feeling, unknown and undivined till then, of completeness, of proportion, of reconciliation, and of ecstatic devotional merging in the highest synthesis of life."

The third kind of experience which helps to communicate Myshkin's vision is a sympathetic identification with the sufferings of Christ. When he talks to the footman (in Part I, Chapter 2), Myshkin links Christ with the man who believes that he is about to be executed.

> Perhaps there is some man who has been sentenced to death, been exposed to this torture and then been told 'you can go, you are pardoned.' Perhaps such a man could tell us. It was of this torture and of this agony that Christ spoke, too. No, you can't treat a man like that! (pp. 20–21)

And later, when he describes the scene which Adelaida might paint, he associates the cross with the image of the man executed at Lyons:

> Paint the scaffold so that only the last step can be distinctly seen in the foreground and the criminal having just stepped on it; his head, his face as white as paper; the priest holding up the cross, the man greedily putting forward his blue lips and looking—and aware of everything. The cross and the head—that's the picture. The priest's face and the executioner's, his two attendants and a few heads and eyes below might be painted in the background, in half light, as the setting. . . . That's the picture! (pp. 60–61)

It is not surprising that when Christ becomes the subject of more extended consideration, he is introduced by means of a painting.

The reader first encounters the copy of Holbein's famous "Dead Christ" during Myshkin's visit to Rogozhin's house in Part II, Chapter 4. Appropriately, the picture represents the *prostrate* figure of Christ and therefore has a "rather strange shape, about two yards in breadth and not more than a foot high" (p. 205). (This picture, incidentally, is reproduced in the *Encyclopedia of World Art*, Vol. III, plate 307.) Myshkin has seen the picture at least once before, during his stay in Switzerland; but he reacts to it strongly, commenting as if with half seriousness, "Why, that picture might make some people lose their faith." And Rogozhin replies, "That's what it is doing" (p. 206). The picture provides the occasion for Myshkin's explanation of what he regards as "the essence of religious feeling," and it is in this chapter that he and Rogozhin exchange crosses. Much later in the novel, Ippolit discusses the picture, which he too has seen at Rogozhin's house. He describes it in some detail—

> the face is fearfully crushed by blows, swollen, covered with fearful, swollen and blood-stained bruises, the eyes are open and squinting: the great wide-open whites of the eyes glitter with a sort of deathly, glassy light. But, strange to say, as one looks at this corpse of a tortured man, a peculiar and curious question arises; if just such a corpse (and it must have been just like that) was seen by all His disciples, by those who were to become His chief apostles, by the women

that followed Him and stood by the cross, by all who believed in Him and worshipped Him, how could they believe that that martyr would rise again? The question instinctively arises: if death is so awful and the laws of nature so mighty, how can they be overcome? (pp. 388–389)

Thus, the images of light and prostration relate the sufferings of Christ to both the epileptic and the people about to be executed. The prostration is accentuated by the strange shape of the Holbein painting, and the *"inner* light" manages even to come through the whites of the dead Christ's eyes, though to the observer it seems "a sort of deathly, glassy light." If one wanted to insist on the autobiographical character of the experiences which Dostoevsky uses to represent Myshkin's vision, he would not have to limit himself to the emphasis upon epilepsy and the feelings of condemned men. Notice, for instance, Aglaia's explanation of why she loves the "poor knight" and "respects his exploits":

> Anyway, it's clear that that poor knight did not care what his lady was, or what she did. It was enough for him that he had chosen her and put his faith in her "pure beauty" and then did homage to her for ever. That's just his merit, that if she became a thief afterwards, he would still be bound to believe in her and be ready to break a spear for her pure beauty. The poet seems to have meant to unite in one striking figure the grand conception of the platonic love of mediaeval chivalry, as it was felt by a pure and lofty knight. (p. 236)

These comments seem a rather thinly veiled description of Dostoevsky's *credo*, set forth in a letter to a woman who had befriended him during the period of his greatest suffering:

> to believe that there is nothing more beautiful, more profound, more sympathetic, more reasonable, more manly, and more perfect than Christ, and not only is there nothing, but, I tell myself with jealous love, there can be nothing. Besides, if anyone proved to me that Christ was outside the truth, and it *really* was so that the truth was outside Christ, then I should prefer to remain with Christ than with the truth.[5]

By combining the two statements we may describe fairly accurately Dostoevsky's purpose in the characterization of Myshkin—"the novelist seems to have meant to unite in one striking figure the grand conception of the redeeming love of Russian Orthodox Christianity, as it was felt by a pure and lofty believer."

The three kinds of experience which Dostoevsky draws upon in order to provide an "objective correlative" of Myshkin's feelings are all autobiographical; they all involve suffering; and they all provide expiation and reconciliation. The condemned man apprehends an "eternity of life" in his final moments; the epileptic is able to grasp in the moment before his fit "a feeling, unknown and undivined till then, of completeness, of proportion, of reconciliation"; and the man who participates in the sufferings of Christ helps to redeem the world from brutality and meaninglessness.

The question naturally arises as to the ultimate meaning of this vision that is "graven on Myshkin's heart," and what relation that vision has (if any) to the Apocalypse, which is referred to so often and so directly in *The Idiot*. Thus far, the only immediate connection we have discovered is Myshkin's statement that in the split second before the onset of an epileptic fit, he seemed "somehow to understand the extraordinary saying that *there shall be no more time*"; and this "saying" is identified by Ippolit as having been spoken by "the great and mighty angel in the Apocalypse." On the other hand, Dostoevsky seems to poke a great deal of fun at this final book of the New Testament. Lebedyev, who is a ludicrous and finally a very cruel character, plumes himself on being expert in the book of Revelation: "Yes, I am a great hand at interpreting the Apocalypse; I've been interpreting it for the last fifteen years" (p. 189); and again, "But in interpreting revelation I am equal to the foremost in the land, for I am clever at it" (p. 190). General Ivolgin, who later becomes the victim of Lebedyev's cruelty, delights in ridiculing Lebedyev's attempts to make sense out of Revelation: "to take up such an extraordinary *intrus* for the interpretation of the

Apocalypse is a diversion like any other, and even a remarkably clever diversion, but . . ." (p. 231). On another occasion the general compares Lebedyev unfavorably to another man he had known:

> I used to know a real interpreter of the Apocalypse, . . . the late Grigory Semyonovitch Burmistrov. He used to make your heart glow. First, he'd put on his spectacles, and open a big old book in a black leather binding, and he'd a grey beard and two medals in recognition of his munificent charities. He used to begin sternly and severely. Generals would bow down before him, and ladies fell into swoons. But this fellow winds up with supper! It's beyond anything. (pp. 361–362)

When Ippolit reads his "Essential Explanation," he parodies the Apocalypse by making a great fuss about whether or not he should "break the seal" in order to read it (pp. 364–366; cf. the Lamb's breaking of the seven seals, Rev. 6: 1–17, 8:1–5); and this parody is based on the same passage which Lebedyev had already quoted from earlier in the novel (pp. 189–190). Ippolit also seems concerned to know whether people are listening as he reads: "If anyone wants to listen, let him" (p. 372); and this sentence echoes the formula "He who has an ear, let him hear," which is repeated seven times in Chapters 2 and 3 of Revelation. Through all of this we are never allowed to forget that Ippolit is an arrogant and callow youth, and Lebedyev a cynical and sneaky old man.

But still, Lebedyev's explication of the "star that is called Wormwood" (Rev. 8:11) emphasizes something which Dostoevsky returned to again and again in his writings, "the whole tendency of the last few centuries in its general, scientific and materialistic entirety" (p. 355). In *The Brothers Karamazov,* the Grand Inquisitor embodies all of Dostoevsky's misgivings about the "scientific and materialistic" tendencies of recent history. And Ippolit's "Essential Explanation," with its emphasis upon "the process of discovering, the everlasting and perpetual process, not the discovery itself" (p. 375), likewise reflects an important Dostoevsky theme. The ending of *Crime and Punishment,* which many critics have found unsatisfactory, may indeed be accounted for by Dostoevsky's placing far less emphasis upon the discovery itself than upon the process by which the discovery was made. What then emerges from this apparently ambiguous attitude toward the book of Revelation, and what connection do these parodies have with Myshkin's vision? Does Dostoevsky, by associating these two overbearing characters with the Apocalypse, mean to make that piece of scripture ridiculous in the eyes of the reader? On the contrary, by so doing he emphasizes the importance of understanding Myshkin's vision rightly and shows the consequences of interpreting *parts* of it in a purely literal way and mistaking those parts for the whole. Lebedyev and Ippolit see only fragments of the vision and therefore are unable to respond to it the way Myshkin does.

Besides the obvious connections between these visions and the Apocalypse which we have already noted (the saying that "there shall be no more time," the "star that is called Wormwood," Ippolit's "breaking the seal," and the like), the essential imagery of Myshkin's vision is borrowed directly from the Apocalypse. The emphasis upon prostration and falling reflects the fact that in the book of Revelation the word *fall* or *fall down* (Greek *piptō*) occurs more frequently than in any other book of the New Testament, at least twenty-one times in all, from the first chapter to the last: "When I saw him, I fell at his feet as though dead" (Rev. 1:17), and "I John am he who heard and saw these things. And when I heard and saw them, I fell down to worship at the feet of the angel who showed them to me" (Rev. 22:8). Likewise, the symbolism of *light* is very important in Revelation, God being the source of all light and Christ being the lamp. When the New Jerusalem descends "out of heaven from God," we are told that "the city has no need of sun or moon to shine upon it, for the glory of God is its light, and its lamp is the Lamb. By its light shall the nations walk" (Rev. 21:23–24). A few sentences later we learn that "night shall be no more; they need no light of lamp or sun, for the Lord God will be their light, and they shall reign for ever and ever" (Rev. 22:5). The Johannine writings are full of the word *light;* John's gospel, which represents Christ as "the light of the world" (John 8:12), uses the word at least twenty times, again more than any other book of the New Testament.

Occasionally in Revelation the images of falling and light are combined, as with the "star that is called Wormwood": "The third angel blew his trumpet, and a great star fell from heaven, blazing like a torch; . . . The name of the star is Wormwood" (Rev. 8:10–11). The first verse of the following chapter also includes the words, "I saw a star fallen from heaven to earth" (Rev. 9:1), and it describes the locusts which descend upon the world: "and they were given power like the power of scorpions of the earth; they were told . . . to harm . . . only those of mankind who have not the seal of God upon their foreheads; they were allowed to torture them for five months, but not to kill them, and their torture was like the torture of a scorpion, when it stings a man" (Rev. 9:3–5). Hence the creature that torments Ippolit in his dream: "I noticed an awful animal, a sort of monster. It was like a scorpion, but it was not a scorpion, it was more disgusting, and much more horrible, and it seemed it was so, just because there was nothing like it in nature, and that it had come *expressly* to me, and that there seemed to be something mysterious in that" (p. 370). Ippolit, unlike Myshkin, is obviously one of those "who have not the seal of God upon their foreheads." But if we undertook to trace all of the imagery and symbolism which Dostoevsky borrows from the Apocalypse, we should never finish.

More important than the apocalyptic imagery is the apocalyptic eschatology. Any discussion of eschatology necessarily involves a consideration of time, with its divisions into past, present, and future, though the use of these terms inevitably confuses the issue. Dostoevsky attempts to transcend these terms by introducing the phrase "there shall be no more time"; but in order to make himself intelligible to his readers, he is forced back upon them. The Apocalypse gets over this difficulty by referring to God (twice in the first chapter) as the one "who is and who was and who is to come." Even critics who say very little about the religious meaning of *The Idiot* are aware that the conception of time is crucial to the book. Edwin Muir, for instance, in *The Structure of the Novel,* has this to say: "No one, perhaps, has understood better than Dostoevsky this naked manifestation of Time at the moment when it is slipping away; and a passage in *The Idiot* describing the feelings of a man condemned to death explains it with great force." [6] But the point is not simply that "time is precious," as Madame Epanchin moralizes when Myshkin is trying to explain himself (p. 56). The point is rather that in the moment of vision one apprehends past, present, and future as a single entity—Christ's sufferings are not past but present, and the judgment upon man is not off in the future somewhere; it is *now*.

But paradoxically, if a man participates in the sufferings of Christ, in the apocalyptic moment he is not only judged, but forgiven; and he is able to share in "a feeling, unknown and undivined till then, of completeness, of proportion, of reconciliation, and of ecstatic devotional merging in the highest synthesis of life." The interrelation of judgment and forgiveness is the subject of more than one conversation in *The Idiot*. Aglaia, on one occasion, accuses Myshkin of judging Ippolit harshly: "I think it's very horrid on your part, for it's very brutal to look on and judge a man's soul, as you judge Ippolit. You have no tenderness, nothing but truth, and so you judge unjustly" (p. 406). And elsewhere, Myshkin suggests that Yevgeny Pavlovitch is similarly unjust to Ippolit:

> "Oh, for my part I forgive him everything; you can tell him so."
>
> "That's not the way to take it," Myshkin answered softly and, as it were, reluctantly, looking at one spot on the floor and not raising his eyes. "You ought to be ready to receive his forgiveness too."
>
> "How do I come in? What wrong have I done him?"
>
> "If you don't understand, then . . . But you do understand; he wanted . . . to bless you all then and to receive your blessing, that was all."
>
> "Dear prince," Prince S. hastened to interpose somewhat apprehensively, exchanging glances with some of the others, "it's not easy to reach paradise on earth, but you reckon on finding it." (p. 324)

Most characters in *The Idiot* are ready to judge, and a few are ready to forgive, but only Myshkin (despite Aglaia's claim) stands ready, by virtue of the vision graven upon his heart, to judge and to forgive, to be judged and to be forgiven.

But let us return to the categories of past, present, and future, and use them for an analysis of the inadequate visions of Ippolit and Lebedyev. Ippolit stands under sentence of death, and he is no less forcefully struck by the Holbein painting than Myshkin is. But he sees Christ as having been crushed by "that dull, dark, dumb force" of nature, which is like "a huge machine of the most modern construction" (p. 389), and he therefore finally regards the sufferings of Christ as meaningless. He foresees his own destruction by that same senseless power, and his response to that fact is a "natural" one: "what need is there of my humility? Can't I simply be devoured without being expected to praise what devours me?" (p. 393). Thus, because the sufferings of Christ are, for Ippolit, off somewhere in the vague and meaningless past, and because his own death is off somewhere in the vague and meaningless future, his present is likewise vague, meaningless, and hateful to him. Lebedyev, on the other hand, though he is fascinated by the Apocalypse, obviously misses the whole point because he merely allegorizes it and uses it (as fundamentalists often do today) to "predict" events that are already taking place and which can therefore be safely "predicted." Lebedyev proudly reports his own proceedings of this kind: "And he asked me when we were alone, 'Is it true that you expound Antichrist?' And I made no secret of it. 'I do,' said I. I explained and interpreted, and did not soften down the horror, but intentionally increased it, as I unfolded the allegory and fitted dates to it. And he laughed, but he began trembling at the dates and correspondences, and asked me to close the book and go away" (p. 190). The Apocalypse is for Lebedyev, as General Ivolgin rightly observes, a kind of parlor game, "a diversion like any other," and therefore ultimately meaningless.

No matter how negatively the individual reader may react to the religious views which find expression in *The Idiot*, there can be no doubt whatever that Dostoevsky's Christianity was biblical. His main inspiration came from the Apocalypse and the gospel of John; but Jesus speaks in apocalyptic terms in all three synoptic gospels (Matt. 24, Mark 13, Luke 21), and the imagery of falling and light (or darkness) appears in those passages, as we might expect: "Immediately after the tribulation of those days the sun will be darkened, and the moon will not give its light, and the stars will fall from heaven" (Matt. 24:29). Indeed, the account of St. Paul's conversion experience is represented in precisely the same kind of language: "Now as he journeyed he approached Damascus, and suddenly a light from heaven flashed about him. And he fell to the ground and heard a voice. . . . The men who were traveling with him stood speechless, hearing the voice but seeing no one. Saul arose from the ground. . . . And for three days he was without sight" (Acts 9:3–9). With this passage compare the description of Myshkin's epileptic fit:

> his soul was flooded with intense *inner* light. . . . Yet he clearly and consciously remembered the . . . scream. . . . Then his consciousness was instantly extinguished and complete darkness followed.
> . . . It seems indeed as though it were some one else screaming.
> . . . Myshkin had staggered away from him and fallen backwards.
> . . . Rogozhin flew headlong downstairs, avoiding the prostrate figure. (p. 222)

The essential details are the same in the two accounts: the suffusion of light, the falling to the ground, the voice which seems to come from someone invisible to observers, and the subsequent total darkness. And of course Myshkin, like Saul, "arose from the ground." (In *The Brothers Karamazov* when Father Zossima is listing the passages of scripture which one should be sure to read, he says, ". . . and then from the Acts of the Apostles the conversion of St. Paul [that you mustn't leave out on any account]," p. 350.)

For Dostoevsky, as for the apostle Paul, the consequence of sharing in the apocalyptic vision was religious conversion; but whereas Paul became the intellectual interpreter of Christianity, Dostoevsky identified himself with the prophetic tradition of St. John the Divine. To insist, as some critics have done, that Dostoevsky's Christianity is "primitive" (R. P. Blackmur) or that it must not be identified with "real Christianity" (D. S. Mirsky) is merely for the critic to say that he himself finds Paul's intellectual interpretation more palatable than John's prophetic revelation.[7] But the implication, completely unnoticed by these critics, that St. Paul was a "real Christian" while St. John was not can hardly be allowed to pass; it is an error of the most elementary kind.

How thoroughly biblical Dostoevsky's vision was may be seen by looking at a good recent commentary on the book of Revelation. Paul S. Minear, in an article called "The Cosmology of the Apocalypse," shows the inadequacy of ordinary time and space conceptions for understanding Revelation. According to Minear, the only categories which are really relevant are the ones which St. John provides, those of "the first and the new creations," and these "cannot be neatly located within a third and independent reality, the earth which the mapmaker knows or the calendar which the businessman obeys. The creations met and diverged on Golgotha; they meet and diverge wherever decisions embody loyalties. And 'time is of the essence' of such decisions, but this very time is unmeasurable."[8] Still more revealing are these statements near the end of Minear's essay:

> The two creations are everywhere juxtaposed, yet only the saint can become aware of their meeting place and time; and such awareness springs from his present choices [cf. Myshkin] and not from calendrical studies [cf. Lebedyev, who "unfolded the allegory and fitted dates to it"]. . . . The shift in vision, produced by the prophet's own struggle of faith, produced a permanent negation alike of timelessness and of endless time. Moreover, it seems to me that John can be safely classified neither among the thoroughgoing futurist eschatologists, nor among the realized eschatologists. . . .
>
> The prophet, then, sees man's history as the coexistence of two mutually exclusive realms, one of which has the enduring stamp of transiency, the other that of newness. . . . These visions express his certainties concerning the human scene, his depth perceptions concerning two realms which are very substantial indeed. Interpreters who take those perceptions seriously will be alert to detect similar cosmological attitudes in other New Testament books. The prophet's world-view is far more pervasive than we often allow.[9]

What Minear says illuminates our understanding of Dostoevsky on at least two important points: he shows that the mode of thought in Revelation pervades more of the New Testament than we usually recognize, and he makes it clear that St. John's eschatology is neither completely "futurist" nor is it fully "realized" in the present. The first point confirms our impression that even if Dostoevsky derives much of his language and imagery from St. John, the content of his writing is more closely related to the New Testament as a whole than most commentators are willing to admit. And the second point clears up much of what critics usually regard as ambiguous in Dostoevsky's eschatology. For Dostoevsky, as for Ippolit and Ivan Karamazov, it is not enough that at some time way off in the future all men will be judged and that "universal harmony" (p. 394) will be established. In this sense, Dostoevsky cannot be classified "among the thoroughgoing futurist eschatologists." But it is equally true for Dostoevsky that no amount of "good works" in the present will ever save mankind—hence his hatred for atheistic socialism. Indeed, for Dostoevsky there can be no *present* morality without belief in the God "who is and who was and who is to come." That is to say, Dostoevsky cannot be classed with the "realized eschatologists" either. The apocalyptic vision fuses past, present, and future in a way which Ippolit, Lebedyev, Ivan Karamazov, and many other Dostoevsky characters who represent "the first creation" cannot comprehend. That vision is reserved for Myshkin, for Alyosha Karamazov, and a few others who also share in "the new creation."

We should test the validity of this hypothesis about *The Idiot* by applying it to some other incidents in the story. If the apocalyptic vision is really central to the book, it should illuminate those incidents in a way that ordinary interpretation fails to do. Let us take two entirely separate episodes, one of which appears to be a digression from the principal story line and the other of which is a climactic event in the main plot. The first is General Epanchin's story (Part I, Chapter 14) told in response to the invitation to relate "something he had done, something that he himself honestly considered the worst of all the evil actions of his life" (p. 133). The second is the scene in which Myshkin is introduced into "society" as the fiancé of Aglaia; he rants about the Roman church and in his excitement knocks the valuable Chinese vase from its pedestal (Part IV, Chapter 7).

When General Epanchin is persuaded to tell about "the worst of all the evil actions of his life," he recalls an experience that he had had as a young lieutenant. He had been living at the house of an old woman, who at "eighty or thereabouts" was "quite alone," having outlived all her family and friends. He quarreled with her just at the time he was transferred to other quarters; and after moving, he learned from his orderly that the latter had left a bowl at the old woman's house, with the result that they now had "nothing to put the soup in." The general continues:

> I was surprised, of course. "How so? How was it the bowl was left behind?" Nikifor, surprised, went on to report that when we were leaving the landlady had not given him our bowl, because I had broken her pot; that she had kept our bowl in place of her pot, and that she had pretended I had suggested it. Such meanness on her part naturally made me furious; it would make any young officer's blood boil. I leapt up and flew out. I was beside myself, so to say, when I got to the old woman's. I saw her sitting in the passage, huddled up in the corner all alone, as though to get out of the sun, her cheek propped on her hand. I poured out a stream of abuse, calling her all sorts of names, you know, in regular Russian style. Only there seemed something strange as I looked at her: she sat with her face turned to me, her eyes round and staring, and answered not a word. And she looked at me in such a queer way, she seemed to be swaying. At last I calmed down. I looked at her, I questioned her— not a word. I stood hesitating: flies were buzzing, the sun was setting, there was stillness. Completely disconcerted, I walked away. (p. 140)

Later that evening he learned that the woman had died: "So that at the very time I was abusing her she was passing away." He reflects upon it thirty-five years later, saying that the worst of it was that:

it was a woman—so to speak, a fellow creature, a *humane* creature
. . . left alone like . . . some fly accursed from the beginning of
time. And then at last God had brought her to the end, as the sun
was setting, on a quiet summer evening my old woman too was passing away—a theme for pious reflection, to be sure. And then at that
very moment, instead of a tear to see her off, so to say, a reckless
young lieutenant, swaggering arms akimbo, escorts her from the
surface of the earth to the Russian tune of violent swearing over a
lost bowl! . . . This incident I honestly consider my worst action.
(p. 141)

The apocalyptic imagery is there of course—the setting sun,
the imminence of death, and the "stillness" broken by the
screams of the outraged lieutenant; and we notice that when the
young officer's anger subsides, his voice is replaced by the buzz-
ing of flies. Also, the woman herself is described as a fly, "accursed from the beginning of time." This image of flies connects
the incident we are considering with both Ippolit's "Essential
Explanation" (pp. 373, 393, 402–403) and that tremendous final
scene in which Myshkin and Rogozhin lie down together in
darkness beside the body of the murdered Nastasya (pp. 579 ff.).
Using the lost bowl and the broken pot as the basis for the
incident may seem arbitrary at first, but when we recall the
shattered vase in the other episode we are to consider, it seems
likely that both incidents are related to this passage in Revelation: "He who conquers and who keeps my works until the
end, I will give him power over the nations, and he shall rule
them with a rod of iron, *as when earthen pots are broken in
pieces,* even as I myself have received power from my Father;
and I will give him the morning star. He who has an ear, let
him hear what the Spirit says to the churches" (Rev. 2:26–29,
italics mine). We recognize the formula about "hearing," which
Ippolit echoes during his "Essential Explanation" (p. 372); the
following chapter of Revelation contains the passage (Rev. 3:14–
17) which Dostoevsky twice quotes verbatim in *The Possessed*
(pp. 663, 699); and the preceding chapter contains the image of
the "sharp two-edged sword" (Rev. 1:16; 2:12) which fascinated

Dostoevsky and which he seems to have equated with "the Russian proverb about 'a knife that cuts both ways'" (*The Idiot*, p. 458).

The meaning of General Epanchin's worst action is perfectly clear in the context of *The Idiot*. Exposure to a situation which almost by accident has the character of an apocalyptic vision makes it possible for him to see himself, even for a moment, as he really is; and though his behavior is, by his own admission, typical of his whole mode of existence at that time and is therefore probably no worse than his conduct upon many other occasions, he judges himself almost without forgiveness. That is, he judges himself with "nothing but truth, and so he judges unjustly." (Cf. Aglaia's statement to Myshkin on p. 406.) Like anyone else who glimpses the apocalyptic vision even for a moment, he feels the necessity for expiation; and he therefore provides, twenty years later, "for two incurable old women in the almshouse, so as to soften the last days of their earthly existence by comfortable surroundings" (p. 141). This expiation is pitifully inadequate and more than slightly late in coming, but it leads one of the general's hearers to accuse him of "cheating," and to comment that "instead of the worst, your excellency has described one of your good actions." For Dostoevsky, the apocalyptic vision makes it possible to transform the worst into the best, to change "meanness that makes one's blood boil" into acts of charity. The general ends by saying that he may extend his provision for the old ladies by "bequeathing a sum of money to make it a permanent charity." The money part is somewhat crass, but the idea of permanence surely had Dostoevsky's approval.

The second episode we are to consider, that of Myshkin's appearance in Petersburg "society" when he lashes out at Roman Catholicism and smashes the Chinese vase, is far more complex; but it yields to the same kind of analysis. General Epanchin's story is obviously a "digression" from the main plot, and the content of Myshkin's monologue on the Roman church in this scene has likewise been accused of being totally irrelevant. According to Murray Krieger, "When Dostoevsky gets off on the problems of Roman Catholicism and of Russian-ness, he seems to lose all aesthetic presence and ventriloquizes freely. I cannot, then, take this passage seriously, as being more than an errant insertion in this book that is so full of them." [10] But Myshkin's charge against Catholicism is that "It preaches the Antichrist, I declare it does, I assure you it does!" (p. 518); and a page later Myshkin declares that "Our Christ whom we have kept and they have never known must shine forth and vanquish the West." The whole point of the Apocalypse is that it offers a prophetic vision of Christ as the "slain Lamb" and represents the warfare between the first and the new creations, the Lamb's chief antagonist being of course the Antichrist. (The term *antichrist* appears not in the Apocalypse, but in the first and second letters of John; but the "false prophet" of Revelation is obviously the same as the antichrist described in the Johannine letters.) The content of Myshkin's diatribe is *not*, therefore, an "errant insertion," but the subject matter which for Dostoevsky is dictated by the apocalyptic imagery which dominates the whole scene.

This imagery appears long before the onset of Myshkin's epileptic fit, and the conditions are such that he actually mistakes his feelings for those he always has just before a fit overtakes him. The shattering of the vase is accompanied by "a general scream of horror"; and all action is arrested, suspended in one of those endless moments:

A crash, a scream, and the priceless fragments were scattered about the carpet, dismay and astonishment—what was Myshkin's condition would be hard, and is perhaps unnecessary, to describe! But we must not omit to mention one odd sensation, which struck him at that very minute, and stood out clearly above the mass of other confused and strange sensations. It was not the shame, not the scandal, not the fright, nor the suddenness of it that impressed him most, but his foreknowledge of it! He could not explain what was so arresting about that thought, he only felt that it had gripped him to the heart, and he stood still in a terror that was almost superstitious! Another instant and everything seemed opening out before him; instead of horror there was light, joy, and ecstasy; his breath began to fail him, and . . . but the moment had passed. Thank God, it was not that! He drew a breath and looked about him. (p. 522)

Because Dostoevsky has by now provided a completely "objective correlative" for the feelings which accompany the apocalyptic vision, there is no longer the problem of "how to draw the face" or "how to describe it"—though Myshkin's feelings are "hard to describe," it is "perhaps unnecessary" to do so.

The imagery which the reader might confidently expect in such a scene by the time he has read five hundred pages is certainly there—the falling, the light, and the scream. And partly for the reason that he has learned to expect it, the reader (like Myshkin himself) seems to have had foreknowledge of what happens in this episode. Indeed, Varya predicts the event more than fifty pages earlier: "They are only afraid he may let something drop or break something when he walks into the drawing-room, or else flop down himself; it's quite in his line" (p. 446). Myshkin's skillful avoidance of anything like that when he enters the salon only augments our suspicion that it will not be long in coming: "He walked in admirably, was perfectly dressed, and far from falling down on the slippery floor, as they had all been afraid the day before, evidently made a favourable impression on every one" (p. 508). When the apocalyptic moment arrives, it comes therefore with extraordinary power and is soon reinforced by Myshkin's fit and the unspoken reference to all the images which identify that experience.

Myshkin is of course painfully aware during the whole episode that he stands under judgment; he is being scrutinized by everyone to see if he is really a suitable husband for Aglaia. But because he is ready both to forgive and to be forgiven, the scene is dominated by light rather than darkness. After the vase has been smashed, he asks Madame Epanchin, "And you forgive me for *everything*? For *everything*, besides the vase?" (p. 523). He begins then to enumerate the virtuous deeds which those present in the room have done at one time or another—the old "dignitary" had "saved a student called Podkumov and a clerk called Shvabrin from exile three months ago" (p. 524). Ivan Petrovitch had given his peasants "timber to rebuild their huts when they were burnt out"; and to Princess Byelokonsky Myshkin says, "And did not you . . . receive me six months ago in Moscow, as though I had been your own son?" They all regard him as "a good-natured fellow but absurd"; and the scene resembles a final judgment in which men are forgiven and reconciled by virtue of the acts of kindness they had at one time or another performed. Still, Myshkin "exaggerates," and we are told that some of the deeds which make it possible to forgive these people even the "worst actions of their lives" are known to him only by "an incorrect rumour that had reached him." It cannot be said of Myshkin at this point as it had been earlier, "You have no tenderness, nothing but truth, and so you judge unjustly." This scene comes to be dominated by a feeling, "unknown and undivined till then, of completeness, of proportion, of reconciliation," which the narrator has told us suffuses the being of an epileptic, just before the onset of his fit. Myshkin's fit therefore appropriately concludes the episode.

Some critics are convinced that because Myshkin does not succeed in changing Petersburg into heaven on earth in any objective, measurable way, the theme of *The Idiot* must be "the inadequacy of mere goodness in the world of today." [11] It is of course true, as Simon O. Lesser says, that Myshkin fails to "make a reasonably normal adjustment to Russian society." [12] But it is true only in the same sense that Antigone fails to "make a reasonably normal adjustment to Greek society." A reader who completely misses the apocalyptic vision embodied in *The Idiot* may tend to think that the Christian naively falls short of self-knowledge. Commenting upon the scene we have just explicated, Mr. Lesser has this to say: "In judging the Epanchins' guests, he is so indulgent that his ingenuousness has precisely the effect of irony. His appraisal of the aristocracy is so at variance with the facts that it makes his listeners more keenly aware of their shortcomings. Instead of providing expiation, it increases their sense of guilt." [13] There is, however, another layer of irony on top of this one. It is precisely the point of Dostoevsky's Christianity that expiation is possible for individuals only *after* they have become "more keenly aware of their shortcomings." This is in fact the significance of the apocalyptic vision. We can be reasonably sure that Dostoevsky was familiar with the words of St. Paul: "If your enemy is hungry, feed him; if he is thirsty, give him drink; for by so doing you will heap burning coals upon his head" (Rom. 12:20; cf. Proverbs 25:21–22). Dostoevsky had no illusions about the immediate social efficacy of the Christian witness. The last chapter of the Apocalypse—a book which, if we may judge by the imagery of *The Idiot*, Dostoevsky knew rather well—contains these words: "Do not seal up the words of the prophecy of this book, for the time is near. Let the evil-doer still do evil, and the filthy still be filthy, and the righteous still do right, and the holy still be holy" (Rev. 22:10–11). In the light of these facts, it is ironic to suppose that Christian experience, as represented in *The Idiot*, involves ironies which were a sealed book to Myshkin and perhaps even to Dostoevsky himself.

As a final point, at least one other image in the book (or rather *pair* of images) deserves explanation. In *Dostoevsky: The Major Fiction*, Edward Wasiolek attaches great importance to the images in question. He says of Ippolit:

> Under the pressure of death, he is struggling between belief in nothingness and belief in beauty and goodness of life. This struggle is caught in contrasting images: the image of Meyer's wall and the Pavlovsky trees. Meyer's wall, outside the window where he lies in sickness, is an image of the blank and meaningless universe. The Pavlovsky trees, which he has come to see for the last time, are an image of a universe with beauty and purpose. It is the wall he finally believes in, and not the trees: "That damned wall! And yet it is dearer to me than all the Pavlovsky trees, that is, it would be dearer if it did not matter to me now!" [14]

Wasiolek is right in his reaction to the images, but he does not give much indication of their meaning in the book as a whole. Ippolit's concern about what Myshkin had "meant by his everlasting 'trees,' and why he keeps pestering me with those 'trees' " (p. 368) is indeed central to the story. Just why it is we may see by consulting Revelation once more.

When St. John describes "the holy city Jerusalem coming down out of heaven from God," he says that "It had a great, high wall" (Rev. 21:12) and that "he who walked with me . . . measured its wall, a hundred and forty-four cubits by a man's measure, that is, an angel's" (Rev. 21:15–17). They proceed to explore the city itself, inside the wall: "Then he showed me the river of the water of life, bright as crystal, flowing from the throne of God and of the Lamb through the middle of the street of the city; also, on either side of the river, the tree of life; . . . and the leaves of the tree were for the healing of the nations" (Rev. 22:1–2). Ippolit, who insists upon the fact that he is not a believer (and therefore dwells *outside* the city which John describes) stares at the blank wall which excludes him rather than going in to contemplate the trees whose leaves "were for the healing of the nations." (Cf. the words which Jesus spoke to Paul at the time of his conversion, "Rise and enter the city," Acts 9:6.) It irritates Ippolit that Myshkin keeps "pestering" him with those "everlasting 'trees.'" But we may be sure that while most of the characters in *The Idiot* bid furiously against each other for Nastasya's favors, Myshkin is within the city, his eyes fixed upon the trees which are nourished by "the water of life without price."

IX

The Grand Inquisitor

"With my pitiful, earthly, Euclidean understanding,
all I know is that there is suffering
and that there are none guilty."
IVAN KARAMAZOV

CRITICS are nearly unanimous in regarding "The Grand Inquisitor" as crucial to any interpretation of *The Brothers Karamazov,* but they are sharply divided as to the meaning of that important chapter and, consequently, as to the meaning of the entire book. Some, notably Berdyaev, identify Dostoevsky with Christ rather than with the Inquisitor, but they point to no cogent and specific reasons within the chapter itself for doing so.[1] Others, including D. H. Lawrence, insist that the Inquisitor's condemnation of Christ reflects "Dostoievsky's own final opinion about Jesus," but they fail to account for Dostoevsky's emphasis upon Christian love throughout the rest of the book.[2] Still others, such as Philip Rahv, believe that Dostoevsky "takes his stand with Christ" not because he was able to refute the Inquisitor's "malign wisdom," but because he would not renounce his long-standing commitment to Christianity.[3] Rahv's conclusion implies a serious flaw in the book, a direct contradiction between the author's realistic view of the world and his apparently unrealistic way of dealing with that world. Even so, this contradiction is perhaps no greater than the ones implied by Berdyaev and Lawrence: Berdyaev fails to convince us that Dostoevsky rejected the reasonableness of the Inquisitor's views, and Lawrence simply ignores the prominence of Alyosha and Zossima as embodiments of Christian love in the novel as a whole.

These three interpretations represent the broad range of critical thought; and two of them assert that the Inquisitor's argument is unanswerable. The third (Berdyaev's) claims, but does not prove, that the Inquisitor's argument is self-contradictory. In *Dostoevsky: The Major Fiction*, Edward Wasiolek summarizes the critical consensus so admirably that he deserves to be quoted at length:

> The Grand Inquisitor's argument is not based on idle rhetoric or cheap tricks. Nor is it contradictory as some have claimed. Logic is on his side, not Christ's, although the truth of each is finally subject to more than logic. Lawrence, Shestov, Guardini, Rozanov, and many other distinguished critics have taken the side of the Grand Inquisitor against Christ because his argument is powerful and indeed unanswerable. And they do this despite the fact that Dostoevsky made the case he wanted to make for Christ. There is no weakness in Christ's argument, and there is no weakness in the Grand Inquisitor's argument. Mochulsky's argument that the Grand Inquisitor is wrong because he argues from love of mankind, yet portrays mankind as weak and slavish is clearly a *non sequitur*. One can love what is weak and slavish, and perhaps love more deeply. Those who try to help out Dostoevsky by showing that the Grand Inquisitor's argument is self-contradictory do not understand the Grand Inquisitor, and they do not understand Dostoevsky. Dostoevsky made the only case he could for Christ, and the truth of Christ he presents does not demolish the Grand Inquisitor's truth any more than the Grand Inquisitor's truth demolishes Christ's truth. We are concerned here with two ways of understanding man's nature, and they are discontinuous; one cannot stand in refutation by the other because there are no common assumptions. This will become clear by seeing and understanding the nature of the Grand Inquisitor's truth, which is consistent and complete and deep in its appeal.[4]

In short, we are told repeatedly that the Inquisitor's argument is logical, consistent, and, in the last analysis, unanswerable.

But the old Jesuit's position compels our assent only if we take everything he says at face value; and if we do that, tremendous contradictions arise not only between this one chapter and the book as a whole, but also within the chapter itself. For instance, the Inquisitor often asserts that Christ rejected miracle, because "Thou wouldst not enslave man by a miracle, and didst crave faith given freely, not based on miracle" (p. 304). And yet, near the beginning of the chapter, the old man first sees and recognizes Christ in the act of performing a miracle, that of raising a seven-year-old child from the dead: The Inquisitor approaches; "He sees everything; he sees them set the coffin down at His feet, sees the child rise up, and his face darkens. He knits his thick grey brows and his eyes gleam with a sinister fire" (p. 296). In terms of the book as a whole, if he shares the Inquisitor's admittedly inescapable conclusion that "beyond the grave [men] will find nothing but death" (p. 308), why does Dostoevsky end the book by having Alyosha (whom he designates as "my hero") declare to the boys: "Certainly we shall all rise again, certainly we shall see each other and shall tell each other with joy and gladness all that has happened"? (p. 940).

As a literary consideration, it seems odd that no one has noted the source of the Inquisitor's most characteristic language and imagery; it comes directly from the book of Revelation, where it is associated with "the false prophet" (Rev. 16:13; 19:20; 20:10). The words *miracle*, *mystery*, and *authority* recur frequently in this final book of the bible. (Greek *sēmeîon* is translated as *miracle* in the King James Bible and as *sign* in the Revised Standard Version.) But their meaning in that context is spurious, referring as they do to the machinations of the Antichrist. One first notices the allusions to Revelation when the Inquisitor speaks of the beast that brings fire from heaven (p. 300; cf. Rev. 13:1–15), of the prophet (St. John the Divine) who describes the "first resurrection" (p. 304; cf. Rev. 20:5–6; 14:1–3), and of "the harlot who sits upon the beast, and holds in her hands the *mystery*" (p. 308; cf. Rev. 17:1–8). These references are unmistakable—nowhere but in the book of Revelation is there mention of a "first resurrection," participated in by twelve thousand from each of the twelve tribes; and nowhere else does one hear of the harlot who sits upon the beast and proclaims the "mystery." If Dostoevsky regarded the Inquisitor as a "true prophet," it seems inconsistent that he should have put into the old man's mouth language which the bible associates with "the false prophet." These literary allusions, then, are another matter which any satisfactory analysis of "The Grand Inquisitor" must take into account.

When we look at the Inquisitor chapter closely, we see how even a careful reader might become lost in the maze of reasoning which the Inquisitor elaborately constructs. There are at least nine separate matters which we have to keep in mind as the argument progresses: the three temptations of Jesus; man's three fundamental needs; and the three ways of satisfying those needs —miracle, mystery, and authority. To complicate matters even further, the whole chapter is drenched in irony; and this irony is unconscious as far as the Inquisitor is concerned, because he does not accept or even know the definitions and clarifications which Dostoevsky provides in other parts of the book.

The Inquisitor simply fails to understand that Christianity, as envisioned in *The Brothers Karamazov*, does *not* reject the view that man's three basic needs are (1) someone to worship, (2) someone to keep his conscience, and (3) some means of achieving universal unity. Moreover, Christianity does *not* reject miracle, mystery, and authority as means of satisfying those needs. As a matter of fact, the Inquisitor reverses the real situation: *he* is the one who rejects miracle, mystery, and authority, and proposes instead to meet man's needs by *magic, mystification,* and *tyranny.* He does his best (which is very good indeed) to conceal from both himself and his listener precisely what he is doing. But Christ is not deceived. Strangely, the old man who professes to love humanity reacts to perfect goodness by condemning it to the flames in an *auto-da-fé;* but Christ responds by miraculously offering love, and this one act is sufficient to make the old churchman almost involuntarily abdicate his inquisitorial authority (tyrannical power) over Christ by telling him to leave, by casting him out into "the dark alleys of the town."

This explanation is of course simply a hypothesis which stands or falls according to whether or not it adequately accounts for the evidence—the events, facts, and statements contained in *The Brothers Karamazov*. In order to test it we must begin with the simplest matters and proceed from there. The first question has to do with the Inquisitor's view of human nature and the extent to which it differs from the Christian view as represented by Dostoevsky. These facts we may ascertain by examining the Inquisitor's argument and juxtaposing it with Dostoevsky's conception of Christianity as expressed elsewhere in the novel. After describing the third temptation, in which Satan offered Christ all the kingdoms of the world, the Inquisitor summarizes man's basic needs: "Hadst Thou accepted that last counsel of the mighty spirit, Thou wouldst have accomplished all that man seeks on earth—that is, some one to worship, some one to keep his conscience, and some means of uniting all in one unanimous and harmonious ant-heap, for the craving for universal unity is the third and last anguish of men" (pp. 305–306). This much is perfectly clear. The question now is how seriously we should take the Inquisitor when he says to Christ, "Man is weaker and baser by nature than Thou hast believed him! . . . Respecting him less, Thou wouldst have asked less of him. . . . He is weak and vile" (p. 304). That is, within the context of *The Brothers Karamazov*, does the attitude of contempt for man follow necessarily from the Inquisitor's analysis of man's fundamental needs?

The answer is an emphatic "No," for the simple reason that Christianity, according to Dostoevsky, perceives and serves these same three fundamental human needs. The chief proponents of Christianity in the book are Father Zossima and his disciple, Alyosha. The Elder is the mature Christian, firm in his faith and perfect in love, while Alyosha is the stumbling, youthful Christian, not always faithful and (until after the death of his elder) sometimes lacking in love. In the chapter called "Elders," very near the beginning of the novel, Alyosha contemplates with satisfaction the attitude of the common people toward his elder:

> Alyosha did not wonder why they loved him so, why they fell down before him and wept with emotion merely at seeing his face. Oh! he understood that for the humble soul of the Russian peasant, worn out by grief and toil, and still more by the everlasting injustice and everlasting sin, his own and the world's, it was the greatest need and comfort to find *some one or something holy to fall down before and worship*. (p. 30, italics mine)

Unless there is some cogent reason for thinking otherwise (and none emerges in the whole book), we may regard this passage as a straightforward expression of the Christian view as it is embodied in *The Brothers Karamazov*.

In this same chapter the omniscient narrator indicates that a particular elder sometimes served as conscience for the people who came to see him.

> Masses of the ignorant people as well as men of distinction flocked, for instance, to the elders of our monastery to confess their doubts, their sins, and their sufferings, and ask for counsel and admonition. Seeing this, the opponents of the elders declared that the sacrament of confession was being arbitrarily and frivolously degraded, though the continual opening of the heart to the elder by the monk or the layman had nothing of the character of the sacrament. (p. 28)

> It was said that so many people had for years past come to confess their sins to Father Zossima and to entreat him for words of advice and healing, that he had acquired the keenest intuition and could tell from an unknown face what a new comer wanted, and what was the suffering on his conscience. He sometimes astounded and almost alarmed his visitors by his knowledge of their secrets before they had spoken a word.
>
> Alyosha noticed that many, almost all, went in to the elder for the first time with apprehension and uneasiness, but came out with bright and happy faces. (p. 29)

The Inquisitor harasses Christ particularly on this matter of conscience. According to the old man, Christ made an incredibly bad mistake in refusing to take over this part of man's existence.

> Nothing is more seductive for man than his freedom of conscience, but nothing is a greater cause of suffering. And behold, instead of giving a firm foundation for setting the conscience of man at rest for ever, Thou didst choose all that is exceptional, vague and enigmatic. . . . Instead of taking possession of men's freedom, Thou didst increase it, and burdened the spiritual kingdom of mankind with its sufferings for ever. . . . In place of the rigid ancient law, man must hereafter with free heart decide for himself what is good and what is evil, having only Thy image before him as his guide. (p. 302)

Because this question is so important, Dostoevsky prepares the reader for it in the chapter called "So be it! So be it!" The issue of crime and conscience arises there in connection with Ivan's article on the relation of church and state. Zossima picks up the question and discusses it from a Christian point of view:

> If it were not for the Church of Christ there would be nothing to restrain the criminal from evil-doing, no real chastisement for it afterwards; none, that is, but the mechanical punishment spoken of just now, which in the majority of cases only embitters the heart. . . . All these sentences to exile with hard labour, and formerly with flogging also, reform no one, and what's more, deter hardly a single criminal, and the number of crimes does not diminish but is continually on the increase. . . . If anything does preserve society, even in our time, and does regenerate and transform the criminal, it is only *the law of Christ speaking in his conscience*. It is only by recognising his wrong-doing as a son of a Christian society—that is, of the Church—that he recognises his sin against society—that is, against the Church. (p. 72, italics mine)

Indeed, from a Christian point of view the attempt to obey the "rigid ancient law" which the Inquisitor prefers to Christ's freedom of conscience is a *source* of misery and sin, not the remedy for them. (*See* Romans 7.)

The third fundamental need, universal unity, is also treated from the Christian viewpoint in the chapter called "Elders." It will be achieved, thinks Alyosha, by the coming of Christ's kingdom through love. Though he foresees the possibility of men's being universally united in Christian love, he is discouraged momentarily because Zossima stands before him as a solitary example, as only *one* just man:

> "No matter. He is holy. He carries in his heart the secret of renewal for all: that power which will, at last, establish truth on the earth, and all men will be holy and love one another, and there will be no more rich nor poor, no exalted nor humbled, but all will be as the children of God, and the true Kingdom of Christ will come." That was the dream in Alyosha's heart. (pp. 30–31)

Ivan similarly stakes the validity of his Inquisitor theory on the existence of *one* such man. When Alyosha insists that not all

Jesuits are like Ivan's old man, that they are not united in "simple lust of power, of filthy earthly gain, of domination," Ivan responds:

> Why can there not be among them one martyr oppressed by great sorrow and loving humanity? You see, only suppose that there was one such man among all those who desire nothing but filthy material gain—if there's only one like my old inquisitor, who had himself eaten roots in the desert and made frenzied efforts to subdue his flesh and to make himself free and perfect. (p. 310)

> And if only one such stood at the head of the whole army, "filled with the lust of power only for the sake of filthy gain"—would not one such be enough to make a tragedy? (p. 311)

Thus, the argument about "one such man," like most things in the novel, is "a knife that cuts both ways," and the hope for Christ's kingdom is no less reasonable than the expectation that man will unite into "one unanimous and harmonious ant-heap."

Juxtaposing passages from other parts of the book with crucial points in the Inquisitor's tirade in no way proves that "logic and the facts of history" are on Christ's side rather than on the Inquisitor's; but it does shatter Wasiolek's assertion that "we are concerned here with two ways of understanding man's nature, and they are discontinuous; one cannot stand in refutation by the other because there are no common assumptions." On the contrary, the assumptions about human nature held by the Inquisitor on the one hand and by Dostoevsky's Christianity on the other are identical. (Christianity has not often overestimated man in his natural condition; more frequently it has taken his depravity for granted.) But this error of observation leads to an error of method on Wasiolek's part. He continues: "The Grand Inquisitor is wrong only if his view of human nature is wrong, and neither logic nor the facts of history are against him." [5] Such an argument leads nowhere because proof that the Inquisitor's view of human nature was wrong would also be proof that the Christian view was wrong, and the confrontation of the two attitudes would be without significance. If we are to choose meaningfully between Christ and the Inquisitor, we must look beyond their shared assumptions about human nature to their highly complex conceptions of miracle, mystery, and authority.

We have already noted the contradiction concerning miracle in the Inquisitor chapter: the old churchman repeatedly asserts that Christ rejected miracle, and yet he first sees Christ in the act of raising a little girl from the dead. This inconsistency serves not so much to prove that the Inquisitor is wrong or stupid as to call attention to the fact that he means by the word *miracle* something quite different from the kind of act that Christ performs when he first appears on the scene. Our problem becomes then one of definition, not only of *miracle,* but of *mystery* and *authority* as well. Just before his account of the second temptation, the Inquisitor declares: "There are three powers, three powers alone, able to conquer and to hold captive for ever the conscience of these impotent rebels for their happiness—those forces are miracle, mystery and authority. Thou hast rejected all three and hast set the example for doing so" (p. 303). We shall take the three terms in order and define each, first according to the Inquisitor and then according to Dostoevsky's view of Christianity.

Describing the second temptation, the Inquisitor analyzes Christ's motives in refusing to be drawn in by Satan:

> But Thou didst refuse and wouldst not cast Thyself down. Oh! of course, Thou didst proudly and well, like God; but the weak, unruly race of men, are they gods? Oh, Thou didst know then that in taking one step, in making one movement to cast Thyself down, Thou wouldst be tempting God and have lost all Thy faith in Him, and wouldst have been dashed to pieces against that earth which Thou didst come to save. And the wise spirit that tempted Thee would have rejoiced. But I ask again, are there many like Thee? And couldst Thou believe for one moment that men, too, could face such a temptation? . . . Thou didst hope that man, following Thee, would cling to God and not ask for a miracle. But Thou didst not know that when man rejects miracle he rejects God too; for man seeks not so much God as the miraculous. And as man cannot bear to be without the miraculous, he will create new miracles of his own

for himself, and will worship deeds of sorcery and witchcraft, though he might be a hundred times over a rebel, heretic and infidel. (p. 303)

Shortly thereafter, the Inquisitor declares, "We have corrected Thy work and have founded it upon *miracle, mystery* and *authority*" (p. 305), and still later describes how he and his cohorts will perform the "miracle" of turning stones into bread.

> Receiving bread from us, they will see clearly that we take the bread made by their hands from them, to give it to them, without any miracle. They will see that we do not change the stones to bread, but in truth they will be more thankful for taking it from our hands than for the bread itself! For they will remember only too well that in the old days, without our help, even the bread they made turned to stones in their hands, while since they have come back to us, the very stones have turned to bread in their hands. Too, too well they know the value of complete submission! And until men know that they will be unhappy. (p. 307)

In short, it will be no miracle at all, but the kind of "sorcery and witchcraft" to which men turn because they "cannot bear to be without the miraculous." What the Inquisitor offers "weak and vile" men is a substitute for miracle; it is magic—and magic of a totally spurious kind at that. (Perhaps the nicest irony in the Inquisitor's analysis of Christ's temptation is his obvious conclusion that Christ performed a superhuman act in rejecting "miracle": "Thou didst proudly and well, like God; but the weak, unruly race of men, are they gods?" That is, *he condemns Christ for performing the miracle of rejecting "miracle."*)

Christ, on the other hand, meets man's need not only by performing a genuine miracle, but by enabling the weakest of men to perform that same miracle himself. At the beginning of the chapter entitled "Rebellion," Ivan says to Alyosha, "To my thinking, Christ-like love for men is a miracle impossible on earth" (p. 281). What Ivan calls "Christ-like love for men" is miraculous for two reasons, both of which are illustrated at the end of "The Grand Inquisitor." It is miraculous first because it is, in a sense, unmotivated. It is offered not because man is lovable; it is offered *in spite* of the fact that he is *not* lovable. Secondly, it is miraculous because it produces a total transformation of the one who gives it and sometimes even of those who receive it. Obviously, if Christ loved the Inquisitor for "what he is," a cantankerous and tyrannical old man, utterly incapable of love even for Christ himself, he would love him not at all. This is the essential difference between Christ and the Inquisitor: the Inquisitor despises the most lovable of men; Christ loves the most despicable. When the token of this love is offered, it electrifies the old man. Unable to respond in kind, he none the less ceases to play God on this occasion and sends Christ out into "the dark alleys of the town."

Again in the chapter called "Elders," the narrator discusses miracle in a way that is very illuminating. He describes Alyosha's physical appearance and then goes on:

> I fancy that Alyosha was more of a realist than any one. Oh! no doubt, in the monastery he fully believed in miracles, but, to my thinking, miracles are never a stumbling-block to the realist. It is not miracles that dispose realists to belief. The genuine realist, if he is an unbeliever, will always find strength and ability to disbelieve in the miraculous, and if he is confronted with a miracle as an irrefutable fact he would rather disbelieve his own senses than admit the fact. Even if he admits it, he admits it as a fact of nature till then unrecognised by him. *Faith does not, in the realist, spring from the miracle but the miracle from faith.* (p. 25, italics mine)

Here we have another key to the difference between Christ and the Inquisitor. When the Inquisitor describes the first temptation, he has Satan say, "Turn [the stones] into bread, and mankind will run after Thee like a flock of sheep, grateful and obedient, though for ever trembling, lest Thou withdraw Thy hand and deny them Thy bread" (p. 300). In other words, *not being a realist*, the old man would "correct Christ's work" by using "miracles" to produce faith (shaky faith admittedly, but faith none the less); whereas Christ, the realist, knows that miracles spring from faith, and not vice versa.

The Inquisitor's reversal of faith and miracle accounts for the difference between him and Christ in the definition of *miracle*. An act which would cause the multitude to run after the Great

Man, "grateful and obedient, though for ever trembling" with fear, would be a magical act, a feat of prestidigitation. Such is not the case with "Christ-like love for men." Throughout *The Brothers Karamazov* there is evidence that this love has the miraculous efficacy which Zossima describes in "Peasant Women Who Have Faith":

> If you are penitent, you love. And if you love you are of God. All things are atoned for, all things are saved by love. If I, a sinner, even as you are, am tender with you and have pity on you, how much more will God. Love is such a priceless treasure that you can redeem the whole world by it, and expiate not only your own sins but the sins of others. (p. 58)

The process which Dostoevsky represents is circular: Christlike love for men is a miracle; behind the miracle is faith; behind faith is penitence; "And if you are penitent, you love"; and the circle begins anew. Thus Ivan is entirely correct when he says, "*To my thinking*, Christ-like love for men is a miracle impossible on earth"—it is indeed impossible for those, like Ivan and the Inquisitor, who have no faith. Ivan is therefore able to represent this love in his poem only by introducing Christ himself into the work, but the end of the chapter is even more ironic than Ivan intends:

> Alyosha looked at him in silence.
> "I thought that going away from here I have you at least," Ivan said suddenly, with unexpected feeling; "but now I see that there is no place for me even in your heart, my dear hermit. The formula, 'all is lawful,' I won't renounce—will you renounce me for that, yes?"
> Alyosha got up, went to him and softly kissed him on the lips.
> "That's plagiarism," cried Ivan, highly delighted. "You stole that from my poem. Thank you, though." (pp. 312–313)

Christlike behavior is plagiarism by definition—Ivan's or anyone else's.

But if the primary Christian miracle is that of love, how does Dostoevsky account for the apparently magical acts recorded in the gospels, such as Christ's turning the water into wine? He makes it perfectly clear that the motive behind such acts is not that of creating faith in the beholders. After Zossima's death, while Alyosha sits by the body praying drowsily, he hears Father Paissy reading about the marriage in Cana of Galilee:

> *"And when they wanted wine, the mother of Jesus saith unto him; 'They have no wine'"* . . . Alyosha heard.
>
> "Ah, yes, I was missing that, and I didn't want to miss it, I love that passage; it's Cana of Galilee, the first miracle. . . . Ah, that miracle! Ah, that sweet miracle! It was not men's grief, but their joy Christ visited, He worked His first miracle to help men's gladness . . . 'He who loves men loves their gladness, too.'" (p. 433)

Such miracles, then, were performed according to Dostoevsky not to create men's faith, nor to alleviate their grief (as the Inquisitor would have it), but to augment their already existing joy.

The meaning of *miracle* in *The Brothers Karamazov* is far richer than this brief exposition would indicate, but we must go on to the second of the three crucial terms, *mystery*. Again we discover a radical inconsistency in the Inquisitor's use of the word. He asserts categorically that Christ had rejected mystery along with miracle and authority (p. 303), but then he says:

> Canst Thou have simply come to the elect and for the elect? But if so, it is a mystery and we cannot understand it. And if it is a mystery, we too have a right to preach a mystery, and to teach them that it's not the free judgment of their hearts, not love that matters, but a mystery which they must follow blindly, even against their conscience. So we have done. (p. 305)

Christ erred, says the Inquisitor, by rejecting mystery; but still Christ presents a mystery, and if *he* did, so can we. (Strange logic indeed.) The passage just quoted makes perfectly clear the difference in the two definitions of *mystery*. For Christianity, a mystery is something contrary to *understanding*—"But if so, it is a mystery and *we cannot understand it.*" For the Inquisitor, a mystery is something contrary to *conscience*—"a mystery which they must follow blindly, *even against their conscience.*" Christ did indeed reject mystification, under the spell of which men would follow him blindly, "like a flock of sheep, grateful and obedient, though for ever trembling" (p. 300).

But he did *not* reject mystery, and the chief Christian mystery is that of immortality. The conceptions of miracle and mystery are of course very closely related; Dostoevsky had perfectly free choice as to the kind of miracle he might represent Christ performing at the beginning of the Inquisitor chapter, but he specifically related that miracle to immortality, raising a child from the dead. And in "Cana of Galilee," against the background of Christ's first miracle (turning the water into wine, John 2:1–11) Alyosha becomes aware that his "resurrected" elder is present with him though the elder's body lies, at the same time, exuding "the breath of corruption" in its coffin (pp. 434–435). "Cana of Galilee" dramatizes the achievement of Alyosha's salvation, which is represented as one kind of resurrection: "He had *fallen on the earth* a weak boy, but he *rose up* a resolute champion" (p. 437, italics mine). Alyosha becomes convinced of Zossima's (and by implication his own) immortality: "he's in the coffin . . . but he's here, too. He has stood up, he sees me" (pp. 434–435). And at the same time Alyosha becomes perfect in love: "He longed to forgive every one and for everything, and to beg forgiveness. Oh, not for himself, but for all men, for all and for everything" (pp. 436–437). The two conceptions of miracle and mystery ("Christ-like love for men" and immortality) are thus inseparable in Dostoevsky's view of Christianity.

The doctrine of immortality, which is indeed contrary to understanding but not to conscience, is specifically labeled a *mystery* in the New Testament. Read, for instance, the words of St. Paul:

> Lo! I tell you a mystery. We shall not all sleep, but we shall all be changed, in a moment, in the twinkling of an eye, at the last trumpet. For the trumpet will sound, and the dead will be raised imperishable, and we shall be changed. For this perishable nature must put on the imperishable, and this mortal nature must put on immortality. (I Cor. 15:51–53)

Almost any reader of *The Brothers Karamazov* is struck and perhaps puzzled by the epigraph of the book: "Truly, truly, I say to you, unless a grain of wheat falls into the earth and dies, it remains alone; but if it dies, it bears much fruit" (John 12:24, R. S. V.). The image of the grain of wheat which dies in order to bear fruit makes only one other appearance in the New Testament, and that is in the chapter of First Corinthians just quoted: "But some one will ask, 'How are the dead raised? With what kind of body do they come?' You foolish man! What you sow does not come to life unless it dies. And what you sow is not the body which is to be, but a bare kernel, perhaps of wheat or of some other grain" (I Cor. 15:35–37). The epigraph, which is taken from the words of Jesus and which symbolizes the mystery of immortality, may surely be taken as evidence that the Inquisitor is wrong in asserting that Christ rejected mystery.

The circle described in connection with miracle begins now to be more adequately defined. In the chapter "A Lady of Little Faith," a woman comes to Father Zossima asking how she can be certain about immortality: "What if I've been believing all my life," she asks, "and when I come to die there's nothing but the burdocks growing on my grave?" (p. 62). Zossima responds:

> "But there's no proving it, though you can be convinced of it."
> "How?"
> "By the experience of active love. Strive to love your neighbour actively and indefatigably. In as far as you advance in love you will grow surer of the reality of God and of the immortality of your soul." (p. 63)

Part of the miraculous efficacy of love is that it creates the conviction of immortality, the mystery which the Inquisitor, not Christ, rejects. Thus, because he loves them with all his heart, Alyosha can tell the boys confidently as they stand by the stone at Ilusha's funeral, "Certainly we shall rise again." And in the chapter called "Over the Brandy," the contradictory answers which Alyosha and Ivan give to their father's questions about the existence of God and immortality (pp. 159–160) mean quite simply that Alyosha loves his brothers and accepts responsibility for them, whereas Ivan does not.

The Inquisitor's third crucial term is *authority*. He correctly observes man's need for submission to something higher than

himself: "Too, too well they know the value of complete submission! And until men know that, they will be unhappy" (p.
307). It is of course true that if there is authority, there must be
submission, but again the Inquisitor reverses things. His logic
involves the fallacy of affirming the consequent. He apparently
reasons thus: "If there is authority, there is and will be submission; there is and will be complete submission; therefore, there
is and will be complete authority—mine!" He seems to define
authority as raw power, concentrated in the hands of one man or
a few men; and this, as we know, is not authority, but tyranny.

Again in the chapter called "Elders," Dostoevsky anticipates
what the Inquisitor says. The narrator tells the story of the monk
who was commanded by his elder to leave the monastery and go
to Siberia. The monk appeals to the Patriach at Constantinople
to release him from the necessity of obeying this command; but
the Patriarch refuses to do so, claiming that no power on earth
could release the man "except the elder who had himself laid
that duty upon him." The narrator continues:

> In this way the elders are endowed in certain cases with unbounded
> and inexplicable authority. That is why in many of our monasteries
> the institution was at first resisted almost to persecution. . . . In
> the end, however, the institution of elders has been retained and is
> becoming established in Russian monasteries. It is true, perhaps,
> that this instrument which had stood the test of a thousand years
> for the moral regeneration of a man from slavery to freedom and to
> moral perfectibility may be a two-edged weapon and it may lead
> some not to humility and complete self-control but to the most
> Satanic pride, that is, to bondage and not to freedom. (p. 28)

Dostoevsky's Christianity in no sense rejects authority; it rejects
only tyranny, the tyranny of men dominated by "the most Satanic
pride"—men like the Grand Inquisitor.

What is authority as understood by Dostoevsky? It is the
power which God has by virtue of the fact that He is God (which
is to say, the power of love). Alyosha learns "humility and complete self-control" by *voluntarily* submitting to the authority of
his elder, Father Zossima. Again in the "Elders" chapter, we read:

> An elder was one who took your soul, your will, into his soul and his will. When you choose an elder, you renounce your own will and yield it to him in complete submission, complete self-abnegation. This novitiate, this terrible school of abnegation, is undertaken voluntarily, in the hope of self-conquest, of self-mastery, in order, after a life of obedience, to attain perfect freedom, that is, from self; to escape the lot of those who have lived their whole life without finding their true selves in themselves. (p. 27)

The authority of elders is of course vicarious, they hold it legitimately in so far as they themselves are transformed by the power of love, and the institution of elders involves a discipline which prepares the young man and teaches him "the value of complete submission." (The Inquisitor is entirely right when he says that "until men know that, they will be unhappy," p. 307.) Christ sets the example for this kind of discipline in the very temptations which the Inquisitor tries to analyze. In response to every one of Satan's offers, he declares that he submits himself to the authority of God and to that authority alone. The Inquisitor, as we would expect, refuses to recognize this and therefore quotes only a part of one reply. He says, "Thou didst reply that man lives not by bread alone" (p. 300) and is careful to omit the rest of the sentence: "but by every word that proceeds from the mouth of God" (Matt. 4:4). When Satan urges Christ to cast himself down, Jesus replies, "Again it is written, 'You shall not tempt the Lord your God'" (Matt. 4:7); and when Satan offers him "all the kingdoms of the world," Christ says, "Begone, Satan! for it is written, 'You shall worship the Lord your God, and him only shall you serve'" (Matt. 4:10). (When Christ speaks of God in these passages, he is obviously *not* referring to himself.)

Submission to this authority is a definition of *faith;* and refusal to submit is *rebellion.* The conception of authority completes the definition of Dostoevsky's circle. One breaks into the circle only by becoming penitent, that is, by assuming responsibility for one's own sins. According to Zossima, "If you are penitent, you love" (p. 58). Ivan declares that "Christ-like love for men is a miracle" (p. 281), and the narrator tells us that "Faith does not, in the realist, spring from the miracle but the miracle from faith" (p. 25). Thus, behind love (miracle) is faith (submission to God's authority), and part of the efficacy of the miracle is that it creates our belief in immortality (mystery), because, as Zossima says, "In as far as you advance in love you will grow surer of the reality of God and of the immortality of your soul" (p. 63).

The Inquisitor, by refusing to put first things first, enters a different circle and ends by substituting himself for God, at least in relation to other men. Being unrepentant, he rebels against the authority of God and is therefore unable either to perform the miracle or to believe in the mystery. Since "man cannot bear to be without the miraculous" (p. 303), he undertakes to perform a spurious "miracle" so that "mankind will run after [*him*] like a flock of sheep, grateful and obedient, though for ever trembling" (p. 300). The only "mystery" about him is his carefully kept secret that he is in league with the devil: "Perhaps it is Thy will to hear it from my lips. Listen, then. We are not working with Thee, but with *him*—that is our mystery" (p. 305). Whatever "authority" he has is therefore presumably derived from Satan. It is interesting to note in this connection that in the book of Revelation, the "false prophet" and the "beast" receive their "authority" from the "dragon" (Rev. 13:2; 13:12–13; 19: 20); and this dragon (or one very much like it) is later identified as "the Devil and Satan" (Rev. 20:2).

The fundamental antagonism in *The Brothers Karamazov* is between belief and love on the one hand, and unbelief and hatred on the other. In the first half of the novel, these two forces are represented most clearly by the Inquisitor and by Father Zossima, who is Christ's representative in the Karamazov world. (In the second half these functions are taken over entirely by Ivan and Alyosha, Dmitri being torn between the two.) The difference between the Jesuit and the elder is quite simply the difference between the cynic and the realist—the realist includes himself in his generalizations about mankind, whereas the cynic does not. The Inquisitor says in effect: All men, except me of course, are weak and vile. Zossima says: All men are sinners, and I am the worst. The Inquisitor's appeal is not simply an alternative to Christianity, one based on different assumptions about man and his needs. It is a total perversion of the Christian gospel itself, a distortion in which all of the crucial terms and processes are reversed. The Inquisitor puts miracle before faith; he makes all men responsible to him; and he would save mankind by having the "church" take over the state, rather than by having the state become Christian, as recommended by Zossima and Paissy (pp. 74–75). The net result is that for the Inquisitor there is no miracle, no mystery, and no authority—only "magic," mystification, and tyranny.

The meaning of the novel's explicit theme, "We are all responsible for all," now begins to emerge. Except for Rakitin (p. 93), everyone in the book accepts the truth of Ivan's conditional statement, "There is no virtue if there is no immortality" (first stated by Ivan himself on page 79). Zossima immediately responds, "You are blessed in believing that, or else most unhappy." Here is the crux of the matter as far as Dostoevsky is concerned. Any student of elementary logic knows that there are two ways to obtain a valid conclusion from a conditional statement; we may either affirm the antecedent, or we may deny the consequent. In its simplest form Ivan's statement is this: If there is no immortality, then there is no virtue (and all things are lawful, even cannibalism). Ivan affirms the antecedent ("There is no immortality"), and concludes validly that there is therefore no virtue, that all things are lawful.

Zossima endorses the conditional statement as a whole in another context: "It is different with the upper classes. They, following science, want to base justice on reason alone, but not with Christ, as before, and they have already proclaimed that there is no crime, that there is no sin. And that's consistent, for if you have no God what is the meaning of crime?" (p. 378). Zossima and Alyosha, however, deny Ivan's consequent by saying in effect, "But there *is* virtue, and all things are *not* lawful, because we are all responsible for all." They conclude, equally validly, that there *is* immortality. (The novel ends on this note when Alyosha tells the boys, "Certainly we shall all rise again.") In these conclusions, which are equally valid from the standpoint of logic, Zossima and Alyosha are "blessed," while Ivan and the Inquisitor are "most unhappy."

Besides the book of Revelation and the story of Christ's temptations (Matt. 4, Luke 4), there are two primary scriptural sources for *The Brothers Karamazov*. One is the verse from John's gospel which stands as the epigraph and appears twice during the novel itself (pp. 339, 370), and the other is Genesis 4, the story of Cain and Abel. In the chapter called "The Brothers Make Friends," Alyosha is talking earnestly to Ivan about their family:

> "What of Dmitri and father? how will it end?" asked Alyosha anxiously.
>
> "You are always harping upon it! What have I to do with it? Am I my brother Dmitri's keeper?" Ivan snapped irritably, but then he suddenly smiled bitterly. "Cain's answer about his murdered brother, wasn't it? Perhaps that's what you're thinking at this moment? Well, damn it all, I can't stay here to be their keeper, can I? I've finished what I had to do, and I am going." (p. 275)

In the structure of the novel, Smerdyakov characteristically echoes Ivan and becomes the instrument for murdering their father; but in this case Ivan is echoing Smerdyakov, who has said only a few pages earlier: "How am I to know about Dmitri Fyodorovitch? It's not as if I were his keeper" (p. 269). And Rakitin gives this attitude its most generalized form when he blurts out at Dmitri's trial, "I cannot answer for all my acquaintants. . . . I am a young man . . . and who can be responsible for every one he meets?" (p. 813).

In the Genesis story, after Cain has asked his famous question in an effort to conceal his guilt for the murder of his brother, we read these words:

> "When you till the ground, it shall no longer yield to you its strength; you shall be a fugitive and a wanderer on the earth." Cain said to the LORD, "My punishment is greater than I can bear. Behold, thou hast driven me this day away from the ground; and from thy face I shall be hidden; and I shall be a fugitive and a wanderer on the earth, and whoever finds me will slay me." Then the LORD

said to him, "Not so! If any one slays Cain, vengeance shall be taken on him sevenfold." And the LORD put a mark on Cain, lest any who came upon him should kill him. (Gen. 4:12–15)

We gain considerable insight into Dostoevsky's view of those who bear the mark of Cain by juxtaposing this passage with the novel's epigraph: "Truly, truly, I say to you, unless a grain of wheat falls into the earth and dies, it remains alone; but if it dies, it bears much fruit." When Cain sows seed in the earth, he will find that it no longer "bears much fruit"; he is henceforth a fugitive and a wanderer—that is, he now "remains alone"; a mark is set upon him so that no one will kill him—he cannot even "fall into the earth and die." This, Dostoevsky indicates, is what happens when we reject our brothers, when we deny that "we are all responsible for all." And the mark of Cain is obtrusively present in *The Brothers Karamazov*—it takes the form of "lacerations."

For Dostoevsky, the words "We are all responsible for all" are not an exhortation or a command, but a simple fact of life. This is why the sentence does not take some such form as "We must all be responsible for all," or even "Let us all be responsible for all." It is a purely indicative statement. To accept it as true, one must welcome suffering; to take one's stand with Cain, as Ivan does, is to precipitate endless torment and self-laceration. Unless one falls to the level of Rakitin and becomes a man without a conscience, there is no third way. ("Life's easy for Rakitin," p. 721.) Why should Ivan be tormented by the ghastly sufferings of innocent children ("Rebellion") if he is not in some sense responsible for those children? Instead of admitting that we are all responsible for all, he says in effect, "God is responsible for all. . . . And I hate Him for all." The Inquisitor, with his penchant for reversing things, says in effect, "All are responsible to me; and I am responsible to no one, for I will be God." Perhaps the most frightful example in the novel of negation and self-laceration is Lise, who imagines herself as helping to crucify a four-year-old child and then sitting, eating pineapple compote, while she listens to the child moaning in agony ("A Little Demon"). She ends by deliberately squashing her finger in the crack of a door, and whispering to herself, "I am a wretch, wretch, wretch, wretch!" (p. 712).

The fact that we are all responsible for all is the reason, Dostoevsky implies, why Christlike love for men is not only a miracle, but an absolute necessity; as the Inquisitor says, "Man cannot bear to be without the miraculous" (p. 303). If we refuse to love those things which are not lovable, we lose the capacity to love those which are. Thus Lise becomes incapable of loving Alyosha. By the same token, if we reject responsibility for those things which are not specifically our fault, we cannot properly assume responsibility for those which are. This happens because when we disclaim, in retrospect, all responsibility for evils and suffering which we did not actually cause, we create, in prospect, evils and suffering for which we *are* to blame. Ivan, cursing God for the sufferings of innocent children, unconsciously poisons the mind of his bastard half-brother, who then actually murders their father (pp. 758, 768). It is also true that unless *someone* accepts responsibility for evils which he himself did not cause, these evils go forever unexpiated. As Dmitri says, "It's for the babe I'm going. Because we are all responsible for all. For all the 'babes,' for there are big children as well as little children. All are 'babes.' I go for all, because some one must go for all" (p. 720).

The two points of view between which tension exists in *The Brothers Karamazov* both follow validly from Ivan's conditional statement. They are most clearly represented in the Inquisitor chapter, and the choice between them is the burden of man's freedom. If he is to be fully human, not just another Rakitin, a man *must* choose between heaven and hell, between being "blessed" and being "most unhappy," between voluntary suffering and excruciating self-laceration. Most critics have observed (correctly) that Dostoevsky loves the Inquisitor, and they have concluded (incorrectly) that he does so because the Inquisitor is so clever. Of course he loves the Inquisitor! If he did not, he would be implicitly denying the thesis of the entire novel which, according to Dostoevsky himself, "serves as an answer" to the powerful negation of God "embodied in the Inquisitor and in the preceding chapter." [6] *The Brothers Karamazov* is after all a thesis novel, no matter how thoroughly dramatized that thesis may be. Differences of interpretation arise not from any dispute as to whether the novel is based on a thesis, but from disagreement as to precisely what that thesis is.

After careful analysis of both the Inquisitor's argument and the novel as a whole, the assertion that "logic and the facts of history are on the Inquisitor's side" seems less accurate than it did at first. From the standpoint of logic, the Inquisitor's most prominent characteristic is a tendency to equivocate and to pay no attention to the distribution of terms. The meaning of *mystery* shifts, in his argument, from something against understanding to something against conscience; and though all mysteries are things contrary to understanding, it is *not* true that all things contrary to understanding (conscience?) are mysteries. From the standpoint of history, men like Mussolini, Stalin, and Hitler have always been able to gain the support of an entire nation; but mankind has deserved the Inquisitor's adjectives "weak and vile" exactly in proportion as it has yielded to the blandishments of demagogues like the Inquisitor himself. These seem poor reasons indeed for our preferring, here and now, the Grand Inquisitor to Dostoevsky's Christ.

X

The Meaning of Christian Tragedy

For while we live we are always
being given up to death for Jesus' sake,
so that the life of Jesus may be manifested
in our mortal flesh.
II CORINTHIANS 4:11

Thomas, called the Twin, said to his fellow disciples,
"Let us also go, that we may die with him."
JOHN 11:16

THE preceding chapters have distinguished two fundamentally different kinds of Christian tragedy: Shakespeare's, which is Pauline and intellectual; and Dostoevsky's, which is Johannine and prophetic. The first adjective in each pair comes from the biblical sources upon which the artist drew most heavily, and the second adjective describes both the religious texts in question and the works that are based upon them. Neither type can be regarded as more "authentic" than the other, unless the critic mistakes his own preferences for historical fact. We cannot claim that St. Paul is "more Christian" than St. John without setting up criteria that many Christians simply would not accept; and we can hardly argue that *Hamlet* is "more tragic" than *The Brothers Karamazov* without imposing our individual tastes upon readers in general. We are now in a position, however, to generalize about our six examples in a way which will clarify the term *Christian tragedy* as opposed to *Greek tragedy;* and perhaps we should begin by indicating what Christian tragedy does *not* mean, since this procedure will help us to avoid confusion later in the discussion.

First of all, the term *Christian tragedy* does not mean that the artist substitutes religious values for the supposedly moral values of Greek tragedy. Tragedy has *always* dealt with unmerited but necessary suffering, and this is a matter which the moralist is simply not equipped to deal with. Contrary to popular opinion, it is the moralist who imposes idealistic demands upon the literary artist, not the religious person. The moralist requires that a simple kind of "justice" should prevail; the religious person knows perfectly well that such "justice" is extremely rare in human experience. From both a religious and a tragic point of view, the death of Cordelia, for instance, is entirely fitting and extremely moving. From a moral point of view, her death is outrageous—Aristotle would no doubt have regarded it as a "revolting spectacle." The moralist posits a world in which people "get what they deserve"; the religious person bears constantly in mind that "the race is not to the swift, nor the battle to the strong."

What does the term *religious* mean as it is used in the preceding paragraph? William James provides what is perhaps the best answer, in an essay called "The Will to Believe." According to James, religion makes two distinct affirmations: first, "that the best things are the more eternal things, the overlapping things, the things in the universe that throw the last stone, so to speak, and say the final word"; and secondly, "that we are better off even now if we believe her first affirmation to be true." [1] As applied to *King Lear*, these statements mean that even though Cordelia dies first, in reality she speaks "the final word." Most people who find that play genuinely moving will admit that this assertion is somehow true, but the moralist will continue to protest that she does *not* have the final word. Such a protest is not, however, a valid objection to *King Lear* as a literary work; it is merely a rebellion against life itself, and against death.

At the heart of the moralistic view of tragedy is the Aristotelian conception of *hamartia*. As we saw in the case of *Hamlet*, *hamartia* may indeed be central in tragedy; but when it is, it does not designate some moral defect peculiar to the hero as an individual. On the contrary, it points to an aspect of human existence that individuals cannot evade by their own efforts, however strenuous.

It is simply a weakness that all "flesh is heir to," and therefore the same kind of dilemma which Hamlet faces plagues the other characters too. No one but the most unsympathetic observer would claim that the tragic hero "gets what he deserves"; and no one but an inveterate moralist would undertake to show that the hero "deserves what he gets." And yet this is precisely what Aristotle's doctrine of *hamartia* purports to show.

Secondly, the writing of Christian tragedy does *not* require the dramatist or novelist to surrender his objectivity. Works which are not objectively written cannot gain acceptance as literature of *any* kind, much less as Christian literature. The popular misunderstanding that is involved here stems from a confusion as to the relation of form and content, means and ends. Literature may be defined, at least for present purposes, as the objective communication (in words) of subjective truth. The form and the means are objective and universal; the content and ends are necessarily subjective and personal. A critic's demand that a literary work should be completely objective is actually nothing more than a requirement that the work should have no content whatever. By a strange paradox, the purist who cherishes the literary work solely as an end in itself, not to be contaminated by narrow-minded propaganda, Christian or any other kind, in reality contends that literature is *not* an end in itself at all, but only pure means. The champion of art for art's sake who condemns all identifiable content as mere propaganda is blood brother to the Puritan who condemns all art as mere froth. In *Hamlet*, Queen Gertrude's request for "more matter, with less art" is simply a courteous way of telling Polonius that his "foolish figures," if completely unchecked, are a complete waste of time; and few people in the audience find her request unreasonable.

The conception of objectivity is best illustrated in the natural sciences; and no one would be so foolish as to claim that the scientist who conducts his experiments objectively and then reaches a conclusion sacrifices or abandons that objectivity by clinging to his conclusion. Unless he does so, there is hardly any point in performing the experiment. In popular language, *ob-*

jectivity has come to be almost synonymous with *indifference*. A scientist behaves, in a sense, as if he were "indifferent" to how an experiment *will* turn out; but he is most emphatically *not* indifferent to how it *did* turn out. A work of literature is like the report of an experiment; we judge the author's objectivity not by his conclusions, but by the honesty and the thoroughness of his method in reaching those conclusions. If an author presses Christianity upon us as a kind of *deus ex machina* which descends out of the blue and provides an unearned solution to an obviously hopeless and merely pathetic situation, then we must regard him as we would a schoolboy who cheats on his arithmetic test—though his answers may be right, we must give him a failing grade.

Christian tragedy does have subjective content, but this content need not be the whole Christian message. That it may come close to that we see in *The Brothers Karamazov*; but on the other hand, this content may be only one part of St. Paul's analysis of the human dilemma, as we see in *Hamlet*. No one preaches the gospel in *Hamlet* or *King Lear*. If, however, one character *does* preach it, as Myshkin and Zossima do in *The Idiot* and *The Brothers Karamazov,* we may be sure that the opposing point of view is eloquently preached in the same work, by Ippolit and Ivan. It is precisely here that Dostoevsky's objectivity may be seen most clearly—he in no way diminishes the power and appeal of nonreligious views. Indeed, he states the case for atheism with much greater force than most atheists could ever do. The fact that intelligent critics, ignoring the whole context of the Inquisitor's tirade, have sided with the old churchman and have claimed, moreover, that Dostoevsky did so too, testifies eloquently to the objectivity of *The Brothers Karamazov*. In similar fashion, the critic's claim that Shakespeare had no more perspective on Hamlet's inability to "hit the mark" than the critic himself does (namely, almost none at all) indicates the extent of that work's objectivity.

Thirdly, Christian tragedy does *not* imply that certain people automatically have at their disposal what Stanley Edgar Hyman calls "otherworldly allies" [2] that will pull them through in spite of everything. Such a view is no more than a caricature of the Christian's position in relation to the world. It suggests that the Christian has (or believes he has) some unfair advantage over mere atheists, that he has special privileges as "a friend of the general" or "a cousin of the president." Indeed, the usual view is far less charitable than these analogies would indicate—to the real skeptic, the Christian seems to be not someone who might have a legitimate relation to the one in power (if such a "person in power" exists). He is more like a hanger-on, a parasite who curries favor in order to secure special privileges; and most people rightly regard such a person as self-deceived and treacherous.

But the Christian—unless, like many other people, he really *is* self-deceived—has no such special claim on anyone or anything. He has only a faith—a faith which is hard to achieve and which affirms little more than this: that Christ has shown by his example that if one loves enough, then the belief that love is stronger than death becomes a part of reality and not just a fine sentiment. The skeptic may assert that Lear is self-deceived when he says of Cordelia that "she lives," and that Alyosha Karamazov is leading the boys astray when he tells them, "Certainly we shall all rise again." The whole point of these works, however, is that such statements of faith are the product of suffering, that they are made not *in spite* of experience, but *because* of it and *out* of it. The affirmations of Christianity must be earned, not merely appropriated; and the function of Christian tragedy is to show how difficult it is to earn them.

Let us proceed now to more positive statements about the nature of Christian tragedy. It is, first of all, based solidly upon the New Testament, which served these writers not merely as the source of a few images or some philosophical commonplaces set forth in biblical style, but as the matrix of the thought which finds expression in *Hamlet, King Lear,* and *Macbeth, Crime and Punishment, The Idiot,* and *The Brothers Karamazov.* The attitude toward human action in *Hamlet*—the futility of works without faith—reflects in detail the analysis which St. Paul sets forth in the book of Romans; in *King Lear* the treatment of love, as well as that of the relation between wisdom and foolishness, between sight and blindness, mirrors conceptions embodied in the Corinthian letters; and the thematic material in *Macbeth* is straight out of Luke's gospel. The vision graven on Myshkin's heart in *The Idiot* comes directly from the book of Revelation; and much that is central in *Crime and Punishment* and *The Brothers Karamazov* is taken from two chapters in the gospel of John. These are not casual borrowings, but the very substance of the works in question. On the basis of our six examples we may even say that Christian tragedy must be securely anchored in the New Testament in order to be Christian tragedy at all. Simply because we encounter in a tragic work an image or a saying which may also be part of the Christian heritage, we should not conclude that the work is therefore a Christian tragedy. Though it may have been written during the Christian era, and though it may do lip service to Christ, it is not for these reasons alone a Christian tragedy.

We learn too from our examples that Shakespeare and Dostoevsky were consistent, as tragic writers, in their preference for certain kinds of biblical material. In general, Shakespeare made elaborate use of the intellectual conceptions that St. Paul articulated most fully, while Dostoevsky found St. John's prophetic mode more congenial to his purposes. This does not mean that they ignored other biblical writings; but when they took their material from other parts of the bible, they treated it in a way which was entirely consistent with their preferred point of view. One would be hard pressed to find another passage in the synoptic gospels which would be more perfectly suited to the Pauline conception of the inwardly divided self than the one containing Christ's statements about "Satan divided against himself," which became the basis for *Macbeth*. And this passage in Luke, to which Shakespeare was apparently attracted by its intellectual similarity to Paul, is even richer in imagery and symbolism than Paul is except upon rare occasions.

Dostoevsky, like Shakespeare, usually stayed with the biblical writer who best reflected his own point of view. But when Dostoevsky turned to another part of the bible, it was, more often than not, to find negative examples of the Johannine attitude. Thus Cain, who murdered his own brother, comes to stand for those who cannot comprehend that "we are all responsible for all." And St. Paul, whose intellectualism leads him to declare that "all things are lawful for me," furnishes some of the rationale for characters like Raskolnikov, Ippolit Terentyev, and Ivan Karamazov, who end in despair. Dostoevsky's attitude differed from Shakespeare's at this point—though the dramatist obviously preferred the Pauline conceptions, he seems not to have regarded alternative Christian views as possible sources of error. There is, to be sure, nothing positively Johannine about his characters who, like Laertes, go seriously astray or who, like Edmund, behave consistently as villains. Such characters place their confidence in strictly nonbiblical postures: Laertes, as we can see by his parting advice to Ophelia, has absorbed at least some of his father's worldly moralism; and Edmund is a devout worshipper of Nature, as befits Gloucester's natural son.

A further difference between Shakespeare and Dostoevsky results from the very character of the Pauline material as opposed to that of the Johannine writings. Because Paul's views are essentially historical, it is possible to borrow his conceptions, to take them over almost completely, without ever mentioning what he gives as the key to the problems which are being analyzed. For instance, another writer can appropriate, as Shakespeare did in *Hamlet*, the view of the human condition as one in which "I can will what is right, but I cannot do it," and then break off shortly before the first verse of the next chapter: "There is therefore now no condemnation for those who are in Christ Jesus" (Rom. 8:1). Paul clearly presents the problem as being insoluble apart from belief in Christ; and when Shakespeare borrows the analysis and neglects to present us explicitly with Paul's key, it is not surprising that critics should find it baffling, especially when they insist upon sloughing off such lines as "There is special providence in the fall of a sparrow" as mere folk wisdom, presumably on a par with most of Polonius's utterances. Shakespeare was no preacher, and he was a shrewd enough observer of human nature to know that if he carefully removed the label, most people would never recognize what he was offering for their consideration. And with the Pauline material, this procedure presented no great technical difficulty.

Dostoevsky, on the other hand, even if he had wanted to, could not have concealed the profoundly biblical character of his vision. So Christ-centered and so unconcerned with analyzing man's dilemma before the appearance of Christ is John's writing that no one else could borrow anything significant from it without also taking what holds it all together, the person of Jesus Christ as the living Lord. There is no Lazarus story without the person who calls the dead man forth from the grave; and without the central image of Christ as the slain lamb, the book of Revelation would be an unintelligible conglomeration of fragments and symbols. But it does not follow that Dostoevsky is a "preacher," while Shakespeare is not. That term, which in literary criticism inevitably has a pejorative connotation, is no more appropriate to Dostoevsky than it is to Shakespeare. We recall that E. M. Forster makes the proper distinction in *Aspects of the Novel* when he calls George Eliot a "preacher," and reserves the term *prophet* for Dostoevsky.[3] This seems eminently appropriate since the Johannine tradition, to which Dostoevsky belongs, is a prophetic one. For the reasons just cited, we may say that Shakespeare and Dostoevsky are both Christian writers, though in quite different ways, at least as far as their surface meaning is concerned. From a literary viewpoint, they both derive much of their material from the New Testament; and this practice connects them so significantly that their very differences become points of contact rather than points of separation.

Secondly, in Christian tragedy all of the characters are implicitly measured by the standards of Christian thought—even the unbeliever is represented by means of Christian categories. Action in *Hamlet* is not any easier for Christians than for non-Christians. All of the characters, including the protagonist, strive to fulfill what they take to be "the law"; but only Hamlet himself ever comes close to achieving what he wants, and ironically even he can do that only after he stops thinking in terms of "the law," the revenge-code in which he puts his faith during most of the play. In *King Lear,* love is not one thing for Lear and another for Cordelia, at least not from the perspective of the whole play. Lear suffers the way he does because he "has not love," because his conception of love falls far below the Christian conception embodied in Cordelia, and consequently, he is "nothing." (We are reminded of Father Zossima's definition of hell—"the suffering of being unable to love," *The Brothers Karamazov,* p. 387.) Cordelia, on the other hand, suffers precisely because she *does* love; for love "endures all things." Symbolically, Lear suffers "in hell," while Cordelia resides "in heaven," as Lear himself says to Cordelia, "Thou art a soul in bliss; but I am bound/Upon a wheel of fire, that mine own tears/Do scald like molten lead" (IV, vii, 46–48). In *The Idiot* and *The Brothers Karamazov,* Ippolit and Ivan are not a different breed of men from Myshkin and Alyosha. They simply "return the ticket," reject their own humanity and their own responsibility to and for others.

Ivan Karamazov perhaps best represents the non-Christian measured in Christian terms. He stakes everything on the formula "All is lawful"; but because he finds no *natural* law (and indeed there is none) that men should love one another, he assumes that there is no reason of any kind why they should. Like the Grand Inquisitor, he uses only the first part of a biblical statement and ignores the rest. According to St. Paul, "All things are lawful for me, but not all things are helpful. All things are lawful for me, but I will not be enslaved by anything" (I Cor. 6:12). And again, "All things are lawful, but not all things are helpful. All things are lawful, but not all things build up" (I Cor. 10:23). For Paul "Christ is the end of the law" (Rom. 10:4), and he of course was referring to the Jewish Law, the Mosaic code. Ivan perceives that there is no *natural* law which will serve as a reliable guide for man, and he therefore concludes that "all is lawful"—with no significant qualification whatever. He pays the price, in lacerations, for his error.

Because the unbeliever is measured by Christian standards and is therefore seen as one who is perhaps trying very hard to live as he believes he should, Christian tragedy does not tend to fall into the error of portraying humanity in terms of good and evil characters, as moralistic literature sometimes does. Even so, the moralistic critic may try to impose this error upon the work, as Doctor Johnson seems to have done when he said that he could not understand "why Shakespeare gives to Oswald, who is a mere factor of wickedness, so much fidelity." *King Lear* is the one work of the six that we have chosen in which the critic is most likely to make this error, but the characters in *Lear* who strike the reader as evil simply rely upon false guides. Edmund, like Gloucester and Lear himself, takes Nature as his goddess, and the point of the play resides partly in the fact that nature is hardly a reliable guide. Goneril and Regan turn out to be motivated by sexual love (for Edmund, who plays them off against each other), rather than by Christian love as represented in Cordelia. Hence, there is some justification within the play for Lear's charge that women are lecherous: "But to the girdle do the gods inherit,/Beneath is all the fiend's" (IV, vi, 125–126); and there is all the more weight to Cordelia's question, "Why have my sisters husbands if they say/They love you all?" (I, i, 99–100). Even Oswald, as we have seen, is partly redeemed by his devotion to Goneril, and not one of these characters can be dismissed as "a mere factor of wickedness"—at least not without betraying the complexity of the play.

The Brothers Karamazov reflects the same analysis of human behavior as *King Lear* does. The division of labor among the characters is a little different, but the same elements are present. In both works, some characters theorize about the basis for action and others implement these theories in their behavior. In *King Lear* the protagonist proclaims his reliance upon Nature, but Edmund is the one who behaves the way we would expect a believer in Nature to do. In *The Brothers Karamazov* Ivan articulates the theory that "all is lawful," but Smerdyakov is the one who acts on that conviction. In *King Lear* the King of France defines *love,* but Cordelia shows us love in action; in *The Brothers Karamazov* Zossima is the teacher who explains what love is, but Alyosha is the major character who becomes the embodiment of Christian love. Seen from this point of view, Ivan corresponds to Lear, Smerdyakov to Edmund, and Alyosha to Cordelia. The most important difference between the two works comes from the fact that in the one case Cordelia is static and Lear is dynamic or changing, and in the other Alyosha is dynamic while Ivan is static. Cordelia does not change significantly from the first scene to the last—she is at all times "perfect in love" from the Christian standpoint. Lear, on the other hand, moves during the course of the play away from the kind of thinking that causes him to err at the beginning toward at least a partial recognition of Cordelia's love. Dostoevsky manages things differently, however, by making Ivan the static character. He is, from his first appearance to his last, purely the tormented intellectual; his torment increases, but his position remains basically unchanged. It is Alyosha who changes in this story; faltering and uncertain at first, he does not become "perfect in love" until after the death of Zossima.

Thirdly, Christian tragedy replaces the "law of retaliation" with the law of love. This characteristic has its basis, of course, in Christ's statements in the Sermon on the Mount:

> "You have heard that it was said, 'You shall love your neighbor and hate your enemy.' But I say to you, Love your enemies and pray for those who persecute you, so that you may be sons of your Father who is in heaven; for he makes his sun to rise on the evil and on the good, and sends rain on the just and on the unjust. For if you love those who love you, what reward have you? Do not even the tax collectors do the same? And if you salute only your brethren, what more are you doing than others? Do not even the Gentiles do the same? You, therefore, must be perfect, as your heavenly Father is perfect." (Matt. 5:43–48)

This attitude is echoed repeatedly in Christian tragedy. When Polonius tells Hamlet that he will treat the players "according to their desert," Hamlet replies, "Use every man after his desert, and who shall scape whipping? Use them after your own honor and dignity. The less they deserve, the more merit is in your bounty" (II, ii, 515–519). And Zossima tells his listeners that "love is a teacher; but one must know how to acquire it, for it is hard to acquire, it is dearly bought, it is won slowly by long labour. For we must love not only occasionally, for a moment, but for ever. Every one can love occasionally, even the wicked can" (*The Brothers Karamazov*, p. 383).

Failure to understand this feature of Christian tragedy leads to gross misunderstanding of the work in question. One commentary on *The Idiot* insists upon "the stupidity and shortcomings of Myshkin" and calls the book "the story of the tragedy they cause." In the same paragraph this critic tells us, as a fact of life, that "the *appropriate* reaction to something hateful is hatred." [4] We could allow this statement to pass if the word in italics were *instinctive* or *natural*. But the whole point of Christian tragedy resides in the recognition that what is instinctive or natural is *not appropriate* for human beings unless they want always to live in a jungle where everything is determined by instinct and nature. Total determinism excludes the possibility of freedom, and in the Christian view the only way to break the deterministic chain is by returning love for hatred, good for evil. No one, least of all Shakespeare and Dostoevsky, claims that this is easy or that it will remedy everything immediately. On the contrary, both writers are concerned to show how horribly difficult it is to reach this perception. Christian tragedy makes its ultimate disclosure when the viewer or reader is able to comprehend that to choose the alternative of returning good for evil is merely to choose, for oneself, decency over spite, humanity over brutality, and Christ over chaos; it is, in short, to choose tragedy over meaninglessness. The moralist urges us, as Polonius does, to treat people "according to their desert"; the religious person replies, as Hamlet does, by pointing out that if we do that, *none* "shall scape whipping." Christian tragedy portrays the effort not to suppress nature, but to transform it; for nature, considered all by itself, is essentially meaningless. It does not *mean* anything; it just *is*.

Fourthly, the *family* is no less real in Christian tragedy than it had been in classical drama, but it becomes symbolic in a way that it ordinarily does not in Greek tragedy. This feature probably derives from the emphasis which the New Testament places upon the fatherhood of God, the sonship of Christ, and the brotherhood of man in Christ. Indeed, Jesus himself put the relationship of men to each other in Christ before family ties. When he speaks of the persecutions which the disciples must face, he says: "Brother will deliver up brother to death, and the father his child, and the children will rise against parents and have them put to death; and you will be hated by all for my name's sake. But he who endures to the end will be saved" (Matt. 10:21-22; cf. 12:46-50). In terms of this statement and the one quoted earlier from the Sermon on the Mount, one's enemies come to be regarded as his brothers; and one's responsibility to and for his enemies is no less than his responsibility to and for members of his own family, as in the case of the Good Samaritan. In Greek tragedy, on the other hand, no such obligation exists. According to Aristotle,

> Now if the action is one of an enemy against an enemy, there is nothing, either in the act or in its intention, to arouse pity, unless it be the mere suffering. The same would be true in the case of those who were neither friends nor foes. But whenever the tragic action is against a member of the family, such as when a brother either kills or intends to kill a brother, a son a father, a mother a son or a son a mother, or does some other deed of this kind, these are the materials which the tragic poet must be on the look-out for. (*Poetics*, section 14, trans. Preston H. Epps)

The accuracy of this statement is verified by the fact that when Oedipus kills a wayfaring stranger, no one is the least concerned —until it is discovered that the stranger was his father.

In Christian tragedy, the "tragic action" continues to be within the family (Claudius and the elder Hamlet, Lear and his daughters, the Karamazovs, and so forth); but this action takes on a symbolic character, and bad relations within the family come to represent bad human relations in general. For this reason, doubt is often cast on the family connection of the one who perpetrates the criminal act; and this doubt is created by means of a taboo or stigma, such as incest (Claudius-Gertrude) or illegitimacy (Edmund, Smerdyakov). Unbridled lust is associated with both: Hamlet dwells on this facet of his mother's relation to Claudius; the first lines in *Lear* place the brand of illegitimacy upon Edmund; and old Karamazov begets Smerdyakov upon Lizaveta in response to "the whimsical inquiry whether any one could possibly look upon such an animal as a woman" (*The Brothers Karamazov*, p. 116). Thus, the family tie is violated or dissolved, and it comes as no surprise when the branded person treats others as if there were no real bond between himself and them. Edmund betrays his father and brother because they in a sense have betrayed him; and since he lives by the rule of nature, turnabout is fair play. Likewise, Dmitri's defense at his trial rests heavily upon the lawyer's contention that old Karamazov was not a "real father."

The point is, then, that in Christian tragedy the conception of what constitutes a real father is radically different from what it had been in Greek tragedy. In at least one sense, the parricide in Dostoevsky's novel is a reversal of the one in *Oedipus the King*. The two murders would have been "excusable" for exactly opposite reasons: Oedipus's deed would have been no crime at all if his victim had *not* been the man who had begotten him and then exposed him to die upon a mountain, whereas Dmitri's defense rests on the fact that old Karamazov had merely begotten him and then in effect left him to die. In other words, the meaning of the term *real father* changes from male parent or begetter in Greek tragedy, to something quite different in Christian tragedy, where it means one who fosters, nourishes, and provides for (his) children. For this reason, one may say with complete accuracy that Laius is Oedipus's real father (Greek view), while old Fyodor is *not* the real father of Dmitri, Ivan, Alyosha, and Smerdyakov (Christian view).

In *The Brothers Karamazov* we can hardly overlook the fact that Ivan's atheism is identified specifically as a rebellion against the authority of God and that the murder of old Karamazov is the direct result of this rebellion. Completely dominated by Ivan's persuasive thinking, Smerdyakov merely puts Ivan's theory into action. As the epileptic bastard tells his intellectual half-brother, "*You* murdered him; you are the real murderer, I was only your instrument, your faithful servant, and it was following your words I did it" (*The Brothers Karamazov*, p. 758). There is no evidence in the book to indicate that the reader should hesitate to take Smerdyakov's statement seriously. Ivan bears the chief responsibility for the old man's death, and the motive is not sexual rivalry, as Freud claimed,[5] but the effort to rebel significantly against the authority of God. The father is, of course, the first symbol of authority which the child encounters; and therefore when one rebels against authority, the father is the first target. But Ivan is far less of a sensualist than either Dmitri or old Fyodor.

The family relationships in *The Brothers Karamazov,* like those in *King Lear,* are no less symbolic than realistic. Ivan's question, "Am I my brother Dmitri's keeper?" with its implied negative answer makes clear Ivan's conception of his relation both to his blood brother and to the children whose sufferings he cries out against ("Rebellion"). His rebellion against the fatherhood of God leads directly to his rejection of all responsibility to and for his brothers, whether they are related to him by blood or not. Similarly, Goneril and Regan's treatment of Gloucester is exactly in keeping with their treatment of their own father. Lear himself equates service with love, forgetting that though all love leads to service, not all service is the product of love—it is sometimes just the policy of those who are currying favor.

Fifthly, Christian tragedy represents human life in terms of reciprocal concepts, but these concepts are *religious,* as with heaven and hell, *not moral,* as with good and evil. The confusion has sprung from the fact that most people, with the all too human tendency to moralize, have identified the Christian conception of heaven with the idea that it is the *place* where the *good* people go, and hell with the grizzly images of Dante's *inferno,* the *place* where the *bad* people go. In Shakespeare and Dostoevsky the conceptions of heaven and hell are perfectly clear: Cordelia is "a soul in bliss" and Lear is "bound/Upon a wheel of fire"; Zossima, who defines *hell* as "the suffering of being unable to love," is denounced after his death by a few envious "fellow-Christians" who gleefully point out that "He followed the fashionable belief, he did not recognise material fire in hell" (*The Brothers Karamazov,* p. 400). The imagery that we associate with the conception of hell comes from Milton, Dante, and ultimately from the book of Revelation; but the conception itself identifies hell as the spiritual condition of those who, in the words of St. Paul, "have not love," or who, in Zossima's formula, are "unable to love." The man whose being is filled with hatred is suffering in hell, and from the Christian point of view it is a disastrous mistake to suffer in hell simply because hatred is the instinctive or the natural response to something hateful.

As we have already seen, these reciprocal concepts figure prominently in *King Lear*. If we respond to the characters in the play by categorizing them as good or evil, we, like Doctor Johnson, will never be able to figure out certain things about the play. The nature of these characters is determined largely by two things: the guides which they choose for their thought and action, and the objects upon which they expend their energies. Those who choose nature, sexual love, and personal gain, are inevitably led astray; those who choose rightly (as Oswald does not) where to bestow their love, belief, and service, suffer and die as anyone else does, but they manage to find genuine significance in human life.

Dostoevsky expresses himself in reciprocal concepts perhaps more consistently than Shakespeare does, and his favorite image for the relation between such concepts is that of "the two-edged weapon" or "the knife that cuts both ways." Zossima juxtaposes the alternatives of heaven and hell when Ivan first expresses his contention that "there is no virtue if there is no immortality" (*The Brothers Karamazov*, p. 79). The monk responds, "You are blessed in believing that or else most unhappy"—"blessed" if he denies the consequent, "most unhappy" if he affirms the antecedent. In other words, the index of his spiritual condition is whether or not he finally believes, beyond the formula, in immortality itself. The moral categories of good and bad are irrelevant at this level. To be sure, Ivan's behavior is "bad" as a result of his "unhappiness," but by then it is purely a matter of cause and effect. The essential irrelevance of good and evil is repeatedly stressed in the Dostoevsky novels, as when Myshkin describes the outcast Marie, whom he had known in Switzerland:

> Then I gave her the eight francs and told her to take care of it, because I should have no more. Then I kissed her and said that she mustn't think I had any evil intent, and that I kissed her not because I was in love with her, but because I was very sorry for her, and that I had never, from the very beginning, thought of her as guilty but only as unhappy. I wanted very much to comfort her at once and to persuade her that she shouldn't consider herself below every one, but I think she didn't understand. I saw that at once, though she scarcely spoke all the time and stood before me looking down and horribly abashed. When I had finished, she kissed my hand, and I at once took her hand and would have kissed it, but she pulled it away. (*The Idiot,* p. 65)

When one sees the "sinner" not as a person who is malicious by choice but as one who is desperately unhappy, charity (that is, love) becomes much easier.

Let us look at one more example of Dostoevsky's use of reciprocal concepts—the contrast between Father Zossima and "Father" Karamazov. The former, a saintly man whose life has been transformed by a spiritual crisis, is Dostoevsky's principal exponent of the Christian gospel. Some readers find him insipid as a character, because (one suspects) the things he says are not what they like to hear; but there can be little doubt that his role is crucial for any understanding of Dostoevsky's full meaning. Old Karamazov, on the other hand, is a reprobate and a debauchee of the most highly developed kind. On superficial examination, it seems obvious that one is good and the other bad. But the reader who responds to them in moral terms will miss the point. Both of these characters represent a kind of perfection. It is no more improbable that Zossima should be the kind of man he is than that Fyodor should be what he is. There is a certain charm to the old sensualist who prides himself on being able to regard Stinking Lizaveta "as a woman," when his companions can think of her only as "an animal." Just as nothing in creation is beyond the scope of Zossima's love, no creature that even remotely resembles a human female is beyond the reach of Fyodor's lust. In brief, while Zossima is "perfect in love," old Karamazov is "perfect in lust."

Sixthly, because Christian tragedy is a comparatively modern development, its form is not restricted, as Greek tragedy's had been, to the drama. The differences of form between the tragedies of Sophocles, Shakespeare, and Racine are sufficient to indicate that tragedy does not depend for its existence upon the writer's adherence to any one form. Even within Greek tragedy itself, we may observe an evolutionary development of form; there is a considerable difference between a dramatic trilogy like the *Oresteia* and a single, compact play like *Oedipus the King.* And paradoxically, as the length of Greek dramatic representations diminished, the number of actors grew. The differences between Euripides and Aeschylus are probably no less significant than those between Shakespeare and Racine; yet all four of them produced works that we accept as tragic paradigms. Moreover, there is no single line of continuous development which we can follow with any confidence that we know what the next evolutionary change will be. Euripides, the last of the great Greek tragedians, was surely more "romantic" than his predecessors; but Racine, who followed Shakespeare by more than half a century, was far more severely "classical" than the greatest of English dramatists.

Obviously, art does not progress in the way that science does. It is therefore impossible to distinguish adequately between cause and effect in the history of art; and we cannot know whether the drama was dominant in the Periclean and Elizabethan ages because certain writers chose it as their vehicle for artistic expression, or whether they chose it because it was the most convenient and practical vehicle for them to use. Though literature does not develop in any predictable fashion, it is clearly linked to historical changes external to itself—it can hardly be accidental that of the first two masters of English prose fiction, one (Defoe) was a journalist and the other (Richardson) was a printer. Thus, however true it may be that the rise of Christianity was a necessary precondition for Shakespeare's tragic art, it is also true that

Christianity's appearance, by itself, is not sufficient to account for that art. Otherwise, why should it have taken fifteen hundred years for the one to produce the other? Similarly, the invention of movable type and the creation of a large literate audience was prerequisite to Dostoevsky's achievement as a novelist; but again the time lag of several centuries demonstrates that the first event was not sufficient to have caused the second.

In short, we can do no more than observe that tragedy continues to engage the imaginations of our greatest writers and that tragedy is subtly intertwined with religious thought and conviction. It should not be surprising then, though it was by no means predictable, that the advent of Christianity between the time of Sophocles and that of Shakespeare should have changed the complexion of tragic literature and that the shift from the drama to the novel as the dominant literary mode between the time of Shakespeare and that of Dostoevsky should have changed its form. Because literary history is so unpredictable, depending as it does upon the appearance of single great writers, we have no way of knowing whether the next significant tragedian to appear will produce non-Christian plays, or novels whose religious character is carefully concealed. Only one thing seems certain: he will not be a moralist who represents the most important human suffering as being the product of man's own conscious and deliberate wrongdoing; and he will not be a nihilist that represents that suffering as being either accidental or inescapable.

These few suggestions about the nature of Christian tragedy are not intended as any kind of definitive statement. They may help, however, to correct the strange belief (analyzed in Chapter I) that Christianity and tragedy derive from mutually exclusive modes of thought. The damage it has done to our understanding of literature is almost incalculable. For instance, one intelligent critic has this to say:

> What is Christian about Christian tragedy is not eschatological but psychological and ethical. Hamlet's was a soldier's burial, not a saint's or martyr's. When in the final scene of *Lear* the King enters

with Cordelia in his arms, Kent, Edgar, and Albany pronounce a choric verdict on the pitiful spectable:

Kent. Is this the promis'd end?
Edgar. Or image of that horror?
Albany. Fall and cease!

The Christian hope is shattered. The promised Judgment confuses evil and good, and both perish. The original terror looms close, all the more shocking and disillusioning by virtue of the high promises of the Christian revelation. In one sense, this *is* the end.[6]

We should analyze this passage carefully because it illustrates so beautifully the consequences of thinking that "Christian tragedy, to put it briefly, is not Christian; if it were, it would not be tragedy" (these two quotations are from the same book). We shall take the statement sentence by sentence.

First of all, these chapters have attempted to show that Christian eschatology has had a more important effect upon tragic literature than have the psychology and ethics which are only byproducts of that eschatology. The reciprocal concepts of heaven and hell, the apocalyptic moment in which the man who suffers with Christ is both judged and forgiven—these are the source of both the psychology and the ethics in works like *King Lear* and *The Brothers Karamazov.* "Hamlet's was a soldier's burial, not a saint's or martyr's" because the dominant metaphor of the play is based upon shooting and "missing the mark." The last words of the final scene ("Go, bid the soldiers shoot") remind us that the soldier must be ready at all times. Hamlet is neither a saint nor a martyr, but a sinner, one who "misses the mark" with disastrous consequences but who finally realizes that "the readiness is all," and who therefore does not die meaninglessly. (For New Testament use of the metaphor of soldiering, *see* Ephesians 6:10–17.)

As for the "choric verdict" at the end of *King Lear,* with the exception of one word, the first line quoted ("Is this the promis'd end?") is identical with a question which is raised in Sonnet 146 ("Is this the body's end?"), and the answer there is perfectly clear:

> Shall worms, inheritors of this excess,
> Eat up thy charge? *Is this the body's end?*
> Then, soul, live thou upon thy servant's loss,
> And let that pine to aggravate thy store;
> Buy terms divine in selling hours of dross;
> Within be fed, without be rich no more;
> So shalt thou feed on Death, that feeds on men,
> And Death once dead, there's no more dying then.

The second line quoted, "Or image of that horror?" recalls the fact that Lear has just asked for a "looking glass" in order to test (by her breath) whether Cordelia is still alive. If we are right in using the Corinthian letters (and especially the thirteenth chapter of First Corinthians) as the frame of reference for *Lear,* we may associate this line with St. Paul's declaration, "For now we see in a mirror dimly, *but then face to face*" (I Cor. 13:12; "in a glass darkly" is the more familiar King James wording). The words "Fall and cease" suggest the apocalyptic moment almost as clearly as anything in Dostoevsky. And we should bear in mind that these three lines are spoken by Kent, Edgar, and Albany, the three characters in the play who come closer than anyone else (except Cordelia herself, on whose death they are commenting) to the high standards of Christianity.

"The Christian hope is shattered," says our commentary. But why should the Christian hope be shattered by the hanging of Cordelia if it is not shattered by the crucifixion of Christ? "The promised Judgment confuses evil and good, and both perish." Kent apparently does not think so; for he says moments later, "I have a journey, sir, shortly to go./My master calls me; I must not say no." How can this be, if his master has perished? "The high promises of the Christian revelation" never indicated that anyone would avoid the kind of death which marks the end of this play. On the contrary, this "high promise" indicates that "unless a grain of wheat *falls into the earth and dies,* it remains alone; but if it dies, it bears much fruit." Indeed, to a person familiar with the terms of that promise, the words "Fall and cease" seem to be a reminder of it, rather than a denial. Of course it is true that "in one sense, this *is* the end." If it were not, the play—and individual lives themselves—would have no ending at all.

Our failure to recognize the profound impress of biblical Christianity upon such works as *Hamlet, King Lear,* and *Macbeth, Crime and Punishment, The Idiot,* and *The Brothers Karamazov* is serious enough in itself. But it is only symptomatic of our inability to comprehend the character of the literary imagination. No less shrewd an observer than George Santayana had this to say of Shakespeare:

> A poet of Shakespeare's time could not have found any other mould than Christianity for his religion. In our day, with our wide and conscientious historical sympathies, it may be possible for us to find in other rites and doctrines than those of our ancestors an expression of some ultimate truth. But for Shakespeare, in the matter of religion, the choice lay between Christianity and nothing. He chose nothing; he chose to leave his heroes and himself in the presence of life and of death with no other philosophy than that which the profane world can suggest and understand.
>
> . . . If Shakespeare had been without metaphysical capacity, or without moral maturity, we could have explained his strange insensibility to religion; but as it is, we must marvel at his indifference and ask ourselves what can be the causes of it.[7]

There has indeed been a "strange insensibility to religion" in our reading of Shakespeare, but that insensibility may be ours rather than his. Nevertheless, we have concurred with Santayana's judgment; we have marveled at what we took to be Shakespeare's indifference and have asked ourselves what can be the causes of it.

Ironically, Santayana himself helps us to understand how this has happened. He tells us that "there are only two or three short passages in the plays, and one sonnet, in which true religious feeling seems to break forth." He cites the one in *Henry V,* spoken by the king after the battle of Agincourt, and then says:

> This passage is certainly a true expression of religious feeling, and just the kind that we might expect from a dramatist. Religion appears here as a manifestation of human nature and as an expression of human passion. The passion, however, is not due to Shakespeare's

imagination, but is essentially historical: the poet has simply not rejected, as he usually does, the religious element in the situation he reproduces.[8]

Santayana then "proves his point" by quoting from the relevant passage in Holinshed. But here is the great fallacy. If we assume that any elements in Shakespearean drama which may be traced to some earlier literary source are *not due to Shakespeare's imagination,* but merely to his finding them in his sources and then "not rejecting them, as he usually does," something very strange may ultimately happen. As we discover more and more about the sources of the Shakespeare plays, not only their plots, but their thought structure and their imagery as well, our estimate of the great poet's "imagination" will shrink farther and farther, until perhaps we reach the conclusion, justified by these premises, that he had no imagination at all. This might, however, be a consummation devoutly to be wished; for it would compel us to evolve a larger and more accurate conception of the literary imagination.

The evidence for a Christian interpretation of Shakespeare's greatest dramas and Dostoevsky's finest novels can no longer be ignored. Paradoxically, what has hindered, or rather prevented, our recognizing and accepting that evidence is the obviousness and the accessibility of the evidence itself. A conscientious scholar will gladly journey hundreds of miles and pore over scores of rare books resurrected from cavernous archives in order to track down a single image or phrase in Shakespeare or Dostoevsky, while an English bible, the source of so many of those images and phrases, lies untouched in his hotel room, or perhaps even back in his own home. Edgar Allan Poe treats at some length the psychological phenomenon we are considering—in "The Purloined Letter" Poe's Detective Dupin amazes the Prefect of Police by recovering a letter for which the Prefect himself had carried on an elaborate search. All the time, of course, the letter has been in plain sight in one of the rooms which the police had gone over with great care; they had missed it only because it was not hidden in a secret compartment or a hollow chair leg. Dupin compares the procedure he uses to a game in which one person asks another to find the name of a town, river, state, or empire printed upon a map. A novice, says the detective, will try to confound the other players by making them find the most minutely lettered names. The adept, on the other hand, selects

such words as stretch, in large characters, from one end of the chart to the other. These, like the over-largely lettered signs and placards of the street, escape observation by dint of being excessively obvious; and here the physical oversight is precisely analogous with the moral inapprehension by which the intellect suffers to pass unnoticed those considerations which are too obtrusively and too palpably self-evident.

Across the pages of *Hamlet* and *King Lear, Crime and Punishment* and *The Idiot,* the words of St. Paul and St. John are written in huge, calligraphic letters.

Notes

I TRAGEDY AND THE GOSPEL NARRATIVES

1. Jaspers, pp. 38–39.
2. Kaufmann, p. 342.
3. Sewall, p. 157, n. 49.
4. Cherbonnier, p. 40.
5. *Beyond Tragedy,* p. 168.
6. Jaspers, p. 40.
7. Niebuhr, p. 155.
8. Cherbonnier, p. 38.
9. Kaufmann, p. 345.
10. Freud, *Totem and Taboo,* pp. 200–202.
11. Kaufmann, p. 343.
12. Cited in the Variorum *Hamlet,* I, 440.
13. Jaspers, pp. 30–31.
14. Lattimore, p. 19.
15. *Ibid.,* p. 21.
16. *Ibid.,* pp. 21–22.
17. *Ibid.,* p. 19.
18. *Ibid. See also* Else, *Aristotle's Poetics: The Argument.*
19. Cooper, *Aristotle on the Art of Poetry,* p. 40.
20. Kaufmann, p. 343.
21. Jaspers, p. 41.
22. Niebuhr, p. 164; cf. p. 155.
23. Cherbonnier, p. 31.
24. *Ibid.,* p. 30.
25. *Ibid.,* p. 35.
26. *Ibid.,* p. 37.
27. *Ibid.,* p. 40.
28. *Ibid.,* p. 46.
29. *Ibid.,* p. 42.
30. Jaspers, p. 32.
31. Cherbonnier, p. 42.
32. *Ibid.,* p. 36.

33. *Ibid.,* p. 35.
34. *Ibid.,* p. 50.
35. *Ibid.*
36. Jaspers, pp. 40–41.
37. *Ibid.,* p. 39.

II THE TWO SOURCES OF CHRISTIAN TRAGEDY

1. Simmons, *Dostoevski: The Making of a Novelist,* p. 70.
2. For the general classification, *see* Scott's *Literature of the New Testament* and Bultmann's *Theology of the New Testament.* As for the Pauline authorship of Ephesians and Colossians, Scott indicates that "the Epistle to the Ephesians has sometimes been denied to him, on grounds which cannot be regarded as decisive"; but, says Scott, "that he wrote Colossians . . . there can be no reasonable doubt" (p. 170). Bultmann, on the other hand, does not hesitate to assign both letters to the deutero-Pauline group (II, 6). In *A Rebirth of Images: The Making of St John's Apocalypse,* Austin Farrer seriously challenges the widely held view that the fourth gospel and the book of Revelation were written by two different people: "St John's activity as a Christian writer began, so far as we know, with the Apocalypse. Initiated by this inspired labour, he proceeded to the tranquil composition of the Gospel" (p. 24). The more conservative attitude on this question is expressed by the editors of the Jerusalem Bible: "Internal evidence shows that the Revelation of John has some affinity with the other Johannine writings, but as it is so sharply distinguished from them by language, style, and some theological positions, notably its view of the *parousia,* it is impossible to identify the author of Revelation as it stands with the author of the rest of the Johannine literature. In spite of that, Revelation is clearly Johannine in inspiration: it was written inside the apostle's immediate circle and is pervaded by his doctrine" (N.T., pp. 427–428).
3. *Cross Currents,* XV (1965), 339–353.
4. Benoit, p. 341.
5. *Ibid.,* p. 346.
6. *Ibid.,* pp. 346–347.
7. I refer to the writings of both Benoit and Bultmann in order to show that the interpretations here offered are not peculiar to either the Roman Catholic or the Protestant tradition. The two interpreters are in clear agreement on all matters that are central to our inquiry.
8. Bultmann, I, 245.
9. *Ibid.,* II, 24.

10. *Ibid.*, II, 25–26.
11. *Ibid.*, II, 25.
12. Benoit, pp. 347–348.
13. *Ibid.*, pp. 348–349.
14. *See* Bradley, *Shakespearean Tragedy*, p. 145.

III HAMLET'S *HAMARTÍA*

1. The Variorum *Hamlet* (1877) devotes forty pages (II, 195–235) to summarizing earlier discussion of the question "Is Hamlet's Insanity Real or Feigned?" What may properly be called Freudian criticism does not begin, of course, until nearly a quarter of a century after that; and Ernest Jones's classic study *Hamlet and Oedipus* was not published in its present form until 1949, though a first version of it had appeared in 1910. Current scholarly journals continue to report the progress of the discussion from both Freudian and non-Freudian viewpoints.

2. Grebanier, p. 139. One searches in vain through the rest of Grebanier's book for an explanation of the word as it is used in the apology.

3. *Hamlet: An Historical and Comparative Study*, p. 27.

4. Alexander, pp. 79–91.

5. The Variorum *Hamlet*, I, 440. Johnson's complaint is quoted by Bradley.

6. *Shakespearean Tragedy*, p. 420.

7. *What Happens in Hamlet*, p. 275.

8. *The Question of Hamlet*, pp. 96, 113.

9. "Hamlet's Hallucination," *Modern Language Review*, XII (1917), 339–421.

10. Besides the evidence which Noble accumulates in *Shakespeare's Biblical Knowledge and Use of the Book of Common Prayer*, we have Baldwin's statements in *William Shakspere's Small Latine and Lesse Greeke:* "If Shakspere reached any Greek author at all, it is a safe assumption that he began and continued on the Greek Testament, with English and Latin translations available and at least partially mastered in previous Biblical work" (II, 627). And again, "There is some not wholly conclusive evidence that Shakspere had read in Greek at least part of the *New Testament*" (II, 661). To anyone who reads the Pauline literature with some care, Romans 7 is only a little less familiar than I Corinthians 13, which Scott, in *The Literature of the New Testament*, calls "the most exquisite passage that Paul ever wrote" (p. 134).

11. Bultmann, pp. 156–157 (emphasis mine).
12. Bradley, p. 145.

IV *KING LEAR* AND THE CORINTHIAN LETTERS

1. Introduction to the Pelican *King Lear*, p. 19.
2. *Shakespearean Tragedy*, pp. 264–265.
3. *Ibid.*, p. 256.
4. *Ibid.*, p. 249.
5. "Shakespeare and the Drama," *Recollections and Essays*, pp. 307–383. *See* especially pp. 307–345.
6. Introduction to the Arden *King Lear*, p. lvi.
7. *Shakespeare and Christian Doctrine*, p. 37.
8. *See*, for instance, the chapter on I Corinthians in Scott's *Literature of the New Testament*. In this letter, says Scott, "Without any attempt at logical sequence, he takes up the various subjects brought before him, turning from one to another with some brief formula (e.g., 'Now concerning')" (p. 136). This statement is followed by a list of ten entirely different topics which Paul discusses at some length in I Corinthians. A similar problem exists in connection with II Corinthians, which is made up of at least two different letters. Scott tries to clarify the relation between the widely contrasting parts of what we call II Corinthians (pp. 129–131); and he also indicates that "many attempts have been made to discover unity in the Epistle just as it stands" (p. 140).
9. "Shakespeare and the Drama," p. 339.
10. Van Doren, *Shakespeare*, pp. 239–240.
11. This passage is sometimes regarded as non-Shakespearean for reasons which Bradley lists in the appendix ("Note v") of *Shakespearean Tragedy*. He himself does not accept the lines as genuine; but the five arguments he offers for rejecting them will not bear scrutiny. He says first that "the scene ends characteristically without the lines." In other words, if they were omitted—as the Lord High Executioner intones in *The Mikado*—"they'd none of 'em be missed!" On this basis we might remove a good many other lines from the Shakespeare plays. Next, says Bradley, "they are addressed directly to the audience." Perhaps, then, the Chorus in *Henry V* should also be rejected as non-Shakespearean. Thirdly, "they destroy the pathetic and beautiful effect of the immediately preceding words of the Fool, and also of Lear's solicitude for him." One could use the same argument to reject almost any comic passage in the tragedies. It is hardly consistent to call such interludes comic relief if we like them, and interpolations if we do not. Fourthly,

Bradley claims that speaking the lines involves a dramatic absurdity; but by no stretch of the imagination can this passage be made to seem as absurd from a dramatic point of view as Gloucester's "leap," which Bradley contends "is not, if properly acted, in the least absurd on the stage." Lastly, we are told that "it is also somewhat against them that they do not appear in the Quartos." In the next paragraph, however, he argues that some other lines in the play which are also suspected of being non-Shakespearean should *not* be rejected and indicates that "the fact that the Folio omits the lines is, of course, nothing against them." In short, since Bradley can give no good explanation of why the Fool's "prophecy" is in the play, he finds reasons for regarding it as spurious. But he reveals his own awareness that these reasons are rather feeble; for he concludes by saying that "at the same time I do not think one would hesitate to accept [the lines] if they occurred at any natural place *within* the dialogue." That is to say, none of the last four arguments have any weight if they are separated from the first one—but apparently that one, by itself, is so weak that the other four must be there to shore it up. One cannot help wishing that Bradley had expended as much scholarly energy in discovering what the lines add to the meaning of the play if they are genuine as he did in constructing arguments for thinking that they are not.

12. Quoted by Bradley, p. 298.

13. Heilman, chaps. VIII, IX, entitled "Reason in Madness" and "Madness in Reason."

14. Bradley, p. 330.

15. The word *endure* (I Cor. 13:7) is used in both the Geneva Bible (1560) and the Bishops' Bible (1568); *patient* (I Cor. 13:4) first appears in the Rheims translation (1582; 2nd ed., 1600). The King James Version (1611) is the first to make use of the word *kind* (I Cor. 13:4); before that, *courteous* (Bishops' Bible) or *benigne* (Rheims translation) was preferred. It is significant, however, that the authors of the King James Version, who were men of Shakespeare's own generation, regarded *kind* as a more appropriate word in this context than either *courteous* or *benigne*.

16. Bradley, p. 316.

17. *Ibid.*, pp. 320–321.

18. Introduction to the Arden *King Lear*, p. lviii.

19. Bradley, pp. 322–323, 324–325, 326.

20. Heilman, p. 83.

21. Stanley Edgar Hyman, "Psychoanalysis and the Climate of Tragedy," *Partisan Review*, XXIII (1956), p. 200.

22. Nietzsche, "First Essay" in *The Genealogy of Morals,* especially sections VII through X.

V MACBETH DIVIDED AGAINST HIMSELF

1. *Coleridge's Shakespearean Criticism,* ed. Raysor, I, 67.
2. *Selections from De Quincey,* ed. Milton Haight Turk, pp. 395–400.
3. *Shakespearean Tragedy,* p. 395.
4. Introduction to the Arden *Macbeth,* p. xxviii.
5. *Ibid.,* p. xxix.
6. *Ibid.,* pp. xxxi, xxxiii.
7. *Shakespeare: The Complete Works,* p. 1198, n.
8. *Shakespeare's Bawdy,* p. 159.
9. Introduction to the Arden *Macbeth,* p. xviii.
10. *The Well Wrought Urn,* p. 31.
11. Introduction to the Arden *Macbeth,* p. xxxiii, n.
12. Bradley, p. 353.
13. *Shakespeare Survey,* XIX (1966), p. 45.
14. *Shakespeare's Bawdy,* pp. 52, 54.
15. *Ibid.,* p. 22.
16. Bradley, p. 379, n.
17. Cited by Kenneth Muir, The Arden *Macbeth,* p. 63, n.
18. *Ibid.*
19. "Psychoanalysis and the Climate of Tragedy," *Partisan Review,* XXIII (1956), p. 200.
20. *Shakespeare's Bawdy,* p. 54.

VI THE NOVEL AS A TRAGIC MODE

1. *The English Novel: A Short Critical History,* p. 7.
2. Hadas, p. 5.
3. *See* the Author's Preface to *Joseph Andrews.* The fifth paragraph, which begins with the words "Now, a comic romance is a comic epic poem in prose," presents a definition in the manner of Aristotle.
4. Trilling, pp. 214–215.
5. Dostoevsky, *The Notebooks for Crime and Punishment,* ed. and trans. Wasiolek, p. 188.
6. *Partisan Review,* XXIII (1956), 199.
7. *Ibid.,* p. 200.
8. The passage is quoted by Philip Rahv in "The Legend of The Grand Inquisitor," *Partisan Review,* XXI (1954), p. 252, n. The italics are mine.
9. Forster, chaps. VII–VIII.

10. Brown, especially pp. 3–59.

11. Sewell, p. 120.

12. Forster, pp. 234–235.

13. Brown, p. 55.

14. *Ibid.,* pp. 50–51.

15. *Ibid.,* pp. 8–9.

16. Forster, pp. 142, 143.

17. *Shakespearean Tragedy,* p. 387.

18. Forster, p. 182.

19. *Freedom and the Tragic Life: A Study in Dostoevsky,* p. 19.

20. In order to avoid confusion, we should distinguish between Forster's word *prophecy* and the word *prophetic* as we have used it to characterize the Johannine writings. (*See* Chap. II.) In neither case is the idea of prediction involved; the root meaning of *prophet* is not foreteller, but *forth-teller.* As applied to St. John, the word *prophetic* emphasizes the poetic and symbolic character of his work, as opposed to the analytic tendency of the Pauline letters and the discursive nature of the synoptic gospels. Hence the abundance of imagery in John and the dissolution of time as we ordinarily conceive it. Forster, in describing the "prophetic novelist," comes back repeatedly to one form or another of the word *sing* (*Aspects of the Novel,* pp. 195–203). He says, for instance, that "what matters is the accent of his voice, his song" (p. 195). In this sense, the distinction between the "prophet" (Dostoevsky) and the "preacher" (George Eliot) is that the first one "sings," while the other merely "drones on." Thus, Forster's term may be applied to the writings of both Shakespeare and Dostoevsky, since they both "sing."

VII RASKOLNIKOV AND THE RESURRECTION OF LAZARUS

1. "Dostoevsky in 'Crime and Punishment,'" *Partisan Review,* XXVII (1960), p. 403, n.

2. *Ibid.*

3. *Dostoevsky: His Life and Work,* p. 312.

4. "Dostoevsky in 'Crime and Punishment,'" pp. 402–403.

5. Dostoevsky, *The Notebooks for Crime and Punishment,* ed. and trans. Wasiolek, p. 91.

6. Of particular interest are the sections headed "Eternal life" (pp. 144–150), "Faith" (pp. 179–186), and "The victory of life over death" (pp. 363–368).

7. Dodd, p. 363.

8. *Ibid.,* p. 367.

9. *Ibid.*

10. *The Notebooks for Crime and Punishment,* p. 11.

11. "[Dostoevsky's Technique of Writing]," in *Crime and Punishment: The Coulson Translation, Backgrounds and Sources, Essays in Criticism,* ed. Gibian, p. 551.

12. Mochulsky, p. 300.

13. *Freedom and the Tragic Life: A Study in Dostoevsky,* p. 7.

14. Dodd, p. 368.

15. *Hudson Review,* XIII (1960), 202–253.

16. *Ibid.,* p. 209.

17. *Dostoevski: The Making of a Novelist,* p. 178.

18. Mochulsky, p. 312.

19. "Dostoevsky in 'Crime and Punishment,' " p. 395.

20. Dodd, p. 366.

21. *The Notebooks for Crime and Punishment,* p. 64.

22. Chulkov, p. 548. The quotations which follow may be found on pp. 548–549.

23. *What Is Art?,* p. 123.

VIII MYSHKIN'S APOCALYPTIC VISION

1. According to the editor of the 1957 Moscow edition of Dostoevsky's works, these letters stand for the words "Ave, Mater Dei," Hail, Mother of God.

2. The words are Dostoevsky's own. *See* Simmons, *Dostoevski: The Making of a Novelist,* Chap. XIII; the letter in which Dostoevsky uses the phrase is quoted on pp. 209–210.

3. *The Tragic Vision,* p. 215, n.

4. "Dostoevsky's Idiot, A Symbol of Christ," *Cross Currents,* VI (1956), p. 375.

5. Quoted by Simmons, p. 72.

6. Edwin Muir, p. 73.

7. Blackmur's essay, "A Rage of Goodness: *The Idiot* of Dostoevsky," is reprinted in *The Critical Performance,* ed. Hyman; *see* pp. 241–242. Mirsky's statement appears in his *History of Russian Literature from its Beginnings to 1900,* p. 288. Blackmur makes a special point of distinguishing Dostoevsky's Christianity, which "united spirit and feeling," from St. Paul's which "united spirit and intellect."

8. In *Current Issues in New Testament Interpretation,* ed. Klassen and Snyder, p. 35.

9. *Ibid.,* pp. 36–37.

10. Krieger, p. 215, n.

11. Simon O. Lesser, "Saint and Sinner—Dostoevsky's 'Idiot,' " *Modern Fiction Studies,* IV (1958), p. 211.

12. *Ibid.*, p. 218.
13. *Ibid.*, p. 223.
14. Wasiolek, p. 93.

IX THE GRAND INQUISITOR

1. Berdyaev, *Dostoevsky*, pp. 188–212.
2. "Preface to *The Grand Inquisitor*," in *D. H. Lawrence: Selected Literary Criticism*, ed. Beal, pp. 233–241.
3. "The Legend of The Grand Inquisitor," *Partisan Review*, XXI (1954), 249–271.
4. Wasiolek, pp. 166–167.
5. *Ibid.*, p. 169.
6. Quoted by Rahv, "The Legend of The Grand Inquisitor," p. 252, n.

X THE MEANING OF CHRISTIAN TRAGEDY

1. *The Will to Believe and Other Essays in Popular Philosophy*, pp. 25–26.
2. "Psychoanalysis and the Climate of Tragedy," *Partisan Review*, XXIII (1956), p. 200.
3. Forster, pp. 183–192.
4. Simon O. Lesser, "Saint and Sinner—Dostoevsky's 'Idiot,'" *Modern Fiction Studies*, IV (1958), p. 212.
5. "Dostoevsky and Parricide," *The Standard Edition of the Complete Psychological Works*, ed. James Strachey, XXI, 177–194. The thesis is stated explicitly on p. 188.
6. Richard B. Sewall, *The Vision of Tragedy*, pp. 73–74.
7. "The Absence of Religion in Shakespeare," *Interpretations of Poetry and Religion*, pp. 152–153.
8. *Ibid.*, p. 150.

Bibliography

Alexander, Peter. *Hamlet: Father and Son.* Oxford, 1955.

Allen, Walter. *The English Novel: A Short Critical History.* New York, 1955.

Aristotle. *The Basic Works of Aristotle.* Edited and with an introduction by Richard McKeon. New York, 1941.

————. *The Poetics of Aristotle.* Translated by Preston H. Epps. Chapel Hill, 1942.

Austen, Jane. *Emma.* Edited by R. W. Chapman. London, 1960.

Baldwin, T. W. *William Shakspere's Small Latine and Lesse Greeke.* 2 vols. Urbana, 1944.

Barnet, Sylvan. "Some Limitations of a Christian Approach to Shakespeare," *ELH,* XXII (1955), 81–92.

Beal, Anthony, ed. *D. H. Lawrence: Selected Literary Criticism.* New York, 1956.

Benoit, Pierre. "Pauline and Johannine Theology: A Contrast," *Cross Currents,* XV (1965), 339–353.

Berdyaev, Nicholas. *Dostoevsky.* Translated by Donald Attwater. New York, 1957.

Blackmur, R. P. "A Rage of Goodness: *The Idiot* of Dostoevsky," in *The Critical Performance.* Edited by Stanley Edgar Hyman. New York, 1956.

Bradley, A. C. *Shakespearean Tragedy: Lectures on Hamlet, Othello, King Lear, Macbeth.* London, 1960.

Brooks, Cleanth. *The Well Wrought Urn: Studies in the Structure of Poetry.* New York, 1947.

Brown, E. K. *Rhythm in the Novel.* Toronto, 1950.

Bultmann, Rudolf. *Existence and Faith: Shorter Writings of Rudolf Bultmann.* Translated by Schubert M. Ogden. Cleveland, 1960.

————. *Theology of the New Testament.* Translated by Kendrick Grobel. 2 vols. New York, 1951, 1955.

Butcher, Samuel Henry. *Aristotle's Theory of Poetry and Fine Art, with a Critical Text and Translation of the Poetics.* New York, 1951.

Cherbonnier, Edmond LaB. "Biblical Faith and the Idea of Tragedy," in *The Tragic Vision and the Christian Faith.* Edited by Nathan A. Scott, Jr. New York, 1957.

Chulkov, Georgy. "[Dostoevsky's Technique of Writing]," in *Crime and Punishment: The Coulson Translation, Backgrounds and*

Sources, Essays in Criticism. Edited by George Gibian. New York, 1964.

Coleridge, Samuel Taylor. *Coleridge's Shakespearean Criticism*. Edited by Thomas M. Raysor. 2 vols. New York, 1960.

Cooper, Lane. *Aristotle on the Art of Poetry*. Boston, 1913.

De Quincey, Thomas. *Selections from De Quincey*. Edited by Milton Haight Turk. Boston, 1902.

Dodd, C. H. *The Interpretation of the Fourth Gospel*. Cambridge, Eng., 1954.

Dostoevsky, Fyodor. *The Brothers Karamazov*. Translated by Constance Garnett. New York, 1950.

———. *Crime and Punishment*. Translated by Constance Garnett. New York, 1950.

———. *The Idiot*. Translated by Constance Garnett. New York, 1935.

———. *The Notebooks for Crime and Punishment*. Edited and Translated by Edward Wasiolek. Chicago, 1967.

———. *The Notebooks for The Idiot*. Edited by Edward Wasiolek. Translated by Katharine Strelsky. Chicago, 1967.

Eliot, T. S. *Selected Essays*. New York, 1950.

Else, G. *Aristotle's Poetics: The Argument*. Cambridge, Mass., 1957.

Encyclopedia of World Art. 14 vols. New York, 1959–1967.

Farnham, Williard, ed. *The Pelican Shakespeare: The Tragedy of Hamlet, Prince of Denmark*. Baltimore, 1957.

Farrer, Austin. *A Rebirth of Images: The Making of St John's Apocalypse*. Westminster, 1949.

Fielding, Henry. *Joseph Andrews*. Edited by Martin C. Battestin. Middletown, Conn., 1967.

Forster, E. M. *Aspects of the Novel*. New York, 1927.

Freud, Sigmund. "Dostoevsky and Parricide," *The Standard Edition of the Complete Psychological Works*, XXI, 177–194. Edited by James Strachey. London, 1961.

———. *Totem and Taboo*. Translated by A. A. Brill. New York, n.d.

Frye, Roland Mushat. *Shakespeare and Christian Doctrine*. Princeton, 1963.

Furness, H. H. *The Variorum Shakespeare: Hamlet*. 2 vols. Philadelphia, 1877.

Grebanier, Bernard. *The Heart of Hamlet: The Play Shakespeare Wrote*. New York, 1960.

Greg, W. W. "Hamlet's Hallucination," *Modern Language Review*, XII (1917), 393–421.

Grene, David, and Richmond Lattimore, eds. *The Complete Greek Tragedies*. 4 vols. Chicago, 1959.

Guardini, Romano. "Dostoevsky's Idiot, A Symbol of Christ," *Cross Currents*, VI (1956), 359–382.

Hadas, Moses. *Three Greek Romances*. Garden City, 1953.

Harbage, Alfred, ed. *The Pelican Shakespeare: The Tragedy of King Lear*. Baltimore, 1958.

———. *The Pelican Shakespeare: The Tragedy of Macbeth*. Baltimore, 1956.

Harrison, G. B., ed. *Shakespeare: The Complete Works*. New York, 1952.

Heilman, Robert B. *This Great Stage: Image and Structure in King Lear*. Seattle, 1963.

Holinshed, Raphael. *Chronicles of England, Scotland and Ireland*. 6 vols. London, 1807–1808.

Hyman, Stanley Edgar. "Psychoanalysis and the Climate of Tragedy," *Partisan Review*, XXIII (1956), 198–214.

Ivanov, Vyacheslav. *Freedom and the Tragic Life: A Study in Dostoevsky*. Translated by Norman Cameron. New York, 1966.

James, William. *The Will to Believe and Other Essays in Popular Philosophy*. New York, 1897.

Jaspers, Karl. *Tragedy Is Not Enough*. Translated by Harald A. T. Reiche, Harry T. Moore, and Karl W. Deutsch. Boston, 1952.

The Jerusalem Bible. Edited by Alexander Jones. Garden City, 1966.

Jones, Ernest. *Hamlet and Oedipus*. Garden City, 1954.

Kaufmann, Walter. *Critique of Religion and Philosophy*. Garden City, 1961.

Krieger, Murray. *The Tragic Vision: Variations on a Theme in Literary Interpretation*. New York, 1960.

Lattimore, Richmond. *Story Patterns in Greek Tragedy*. Ann Arbor, 1964.

Lesser, Simon O. "Saint and Sinner—Dostoevsky's 'Idiot,'" *Modern Fiction Studies*, IV (1958), 211–224.

Levin, Harry. *The Question of Hamlet*. New York, 1959.

Liddell, Henry George, and Robert Scott. *A Greek-English Lexicon*. Oxford, 1951.

Mackinnon, D. M. "Theology and Tragedy," *Religious Studies*, II (1967), 163–169.

Melville, Herman. *Moby Dick: Or, The Whale*. Introduction by Leon Howard. New York, 1950.

Minear, Paul S. "The Cosmology of the Apocalypse," in *Current Issues in New Testament Interpretation*. Edited by William Klassen and Graydon F. Snyder. New York, 1962.

Mirsky, D. S. *A History of Russian Literature from its Beginnings to 1900*. New York, 1958.

Mochulsky, Konstantin. *Dostoevsky: His Life and Work*. Translated by Michael A. Minihan. Princeton, 1967.

Muir, Edwin. *The Structure of the Novel*. New York, 1929.

Muir, Kenneth. "Image and Symbol in 'Macbeth,'" *Shakespeare Survey*, XIX (1966), 45–54.

——, ed. *The Arden Shakespeare: King Lear*. Cambridge, Mass., 1957.

——, ed. *The Arden Shakespeare: Macbeth*. Cambridge, Mass., 1957.

Niebuhr, Reinhold. *Beyond Tragedy: Essays on the Christian Interpretation of History*. New York, 1937.

Nietzsche, Friedrich. *The Birth of Tragedy and The Genealogy of Morals*. Translated by Francis Golffing. Garden City, 1956.

Noble, Richmond. *Shakespeare's Biblical Knowledge and Use of the Book of Common Prayer*. London, 1935.

Partridge, Eric. *Dictionary of Slang and Unconventional English*. New York, 1938.

——. *Shakespeare's Bawdy: A Literary and Psychological Essay and a Comprehensive Glossary*. New York, 1960.

Rahv, Philip. "Dostoevsky in 'Crime and Punishment,'" *Partisan Review*, XXVII (1960), 393–425.

——. "The Legend of The Grand Inquisitor," *Partisan Review*, XXI (1954), 249–271.

Santayana, George. *Interpretations of Poetry and Religion*. London, 1900.

Scott, Ernest Findlay. *The Literature of the New Testament*. New York, 1936.

Sewall, Richard. *The Vision of Tragedy*. New Haven, 1959.

Sewell, Arthur. *Character and Society in Shakespeare*. Oxford, 1951.

Simmons, Ernest J. *Dostoevski: The Making of a Novelist*. New York, 1940.

Snodgrass, W. D. "Crime for Punishment: The Tenor of Part I," *Hudson Review*, XIII (1960), 202–253.

Steiner, George. *The Death of Tragedy*. New York, 1961.

Stoll, E. E. *Hamlet: An Historical and Comparative Study*. Minneapolis, 1919.

Tillyard, E. M. W. *Shakespeare's Problem Plays*. Toronto, 1949.

Tinsley, E. J. *Christian Theology and the Frontiers of Tragedy*. Leeds, 1963.

Tolstoy, Leo. *Recollections and Essays*. London, 1937.

——. *What Is Art?* London, 1930.

Trilling, Lionel. *The Liberal Imagination*. Garden City, 1954.

Van Doren, Mark. *Shakespeare*. New York, 1939.

Wasiolek, Edward. *Dostoevsky: The Major Fiction*. Cambridge, Mass., 1964.

Weigle, Luther A., ed. *The New Testament Octapla*. New York, 1962.

Wilson, J. Dover. *What Happens in Hamlet*. Cambridge, Eng., 1962.